Management Theory

Narrative approaches to organization and management studies are very much in vogue. Offering a new challenge to management scholarship, *Management Theory: A Critical and Reflexive Reading* exposes the subtexts of five influential texts by Taylor, Follett, Drucker, Mintzberg and Kanter. In doing so, it encourages readers to recognize the stories that management theories tell and, more significantly, those that they exclude.

The book has been constructed as the story of the author's own research journey, using a unique blend of management theory and poetry. The resulting work is an academically rigorous and clearly described postmodern method of text analysis that draws on a wide range of literary theory. *Management Theory: A Critical and Reflexive Reading* provides novice researchers and teachers with a transparent view of the researcher's methodological workshop, while also modelling an alternative narrative mode of reporting.

Nanette Monin lectures in management and organization studies at Massey University, New Zealand.

Management, Organizations and Society

Edited by Professor Barbara Czarniawska, *Göteborg University, Sweden* and Professor Martha Feldman, *University of Michigan, USA*

Management, Organizations and Society presents innovative work grounded in new realities, addressing issues crucial to an understanding of the contemporary world. This is the world of organized societies, where boundaries between formal and informal, public and private, local and global organizations have been displaced or have vanished, along with other nineteenth-century dichotomies and oppositions. Management, apart from becoming a specialized profession for a growing number of people, is an everyday activity for most members of modern societies.

Similarly, at the level of enquiry, culture and technology, and literature and economics, can no longer be conceived as isolated intellectual fields; conventional canons and established mainstreams are contested. **Management, Organizations and Society** will address these contemporary dynamics of transformation in a manner that transcends disciplinary boundaries, with work which will appeal to researchers, students and practitioners alike.

Management Theory
A critical and reflexive reading

Nanette Monin

LONDON AND NEW YORK

First published 2004
by Routledge
2 Park Square, Milton Park, Abingdon, Oxon, OX14 4RN

Simultaneously published in the USA and Canada
by Routledge
270 Madison Ave, New York NY 10016

Routledge is an imprint of the Taylor & Francis Group

Transferred to Digital Printing 2007

Typeset in Sabon by Keystroke, Jacaranda Lodge, Wolverhampton

British Library Cataloguing in Publication Data
A catalogue record for this book is available from the British Library

Library of Congress Cataloging in Publication Data
Monin, Nanette.
    Management theory: a critical and reflexive reading/by Nanette Monin.
        p. cm. — (Management, organizations and society)
    Includes bibliographical references and index.
    1. Management. I. Title. II. Series: Management, organizations
    and society (London, England)
    HD31 .M6165 2004
    658'.001—dc21   2003010705

ISBN10: 0–415–32399–1 (hbk)
ISBN10: 0–415–43988–4 (pbk)

ISBN13: 978–0–415–32399–4 (hbk)
ISBN13: 978–0–415–43988–6 (pbk)

Printed and bound by CPI Antony Rowe, Eastbourne

For Konrad John

Contents

Illustrations

Figures

Table

Acknowledgements

I would like to thank the many friends and colleagues – especially David Barry, Brad Jackson and Barbara Czarniawska – who have played a crucial role in the shaping and writing of this book. It is more than two years since the completion of my PhD thesis, on which it is based; almost eight years since I first began to plan for it; and a life-time since I first read some of the texts that have played an integral part in its genesis.

For his warm support and critical acumen, my deepest thanks, as always, to John.

Permissions acknowledgements

I would also like to thank the publishers who have generously given me permission to reproduce the following material:

Carcanet Press for permission to reprint *In Broken Images*, and four lines from *Forbidden Words*, by Robert Graves

The Journal of Management Studies for permission to reprint part of an article published in 2003 as 'Toggling with Taylor: A different approach to reading a management text' (40(2): 390–6).

In Broken Images

He is quick, thinking in clear images;
I am slow, thinking in broken images.

He becomes dull, trusting to his clear images;
I become sharp, mistrusting my broken images.

Trusting his images, he assumes their relevance;
Mistrusting my images, I question their relevance.

Assuming their relevance, he assumes the fact;
Questioning their relevance, I question the fact.

When the fact fails him, he questions his senses;
When the fact fails me, I approve my senses.

He continues quick and dull in his clear images;
I continue slow and sharp in my broken images.

He in a new confusion of his understanding;
I in a new understanding of my confusion.

Robert Graves, 1959

1 Writing what I have written

There is nothing either good or bad, but thinking makes it so.
Hamlet, II, ii, 259

I read poetry and I read management theory. Sometimes I read poetry in search of a good theory and sometimes I read management theory as if it were a poem.

The poetic texts I read speak to me across centuries of human inquiry in the words of authors who are sometimes profound and sometimes clichéd, but whatever their aesthetic quality, these texts also seem to me to speak to each other as they contribute to the social construction of my world. In sixteenth century blank verse, for example, when I share Hamlet's perception that his agonized relationship to the world of affairs is the product of his own imagination, I feel that I am also sharing both Shakespeare's intuition of the 'social construction of reality', and an echo of Descartes' existential '*cogito ergo sum*' (I think therefore I am). So I, the reader, become the 'writer' of my own text: I see myself as a co-producer, with the author, of textual meaning because my reading can only connect with the life I have lived, the thoughts I have felt, and the emotions I have experienced.

If it is 'thinking' – our perception of the way the world is – that is the rational force that constructs our values, 'good or bad', then the texts that create and convey that thinking have a key role to play in our constructions. If it is through our texts that we make sense of our experiences, then these same texts become the progenitors of the shared values that knowledge-making in our communities presumes. And because throughout the twentieth century the discipline of management has had exceptionally wide-ranging influence on the thinking and living of people all around the globe, management theory texts have had a particular role to play in the shaping of communal values and knowledge. It is for these reasons that I see the exploration of meaning in the theory texts of management, and the textual strategies that might persuade readers to identify with these meanings, as an important task.

If it can be demonstrated that management theory texts are more multi-layered and plurivocal than is commonly recognized, then it seems to me that the discipline of management will be the richer for knowing itself a little better. The authors of these texts too might wish to more fully recognize the personal worldview that determines the world that they represent, and they might wish to better understand the strategies that they have employed in promoting it. Their readers may wish to unpack the messages they receive, and to decipher the persuasive strategies in which they are couched.

My quest and questions

My interest in conducting an inquiry into the functioning, and the reading effects, of management texts stems from several different but converging strands of engagement. It was first sparked by my bringing to my reading of management theory a critical approach transported from my understanding of the theories of literary criticism, and practice in reading literary texts. Initially, as I read, for example, Gareth Morgan's *Images of Organizations* (1986), and then turned to some of the debate on the role of metaphor in the writing of theory that preceded it,[1] I sensed a vacuum: where, in discussions of management scholarship generally, was there any hint of the vast contribution that the philosophy of language and literary criticism might make?

As management scholarship progressed through the 1990s, and critical approaches to management theory based in a postmodern sensibility developed, I noted that although this movement established a growing confidence in placing texts at the centre of a small, but significant, body of management inquiry, it was not yet supported by accessible methods of text analysis. It seemed that close text analysis was in danger of being dropped into the 'too hard basket' or the 'not relevant basket' before being allowed to enjoy its brief outing.

But, as we approached the third millennium, another strand of the interests that, for me, came together in this research project was growing. A number of academic publications began to appear which took as the subject of their critical inquiry, the popular writings of management gurus. During the same period I was teaching business and society classes. Management students participating in these classes, where much of our discussion returned in one guise or another to values, personal, organizational and societal, spoke of course in a multitude of voices conveying numerous worldviews. But perhaps because I had moved from the humanities to a business faculty, I began to wonder about the formative impact that readings of management theory might be having on the learning experience of these students. I began to pose questions such as: Why are some theorists more fashionable than others? Is there always a clear distinction between a management fad and a management theory? Might readers of these texts be absorbing the worldview conveyed by them without overt awareness of its fuller import?

As I began to pursue these ideas and questions, I recognized that any inquiry that stemmed from them would be premised on the notion that scholars write rhetorically. Management inquiry is rhetorical because all texts are rhetorical. In the world of management, our texts include sales talk and statistics, definition and declamation, explanation and anecdote. Our texts are the interchanges and exchanges of our human interactions and actions, from the casual and the ephemeral to the concretized foundations of the discipline itself, and our texts are language dependent.

In a constructivist worldview,[2] it is generally understood that the image of reality to which we subscribe, and that we therefore experience, is created and maintained in the language of our texts. Our texts, spoken, written and enacted, from the social and pragmatic to the scholarly and poetic, are the communications through which we live the life of humankind.

Nelson and Megill capture this worldview in a paragraph which I think demands more attention and emphasis that they have given it, so I have chosen to reformat their words as below:

> Our world is a creature and a texture of rhetorics:
> of founding stories and sales talks,
> anecdotes and statistics,
> images and rhythms;
> of tales told in nursery,
> pledges of allegiance or revenge,
> symbols of success and failure,
> archetypes of action and character.
>
> Ours is a world of
> persuasive definitions,
> expressive explanations,
> and institutional narratives.
> It is replete with figures of truth,
> models of reality, tropes of argument,
> and metaphors of experience.
> In our world, scholarship is rhetorical.
>   (Nelson and Megill 1986: 36)

Management texts of every flavour and hue are mixed through Nelson and Megill's smorgasbord. They function in a multiplicity of contexts: in the workplace and across stakeholder relationships, in the popular literature of the 'business books' marketplace, and in the scholarly books and journals produced by management academics. The new millennium has opened on to a table of texts in which the ideas and social norms that inform an increasingly global society are increasingly sourced from the discipline of management. For business books are big business. Classroom texts, based on both foundational and contemporary management theories, are bought in vast numbers to feed the masses who enrol in business college courses, and business practitioners everywhere line their bookshelves with the latest promotions. If as widely read as bought, these texts might well be as powerful an influence on the development of societal values, practices and mores as they are on the working environment of people in all the diverse roles of organizational life.[3] To the extent that management theory continues to influence society's assumptions and values, it also inspires the actions on which these beliefs are based. So it seems to me that the more completely we understand our management texts, the better equipped we are to debate, and to accept or reject, the ideas and beliefs that they promote.

If we accept that management texts influence the shaping of values, individual and societal, then the first issue of concern that interests me revolves around our ability to distinguish multiple layers of meaning and a diversity of voices, heard and unheard, in our texts. If, for example, what the text has popularly been assumed to say has been concurred with in any measure because of the way the message has been expressed, because of how the message has been conveyed, then an inquiry that provides a means of identifying this link would be useful. At the same time, if there are subtexts, meanings that act in disguise beneath the most accessible layers of the text, and that may be absorbed into the worldview of the unwary receptive reader, along with the more easily recognized surface meanings, then these too would provide a quarry of interest.

It was primarily from these two considerations that questions which have shaped and directed this book emerged. My first exploratory question, 'How can text analysis and an interpretation of management theory texts reveal and explicate subtexts previously unrecognized in standard interpretations?',[4] immediately presented itself as suggesting two very broad directions. If read with an emphasis on the 'how can' then the question would challenge me to discover a method of text analysis that would enable management scholars to recognize previously unrecognized meaning in management theory texts. This I saw as dependent upon an acceptable importing of literary epistemology into the halls of management scholarship. If read as emphasizing the discovery of 'more' meaning in management theory texts, then I would find myself in the 'what' territory of meaning-making, intent upon a search for buried treasure, for meaning encased in the creases, the linings, and the folds of language that has been ironed smooth by the familiarity of repeated readings.

At this stage of my inquiry I had no preconceived conceptualization as to which critical approach to text analysis would be the most appropriate to import into the environment of management. Nor had I envisioned what, as yet undiscovered, meaning my inquiry might reveal, so I decided to explore both roads, the 'how' and the 'what' routes to textual meaning. I would search for, develop if necessary and apply an approach to text analysis in management. Then I would read management theory texts following the described approach in order to see if more meaning would emerge from my analysis.

My thinking was very focused on the connections and/or ambiguities that I might discover linking the expression and the interpretation of meaning. I planned to explore the ways in which how something is said or written contributes to what is understood. I wondered if there might be discernible patterns of rhetorical persuasion in the texts of management theory that might be influencing the interpretation of meaning in them.

But I also saw that the notion of texts about management theory is very broadly inclusive. As already noted, management texts are not designed to be read only in the theory-driven cloisters of academe: they also act in the world of affairs. Management theorists write texts which academic teachers promote, and which may guide the values and actions that students take out into the workplace and the community. Management scholars provide the research publications on which teaching texts are based; and some of them also write or orate 'guru' texts that are the bases for the books and presentations that feed the hunger of the business practitioner world.

As I reflected on my interest in the worldviews that management texts portray, I became curious about what possible links or differences there might be in the subtexts of a wide range of this influential theory. If there is more meaning than has yet been recognized in these texts, then what common assumptions and values might I find in their spaces, their margins, and their hushed-down voices? So I saw my exploratory path building up on a three-tiered foundation. First I wanted to discover whether there are subtexts, assumptions and values, embedded in management theory. Then I wanted to determine whether there are previously unrecognized subtexts common to a range of influential management theory texts and to note intertextual links that span a range of classical and contemporary theory. Finally I was looking to discover examples of common rhetorical strategies that might bring about reader identification with the worldviews discovered in these texts.

I saw these explorations as being important in the context of both management scholarship and management practice. If there is meaning in management texts that has not been previously recognized, then the discovery of this meaning would contribute to our knowledge of both our classroom scholarship and of the worldviews in the workplace that it has played a role in constructing.

In a final step my thinking on these issues came back to the 'how' of a still overarching question: 'How can text analysis and an interpretation of management theory texts reveal and explicate subtexts previously unrecognized in standard interpretations?' I saw that I would need to seek out or develop a critical approach to reading management theory texts that I could share with my management readers, and so I added a further, and quite distinct goal to my quest: to explain, perhaps discover a method of critical analysis that I could make transparent to the management community.

As I completed the first draft of my thinking as outlined above, I was painfully aware of the potential enormity of the inquiry I planned to begin, and it seemed that I was embarking on an inquiry with few signposts in the scholarship of management.

I wondered if this territory was largely unmapped because, as Kilduff, one of the few management scholars who have deconstructed a management theory text, suggests, many of our theory texts tend to 'give the appearance of straightforward objectivity' (Kilduff 1993: 13). I wondered if classical theory texts in other disciplines had, like management, largely escaped the scrutiny of the textual critic and so I began to read across the disciplines. I was reassured to find that researchers in a wide range of disciplines other than management have published rhetorical analyses of their own theory texts: papers on, for example, science, philosophy, anthropology, mathematics, psychology, history, law and economics. There were pioneers out there, some of whom have had a profound impact on the scholarship of their own disciplines,[5] and I was encouraged by the excitement generated by their work.

Mapping my way

I have already begun to shape this research narrative around a journey metaphor. While the chronology of 'what happened' inevitably drives the narrative action forward, this 'plot' also allows me to look back and look forward, to move out from, and back in again, to the determining time-frames. It provides me with the opportunity to reflect on readings from the distant as well as the more recent past, to make connections across the disciplines and to dialogue with my readers, through every step of the process of my decision-making and discovery.

Moreover, and of seminal importance to me, as both the narrator of, and the protagonist in, this research narrative, I find that this mode of report allows me to speak in all of my own diverse voices. Some of the stopovers in my journey occur when my mode is expositional, some when my research role seems to call up a certain distancing of my analyst-self and my author-self, and some when the images and metaphors of my writing seem to dance beyond my rational narrative. All of this I planned to signpost so that my readers could follow the roads taken and not taken.

Retrospectively, my own image of my research experience in undertaking this journey is that of a tourist who sets out to explore two vast pyramids: the theory of literary criticism is the base of one, and foundational management theory the base of the other. They are quite distinct pyramids and yet, as I explored the mazes within their giant architectures, and surveyed their monolithic outlines from distant vantage points, I began to note the refracting shadows and illuminations, the kaleidoscopic shades of meaning discovered in the play of thought on thought, image on image, image on thought and thought on image – until I sensed a substantive commonality at work. With this intuition, I saw that perhaps I could move these two vast structures a little closer to each other, to a point where, as their giant sides meet, and boundaries blur, the theories and practices of literary criticism and management theory would be more accommodating of the interdisciplinary dialogue I have enjoyed.

The metaphor of the journey is one that many qualitative researchers adopt when reporting on an inquiry. Though it is the overarching (it is so conspicuous I hesitate to describe it as embedded!) metaphor in which I am writing, many other metaphors play through my words. There is intent in this. Oswick and Grant[6] in a summing up of metaphor research in organization studies, have suggested that we should consider 'using metaphor as a vehicle for, rather than target of, research'. Although, in explaining what they mean by this, they do not specify the writing up of research, they do claim that 'it is possible to think of them [metaphors] as a device for enhancing . . . research [to] provide a means to an end rather than being an end in themselves' (Oswick and Grant 1996). My own thinking, following on from this, is that metaphor's 'vividness' and 'compactness', and especially metaphor's 'ability to convey the inexpressible', are of invaluable assistance to the researcher who hopes to convey something of the endless complexity of the role of language in management theory. In the pages that follow, metaphors, my own inventions and some borrowings from the poets, carry meaning that I cannot express otherwise.

As a summary map of the roads taken, I have also sketched an outline of the structure that supports this account of my research. I began this first chapter with a sketch of my thinking, as I untangled the interweaving strands of the questions that would design and fill in the tapestry of the text I was planning. I teased out my reasons for seeing my questions as relevant and interesting, and then eased out into a broad discussion of the regions into which my inquiry will venture, the canvas that will depict it, and the journey metaphor that will carry the narrative.

Chapter 2 is the first of two chapters devoted to a review of comment, argument and knowledge in the contemporary scholarship that relates to my inquiry. I explore my topic from a number of different angles. I begin with the research of a coterie of management scholars who employ a range of critical approaches to analyse the texts of management theorists. Not finding in this literature any particular critical approach that would provide me with a method of analysis that would reveal the plurivocality of texts, I then explore more widely, searching out examples of text analysis of theory texts across the disciplines.

In this interdisciplinary territory, I found myself to be in very reassuring company, although I did not meet with any fellow tourists from management. It was here that I became better acquainted with the scholars who have been collectively engaged in the so-called Project on the Rhetoric of Inquiry (POROI), some of whose objectives seemed to parallel mine. I found that some of their number were intent upon exposing the performative aspects of rhetoric, but few of these authors seemed inclined to engage as closely with the text as I aimed to do, and there was little evidence of analysis that treated textual performance and textual perspective as aspects of each other. This suggested to me that I should introduce a methodology from literary criticism into my reading of management theory.

At this point in my review of the literature, I faced a decision-making challenge: given the vast and hugely contended arena of literary criticism I could either bed down in the comfortable confines of one recognized methodology or I could decide to cut and stitch a bespoke critical methodology, one which would draw on a variety of aspects from different methodologies. I postponed my decision until, as I completed my reading of this literature, I understood that as a reader-response critic I have my own unique method of reading, but that it is a method which shares perceptions and strategies common to many other diverse readers.

Given that one of my objectives is to provide a method of text analysis that could be replicated by other management researchers, also a heterogeneous community, the latter option, a method that embraced methodological diversity, looked more appropriate. Yet it still seemed problematic in that providing a theory base for a synthesis of methodologies initially seemed to spin me out beyond the scope of this inquiry. My solution to this dilemma has been to provide, in Chapter 3, a skeletal synopsis of twentieth-century movements in literary theory, sufficient to indicate the epistemological differences between them, but only in so far as is strictly necessary in order to provide a theory base for the approach to reading that I have developed. As I completed the reading that forms the basis of this section of my inquiry I was able to clarify my own methodological position, and to draft an outline of the approach to reading, the method, that I would adopt when analysing management theory texts.

With this base in place, I then drafted and developed the method of text analysis described in Chapter 4 and coined the term 'scriptive' to denote it. 'Scriptive reading' embraces an eclectic mix of the critical theories and critical practices described in the earlier chapters and while reflecting my own reading experience and borrowings, also allows for individual interpretation of the process that it entails. It recognizes that all readers 'write' their own texts as they construct meaning from 'the black marks' on white paper before them (Derrida 1972: 203). 'Scriptive', derived from the Latin word 'scribere', to write, suggests the paradoxical notion that to read is to 'write': that if the writer is understood as, in the Aristotelian sense of ποιητής – 'poetas' translates as 'maker' – of the text, then the reader participates in this writing act. In the reading of the text meaning is created, much as it is in the writing of it. I see both the reader and the writer as text-makers, and when discussing their roles I describe them as 'text-making'.[7]

My methodology is not prescriptive: it does not set out 'rules' of interpretation. I prefer to describe it as rescriptive for it assumes sense-making that allows for multiple interpretations and an infinity of the combinations of interpretive strategies that lead to a multiplicity of interpretations.

The scriptive reading model that I have developed maps this approach. The selection of interpretative strategies that I have culled from literary criticism, and applied to the management theory texts I have analysed is, I believe, best understood in my demonstration of criticism in action. However, mindful of management readers for whom these strategies may be unfamiliar, I have sought to both avoid esoteric terminology, and to explain, where I have thought it helpful, in the context of the analysis, any particular words or constructs that seem, in an interdisciplinary context, to demand this. Finally in Chapter 4, I provide a rationale for the selection of subject texts that I will analyse.

Chapter 5 is particularly long because it is devoted to my scriptive reading of the selected management theory texts, works by Frederick Taylor, Mary Follett, Peter Drucker, Henry Mintzberg and Rosabeth Kanter. It leads into a further chapter where I pull together the various ideas and themes that have emerged from the analysis, and provides the supporting material for two final chapters in which I review my inquiry.

In summary, this first chapter offers an overview of the first phase of my inquiry. I have described the origins of my interest in my subject, management theory; outlined some important issues that aroused my curiosity; noted questions that these issues suggested, and have explained the role I have assumed as author of this research narrative. I have also sketched the structure of the narrative that my readers may expect to discover in the pages ahead.

2 Pre-cedents in management theory

Heard melodies are sweet, but those unheard
Are sweeter; therefore, ye soft pipes, play on;
Not to the sensual ear, but, more endeared,
Pipe to the spirit ditties of no tone.
    John Keats, 'Ode on a Grecian Urn', 1819

Recognition of the role of texts, and text analysis, in management theory has a short history. It is not yet two decades since *Organization Studies* published a series of papers that introduced readers to the influential work of French philosophers Jacques Derrida (Burrell 1989) and Michel Foucault (Cooper 1989). Five years earlier an attempt by Gibson Burrell to publish in this area was repulsed with scorn by another prestigious journal:

> In 1984 . . . a piece written on Foucault's contribution to organizational analysis was submitted to ASQ. I treasure its referees' comments to this day, for all three questioned the relevance of 'an unknown French philosopher' and asked 'what could an American audience learn' from such thought.
>
> (Burrell 1996: 652)

The history of organizational theory and analysis in the 1990s has rewritten that response, for despite its short history, the study of texts[1] in management research has rapidly gained recognition beyond a coterie of pioneering scholars.

In this chapter, I trace examples of comment that demonstrates a contemporary, burgeoning interest in the language of our texts back to its origins in discussion on the metaphors in management texts in the early 1980s. By the end of that decade postmodern inquiry was challenging established perspectives on the construction of meaning in management theory, and my narrative lingers on critical readings that were completed in the early 1990s. During this period an interdisciplinary inquiry into the rhetoric of inquiry was also gathering momentum and I place management in this environment before moving on. The 1990s was a decade during which management discourse was increasingly promoted as a valid and important site of future research attention,[2] and this profiling sparked a flurry of activity on the conference circuit,[3] as well as prompting special issues of journals.[4] Finally, I explore initiatives that have begun to bring the diverse methodologies of literary criticism to the attention of management scholarship.

Specific suggestions that the appropriation of literary theory will emerge as an avenue likely to bring forth new insights into, and advances in, our understandings of organizations and their management have emerged from this research track.[5] More broadly, it has been widely suggested that as our theories of organization emerge from our language practices (discourses), discursive approaches to understanding our theories will be the central research issue in the third millennium.[6]

From images to deconstruction

> ... the question of the discourse of the human sciences requires us to come to terms with metaphor.
>
> (Bruns 1987: 241–2)

Metaphor theory

To launch my discussion of the scholarship on texts in management theory with an exploration of comment on metaphors in management theory texts seems appropriate for several reasons. Metaphor is the place where all textual inquiry begins, and to which it always returns, because the study of metaphor is generally thought to beat at the heart of all rhetorical sense-making (Gibbs 1993). It is the place where I began my personal inquiry into the texts of management, and it is also the place where the discipline of management first critically engaged with its own rhetoric.[7]

In the language of management then, as in all discussions of language, we must 'come to terms with metaphor' because it is the master trope,[8] the most fundamental form of figurative language. Tropes are figures of speech, linguistic turns, that enable words or phrases to seem to say something other than what they literally mean. When we give something a name that belongs to something else, we highlight certain attributes of the first thing, the subject, by linking it to the second thing, that with which the subject is compared. Kenneth Burke identifies four master tropes (metaphor, metonymy, synecdoche and irony) yet still sees the role of metaphor as 'primary' in our pursuit of the special character of things, and ultimately in our search for the essence of whatever it is we think we know. He characterizes metaphor itself as simply

> a device for seeing something in terms of something else. It brings out the thisness of a that, or the thatness of a this.
>
> (Burke 1989: 247)

Consistently, in extensive interdisciplinary literature, metaphor is discussed as an analogue in relational terms, but the terms that denote the 'this' (the subject) and the 'that' (to which the subject is compared) are as varied as 'tenor' and 'vehicle'; 'topic' and 'ground'; 'focus' and 'frame'; 'source' and 'target'; and 'X' and 'not-X'.[9]

Whatever the terminology employed, metaphors speak of one thing in terms of another so that a manager, for example, may be referred to as a slave driver or perhaps a lame duck. In either case the reader is expected to link some of the manager's attributes to the substitution but not others: in the latter case it might be assumed, for example, that the reader imaging the manager as a lame duck would picture her as unable to keep up with her field, or function in her role, but not as having wings and/or webbed feet. Less predictably, the reader might feel pity, distaste or even contempt for the maimed creature-manager. Metaphors move us to form perceptions of the subject, as for example the manager described above, which are dependent upon these linkages and the emotive responses evoked.

The word metaphor comes from the Greek word μεταφορα derived from μετα meaning 'over' and φερειν 'to carry'. So a metaphor is a particular set of linguistic processes whereby aspects of one object are 'carried over' or transferred to another object: that the second object is spoken of as if it were the first, is an understanding that has become commonplace in the literature of management.[10] What is perhaps not so well understood is that the transference is idiosyncratic: individual readers transfer diverse attributes of the illustrative object back to the subject with varying levels of intensity and identification. So whether we understand metaphor as the 'dreamwork of language', as a 'peremptory invitation to discovery', as a conduit, as spellbinding, or as a 'weapon', and whether we find them to be fun or deeply challenging, tricksters or friends,[11] metaphors become fascinating and contentious when it is understood that different readers link different attributes across the domains: that interpretive reconstructions of metaphorically made meaning is infinitely variable.

While the etymological explanation of the Greek origin of the word metaphor explains the process of metaphorical meaning-making, it does not elucidate its ontological significance. It is this latter area that is much debated in the literature of metaphor theory. Interpretation and definition of what a metaphor is, range from the so-called Aristotelian view that perceives it to be decorative ornamentation, extrinsic to meaning-making, to the so-called Platonic perception that all words are metaphors, and reality a symbolically fashioned construct dependent upon the polysemous play of metaphorical connection and classification.[12]

In critical discussions of management theory, much of the credit for sparking and fuelling awareness of the part that metaphors play in the construction of meaning is attributed to Gareth Morgan's seminal work on metaphors of organizations, *Images of Organizations* (1986), a book which effectively clinched his winning stance in a debate he had conducted with Pinder and Bourgeois in the pages of *The Administrative Science Quarterly*.[13] It was a debate that honed in on dramatically opposed views as to the perceived role of metaphor, as described above. Pinder and Bourgeois, Aristotelian interpreters of metaphor, regard it as a departure from ordinary modes of language, as a fanciful 'embroidery' of the facts. They see metaphors as an 'add-on', something additional to meaning. In Morgan's Platonic view, metaphor is understood as a holistic device, and is seen as a means through which we experience the facts: 'a basic structural form of experience through which human beings engage, organize and understand their world . . . [these] tropes . . . are crucial in structuring conscious and unconscious activity' (Morgan 1983b: 601–2).

As I read it, the acerbic exchange was not just about the role and function of metaphor as a trope, though that of course still continues to be the site of an on-going intellectual contest,[14] but was the site of a struggle to present a dominating worldview to readers; and although theoretical debate on an 'approved' role for metaphor in the texts of management was a new and exciting development in the management scholarship of the 1980s, other disciplines, philosophy, psychology and literary criticism for example, had long been engaged in this exploration.[15]

Gareth Morgan's early work on the place of metaphor studies in management theory marked out the base territory from which almost all subsequent work in this area has proceeded, but in 1986 the publication of his *Images of Organizations* signalled a seismic shift in the ontological foundations of organization theory. Morgan demonstrated not only that a variety of perceptions of what an organization is, may be conveyed metaphorically (it may be described as a machine, an organism or a brain, as culture, a political system, or a psychic prison, and as flux and change or as an instrument of domination), but that persistent use of one or other of these metaphors also leads to the institutionalizing of the perspective the metaphor represents.

Institutionalized themselves, these metaphors, now root metaphors permanently embedded in the language of organizational theory, have faded into the assumed worldview they convey, and despite the plethora of metaphor studies that have crowded into management studies through the last two decades, have remained largely undisturbed.

Studies of organizations based on interpretation and analysis of metaphor, which sailed in the choppy wake of Morgan's seminal work, range from Tsoukas' (1991) theory of the transformational knowledge function of metaphors in organizational science, to Dunford and Palmer's (1996) empirical analyses of metaphors in popular management discourse, and include an extensive and still growing literature. Some papers within this extensive literature attempt to impose taxonomies of the assumptions underlying the use of metaphor in the literature of organization studies (Inns 2002), others have continued to punch their way through the ontological debate already outlined (Alvesson 1993), and others again have sought to bring their work on metaphor into the more contemporary arena of postmodern discussions of language in our theory-making (Parker 1993). It is the third group that provides comment most pertinent to my present inquiry, for it is a literature that returns to interdisciplinary work on metaphor theory and introduces the concept of root metaphors – one of the few areas of inquiry into metaphors in management theory, identified by Oswick and Grant (1996), which is not yet exhausted.

Root metaphors

Christopher Norris (1988) has suggested, with more than a tinge of sarcasm, 'that Derrida has shown that (hasn't he?) there is really no difference between philosophy and literature; that all philosophical concepts come down to metaphors in the end; and that therefore we had much better . . . read all texts with an eye on their covert structures of figural meaning' (p. 12). Lennie (1999) too cites Derrida, when in the context of a reminder of Derrida's 'there is nothing outside the text', that 'all experience is textual in character', and that this 'uncompromising textuality is, in essence, metaphoric', he recalls Derrida's 'what we take to be a concept . . . is a metaphor whose metaphoricity we have conveniently forgotten' (p. 44).

In order to address Norris' rhetorical query, and also the gap in management theory identified by Oswick and Grant as above, I think we 'had better' read metaphors with 'an eye' on the philosophical concepts that they represent.

In *World Hypotheses* (1942), Stephen Pepper argued that the great philosophies all depend on one of four root metaphors (formism, mechanism, organicism and contextualism) and they are great because they have so far survived the criticism of rival metaphors. Each view of the totality of things claims supremacy, but none has been able to annihilate the others. His root metaphor theory 'is the theory that a world hypothesis to cover all the facts is framed in the first instance on the basis of a rather small set of facts and then expanded in reference so as to cover all the facts. The set of facts which inspired the hypothesis is the original root metaphor' (Pepper 1972: 19–20). While such a boast and a classification must necessarily, in a postmodern age, be seen as marginalizing individual interpretation, and exclusive of the infinity of other possible classification types and patterns, yet Pepper's work continues to focus attention on the function of root metaphor in both the conveying and the forming of worldviews.

It is the holistic or gestalt view of metaphor, described above as Platonic that underpins Pepper's notion of root metaphors. In his philosophy root metaphors are understood as more than tropes: they are metaphors which suggest an abstraction, at a 'third remove' from the perceived world of sensible interpretation, and they relate, at a profound level, to values and aesthetics rather that the perceived world of the senses.

Kenneth Burke (1989) identifies with this view of the profound functioning of metaphors. He says of them that his 'primary concern . . . will be not with their purely figurative usage, but with their role in the discovery and description of "the truth"'. When differentiating the four tropes, he also says of metaphor that its particular function is to represent perspective: 'for metaphor we could substitute perspective' – by which I understand him to mean 'worldview' (pp. 247–8). I do not see 'metaphor' as a substitute for 'perspective', 'worldview' or for that matter 'paradigm', but I do see it as both representing and promoting a perspective, or worldview. I also see this perception of the role of metaphor as basic to any reading that acknowledges the seminal role of metaphor, particularly root metaphors, in the construction and interpretation of texts.

Morgan too, in his early work, understood root metaphors as 'a basic structural form of experience through which human beings engage, organize and understand their world' (1983b: 601). In his frame-breaking *Images of Organizations* (1986), he acknowledges his debt to Pepper's philosophical treatise on root metaphors; and his prismatic reconstruction of management theory, based on Pepper's notion of root metaphors, has become the 'sandcastle' (Oswick and Grant 1996: 214) that neither attack nor siege can wash away.

Turner explains the root metaphor that creates perspective or world view as a system, a rhetorical construction which is based on a 'sentence level "root metaphor" from which grows "many shoots" and which, taken as a whole, constitutes an entire system or way of looking at things'. As Turner explains it, constructions of root metaphors 'capture' meaning and shape it much as the shaping of meaning is accomplished by the archetypal thinking established in myth. In both processes, meaning evolves through building a system of connections that are based in the unique experience of the individual but gain coherence and legitimization in the common acceptance of imaginative linkings.[16]

Ricoeur describes this 'network' of meaning-making as 'intersignification': 'Metaphorical functioning would be completely inadequate as a way of expressing the different temporality of symbols' if it were not for 'a whole array of intersignifications . . . one metaphor in effect calls for another and each one stays alive by conserving its power to evoke the whole network'. This network, which he also describes as root metaphors, engenders both assembly and scattering:

> The network engenders what we can call root metaphors, metaphors which, on the one hand, have the power to bring together the partial metaphors borrowed from the diverse fields of our experience and thereby to assure them a kind of equilibrium. On the other hand, they have the availability to engender a conceptual diversity, I mean an unlimited number of potential interpretations at a conceptual level. Root metaphors assemble and scatter.
>
> (Ricoeur 1976: 64)

Reading at a deeper level excavates this web, this play of meaning, which weaves through the connotations of words with emotive links to other texts within the text and beyond it. Bringing this web, this 'network' to light exposes the 'assembly' in the subtext. When revealed, root metaphors, portray a worldview which may otherwise be disguised by an espoused narrative, and in so doing, fragment the meaning of the dominant text: 'Root metaphors . . . assemble subordinate images together, and they scatter concepts at a higher level' (ibid.). It is in the archaeology of a rhetorical or deconstructive reading that we find root metaphors: metaphors that work together to create Turner's 'system' of meaning.

This is an image of metaphors working together in a discursive system (I prefer to think of it as a pattern) that depends upon their interaction to make meaning, and ultimately to portray a worldview; for root metaphors elaborate, extend and refine the connections forged in the initial comparisons suggested by individual metaphors. Working together they image aspects of a worldview. Root metaphors, as discursive patterns, are representations of meaning that operate within paradigms or worldviews.

I do not see root metaphors, understood in this way, as equating to an abstract philosophical stance, 'worldview' or 'world hypothesis' as described by Pepper and discussed by Tsoukas,[17] rather I do see them as manifestations of perceptions and constructions of our world, as the expressive means by which worldviews are revealed to us. They are to be discovered in the language of the text: not extrapolated from philosophical ideas about the genesis and promulgation of meaning. As I understand them, they do not pre-exist as an abstract, absolute form of knowing as Pepper's use of the term 'root metaphor' seems to suggest.

In the literature of management, Morgan's work has ensured that root metaphors are generally now recognized for the role they perform in the formation, and in the breaking, of frames and paradigms. In even the most seemingly scientific texts, root metaphors may be seen to inform the position taken by the author. Thus root metaphors are not frames, or lenses, or paradigms or conduits: but frames, lenses and conduits have all been called into service as metaphors for our manner of perceiving abstract notions, such as organizations.[18] Nor are all metaphors root metaphors, though in any given text many of the metaphors employed may well find a place in the larger, perhaps not so visible, construction, representation and communication of perspective or worldviews.

Root metaphors are not the figurative devices that appear on the surface of the text, the metaphors visible when the reader looks at the text. Root metaphors gradually emerge from the subtext when the reader looks through the text and into the conceptual understandings suggested by the play of meaning dancing beyond the familiar signifiers, and their linking attributes, in the surface text. Looking at the text, we find images of a familiar world, representations of what we already know, much as a mirror reflects the expected but also adds detail, luminosity and perhaps magnification. To look through the text requires an act of the imagination, a walk with Alice as she steps through the looking-glass. There, where logic is paradoxical, dialogue is multivocal monologue, law is contrary, and physical form is deceptive, her explorations lead her haphazardly towards the abstract 'reality' of Plato's third remove.

Yet if root metaphors beat at the heart of expressed meaning-making then the root metaphor which expresses the source of the coherence of described experience, may also, when uncritically accepted by the reader, become the vehicle that persuades the reader to identify with the worldview of the writer. It is in this role that we may also see them as the begetters, and perhaps colonizers, of the reader's worldview, as well as the purveyors of the writer's philosophy and belief.

In a deconstructive reading the root metaphor is exposed: when the covers of its contextual bed are drawn back, the nakedness of its primitive identity is revealed. The function of metaphor is seen to not only prompt new perceptive insights, but also to lead continually to other associations. Metaphor shows how meaning is not contained in a sign but refers endlessly to other signs, other meanings – creating what Lacan (1977) describes as a 'chain of signifiers' (p. 154), leading to his notion of the ephemeral, floating nature of meaning: the possibility of signifying 'this' while writing 'that'; of an intended 'that' being interpreted as a 'this' determines multiple autonomous meanings. I see root metaphors – as discussed above – as providing the conceptual basis from which much of my textual interpretation and analysis stems, and despite the extensive literature on metaphors now completed in management studies, there has, as yet, been little exploration of their role in the construction of management theory.[19]

Cazal and Inns (1998) display much of the ambivalence towards metaphor that permeates comment on it by management theorists. On the one hand they are generally inclined to nod obeisance to ambiguity, paradox and play, but on the other, prompted by a knee-jerk reaction, they harbour a forlorn hope that metaphors can be tamed. Somewhere, somehow there must be a system, an 'organization of metaphors' that will retain and control them. They cite their reading of Lacan, Ricoeur and Saussure as they explain that metaphors are ambiguous, complex and multilayered, but creeping through in the subtext is a continuing worry: they cite Rapport's accusation that metaphors are 'mixed up' in the 'sharp practice' of rhetoric; they cite Schlanger as they warn that metaphors 'unlock new issues . . . but they do not give us answers'; and finally they warn that 'metaphorization leads the way for new perspectives, but it does not in itself directly provide or generate knowledge; this makes it both fecund and dangerous' (p. 190). Their fear reminds me that Plato banned poets from his ideal republic because they are dangerous.[20] The words of poets incite and excite. They appeal to the emotions: rationality may be threatened. Although it is perhaps more fashionable now to seem to be on the side of metaphor, a positivist suspicion of a world and worldview that cannot be fixed still generates antagonistic fear, a fear that masquerades as the champion of postmodern sensibilities, but is still covertly expressed.

Some of the significant theoretical work that has followed in Morgan's wake has been collected in the volume edited by Grant and Oswick (1996b). It provides a comprehensive, yet succinct, summary of the various routes that metaphor research in organization theory has travelled through the last two decades. The editors pay tribute to the 'amount of ground covered' by Gareth Morgan's research, from the general role and scope of metaphor to the application of specific metaphors to organizations and organizational processes, and detail the 'sand castle' wars in organization theory that his work sparked. They note that he has been accused of 'going too far', in attributing ways of thinking to metaphor, that organization theory is now just a plethora, a 'supermarket' (Reed 1990) of metaphors, as well as of having failed to go far enough; that the metaphors he proposed now 'reify and ideologically distort' organizational theory, and that metaphors distort scientific knowledge. But despite the criticism, they conclude that through all of this Morgan's sand castle has survived relatively intact.

Oswick and Grant also arrive at two more general conclusions pertinent to my inquiry: first that many organizational researchers 'have experienced difficulty in disentangling the concept of metaphor from its original roots in philosophy and linguistics' and therefore tend to generalize the 'organization of metaphors' rather than 'metaphors of organizations'; and secondly that researchers tend to adopt polarized philosophical positions, along the lines that I have described above as Aristotelian or Platonic.

Noting Oswick and Grant's elaboration of the first point, that 'metaphors of organizations', variously named as 'dominant metaphors, root metaphors, embedded metaphors or meaningful metaphors' are still very inadequately understood, I firmed up my intention to make more 'transparent [some of] the metaphors and groups of metaphors' I might discover in my reading of the management theory texts selected for analysis. I saw my own reading of metaphor theory,[21] sourced from philosophy and linguistics as well as literary theory, as immediately pertinent to this intention.

Oswick and Grant's second point, that organizational research on metaphor has become a divisive exercise as opposing camps line up artillery with which to mow down the opposition, portrays confrontational stances to which my inquiry will offer an alternative. I will discuss in my next chapter literary theory that recognizes the plurivocality[22] of texts, and the participation of the reader in textual meaning-making. Postmodernism has now brought metaphor into an enlarged arena where it takes its place in broader discussions of language in management theory-making.

Morgan, who had 'more or less refrained from reading and writing about metaphor in recent years in favour of what he calls the praxis of 'doing metaphor', was persuaded to contribute an 'afterword' to the Grant and Oswick volume, which he subtitled 'Is there anything more to be said about metaphor?' (1996: 227–8). He makes two points that particularly support the emphasis I have placed on the central role of metaphor in the rhetoricity of texts: 'metaphor as a primal process is ontological' which he describes as belonging to 'the realm of being'; and metaphors are also epistemological, 'they give us specific frames for viewing the world'.

It is the latter view that underpins a consensual position that recognizes the plurivocality of our texts, for although many of wavelets of a literature once swelled by papers on metaphors in management theory were still washing shorewards in the late 1990s, by then a deeper current was making itself felt: a profound and increasingly vocal text-based challenge to modernism was gathering momentum.[23] Much of the questioning of assumptions, and the positing of different and multiple worldviews that this challenge, and the on-going ontological debate that has ensued, are beyond the scope of this inquiry, but to the extent that this literature has focused scholarly attention on language and text, it is very relevant.

Management theorists on deconstruction

In so far as text analysis in management has aimed to deconstruct disciplinary norms and statements, and has aimed to do this through overturning established textual hierarchies and articulating multiple meanings, it may be regarded as experiencing a postmodern phase. It is a phase that is characterized by strategies that enable the recognition and articulation of the plurivocality of texts.

At a very broad level, postmodern inquiry in management theory is adeptly summed up by Karen Legge.[24] She argues that whereas modernists believe in fundamental truths 'out there', empirically discovered, deductively reasoned, and represented in a language 'subservient to this reality ('logocentrism')', postmodernists subscribe to the theory that meaning is ultimately undecidable and uncontrollable. In support of this latter view, Legge – citing extensive reading of Derrida, and Cooper's 1989 analysis of Derrida's ideas – isolates the binary oppositions around which texts are structured. She also emphasizes the deconstructive reading of texts, a continuous 'process' that is the essence of undecidability, as a determinant of postmodern epistemological positioning.

I will shortly turn to some examples of the deconstruction of management theory, but first, because some of the examples of deconstruction by management theorists that I have discovered seem to recognize binary oppositions in texts, but not the ultimate 'indecidability' of texts, it is significant that Legge has this to say:

> That meaning is ultimately 'undecidable', is because not only are texts structured around binary oppositions ('good'/'bad', 'formal'/'informal') in which one term dominates the other ('male'/'female') but the relationship between opposing terms is one of mutual definition ('black'/'white'). To use Cooper's (1989: 483) expression they 'inhabit' each other. Hence individual terms 'give way to a process where opposites merge in a constant undecideable exchange of attribute' (Norris 1987: 35, cited in

Cooper 1989: 483). Derrida shows, for example, how the ancient Greek term pharmakon is intrinsically undecidable since it could mean both remedy and poison and good and bad simultaneously (Cooper 1989: 486).

(Legge 1995: 302)[25]

Comment on postmodernism in management theory tends to concur with Legge's view that, whereas modernism insists that the only legitimate reading of a text is one which centres the subject of the writing as intended by the author, postmodernism decentres the subject and asserts the primacy of the reader(s). The latter, Derridean, position allows for multiple readings of a text – allows each reading its own validity.

Yet the 'undecidability' of textual meaning should ensure that the deconstructive overturning of textual hierarchies does not simply install a new, reversed, hierarchy, and thus continue the prioritizing of structure over a reading process that is infinitely incomplete:

> Further, in reading a text, a reader might choose to deconstruct or overturn the hierarchies within it ('her'/'his'). But the reflexive logic of deconstruction does not allow this reversal to result in a new and permanent, if opposite, hierarchy. This would be merely another instance of prioritising structure over process, in which opposing terms are kept separate and discrete rather than inhabiting each other. The process of deconstruction must be continuous – a process Derrida terms 'metaphorisation'.

(ibid.)

In the scholarship of management, Robert Chia[26] not only most clearly spells out the indeterminacy that 'adheres in writing's very essence', the metaphorization of endlessly morphing meaning, but is also alert to Derrida's reluctance to suggest even an approximate definition of deconstruction in conceptual, methodological or 'even' philosophical terms. On this latter issue he cites Derrida (as cited in Wood and Bernasconi 1985):

> All sentences of the type 'deconstruction is X' or 'deconstruction is not X' a priori miss the point, which is to say that they are at least false. As you know one of the principal things at stake in what is called in my texts 'deconstruction', is precisely the delimitation of ontology and above all of the third person present indicative: S is P.

(Chia 1994: 785)

The point here is of course, as Chia further explains, that wherever deconstruction begins to be thought of as an 'is' or 'is not', we are pulled back into 'the organizing force behind western logocentric thinking'.[27]

To illustrate what is to be avoided in 'logocentric thinking' (the belief that our ideas, thoughts, and actions are grounded in a world circumscribed by original and indubitable facts) Chia helpfully recalls Fenollosa's image of western languages as shaped by a 'medieval' 'brickyard' logic:

> . . . thought is a kind of brickyard. It is baked into little hard units or concepts. These are piled in rows according to size and then labeled with words for future use. This use consists in picking out a few bricks, each by its convenient label, and sticking them together into a sort of wall called a sentence, by the use of either white mortar for the positive copula 'is' or of the black mortar for the negative copula 'is not'.
>
> (ibid.)

My reading of the few examples of deconstructive analyses of text attempted by management theorists, as discussed in the next section of this chapter, suggests that the argumentative is/is not dichotomy postmodern management theorists proclaim against is, in practice, often uncomfortably close to the nub of their critical practice, and this despite claims to espouse a theory base that eschews such an outcome.

Chia himself, for example, argues for this not that, that 'this' is better understood as 'that'. He says in his abstract 'I argue here that decision is better understood. . . .' He seems to be thinking and writing of an either/or world, setting up dichotomous constructs which we expect to compete, assuming that one will be seen to win out against the other. Yet in a footnote he insists that the formation of dualities through the constant usage of oppositional terms suggests a world of strong unchanging properties; and takes up a critical perspective on this. In his attempt to dislodge the endless debate based on antithetic stationary positioning that he describes as failing to examine 'the relationship between that which is treated as separate and opposing', he cites the provocative phrase given us by Elias (1992): 'intellectual apartheid'.

An alternative worldview that Chia theorizes, even while operating otherwise, returns us again to Ernesto Fenollosa who based his observations on a comparative study of Chinese and European languages. Fenollosa (1969) argues that poetry and music, like the Chinese language, because they are not 'overly dependent on grammatical logic' are able to deal with the 'concrete of nature', not 'with rows of "separate" particulars' (p. 377). To the extent that Chia's work endorses poetry and art as an enabling approach to an aesthetic logic, 'one that escapes the rigid is/is not and either/or conceptual categories of grammatical logic', when reading this paper I felt myself to be in congenial company.

It is a paper that anticipates his later book, a much more sustained attack, on representationalism.[28] In his review of the book Tony Watson highlights Chia's suggestion that representationalism, as witnessed in organization theory, refers to 'attempts to accurately capture and represent an already constituted external reality', and that 'out there' is in some sense independent of the language or 'texts' which are deployed to relate to it. But Watson also notes, creeping into Chia's tone, the 'paranoia' of the postmodernist writer whose tone suggests a perception that s/he is operating in a milieu unsympathetic to postmodernism. I, like Watson, am more comfortable identifying with the Chia who sees himself as 'swimming upstream' where 'theorising is deemed to be exploratory, emergent and processual in character'. And I also concur with Watson in particularly liking Chia's description of research and inquiry as 'a matter of continually reweaving webs of beliefs to produce new and novel insight into the human condition' as we increasingly abandon attempts to 'converge at a single point called truth'.[29]

Other critics and commentators who have embroiled themselves in controversy over deconstructive readings of management texts have also hit upon Chia's paper, but there is general agreement that it is a timely publication because it challenges styles of thinking that have been taken for granted.[30] Weiskopf and Willmott for example, in their critical appraisal of Chia's book, find an 'either/or dichotomy of orthodox/deconstruction or modern/postmodern styles of thinking' that suggests the difficulty of 'escaping the problematic of dualistic thinking and theorising'; and they prefigure the position that I will read and write from in my analysis when they point to the contrast of their own positioning with that of Chia's:

> In contrast to Chia, we assume the necessity of positioning ourselves . . . observers/subjects/representors in relation to the observed/object/ reality of the texts which we interpret and criticise. If this view is accepted, then the attempt to replace 'modern mainstream analysis' with 'postmodern reflexive analysis' is futile. It is necessary to acknowledge their continuities as well as their differing – positive and deconstructive – emphases.
>
> (Weiskopf and Willmott 1997: 7)

As the 1990s drew to a close, this response to Chia's book typifies the moves towards a wider recognition of, and welcome for, the multiple perspectives, inclusivity and subjectivity of interpretivism that underpin glimpses of a linguistically constituted future for management theorists. Tsoukas[31] had firmly ensconced language centre stage in 'the latest thinking in organizational behaviour' when he declared the main message of his book to be 'the increasing appreciation of language and, thus interpretation in shaping social reality', adding, 'The kind of thinking that places interpretation right at the centre of management is relatively new and its consequences are important'.

And yet, although the closing years of the second millennium at least succeeded in pushing text analysis towards the centre of theory discussion in management scholarship, it should be clearly acknowledged that those who position postmodern sensibilities at the centre of organizational theorizing are still engaged in heated debates,[32] debate that tends to centre on the simplistic question of whether or not postmodernism gives up entirely on notions of 'truth' and 'progress'. At a more generalized level, it reflects debate between the New Humanists and poststructuralists that has raged through the closing decades of the twentieth century: is there, or is there finally not, textual meaning on which readers can/should agree? In the next chapter I will outline my position on this, supported by the literary critics with whose theorizing I identify.

For the moment, and in company with other management theory readers I find myself beset by the 'various and slippery meanings – not all of them compatible – ascribed' to the terms modernism and postmodernism and the 'contradictions and confusions [that] are created making it difficult to express something meaningful'. I also concur with Alvesson's further claim that:

> The persistent and expanding literature that includes references to these elusive concepts often clouds and distorts new ideas for understanding contemporary phenomena and for carrying out social research [because] the words seem to invite sweeping statements and thereby muddled thinking.
>
> (Alvesson 1995: 1047)

Nevertheless, no matter what names it goes by, nor what generalized fashion and befuddlement it is dressed in, the 'postmodern' scholarship emerging from these contested fields has, couched within it, theory-building argument that takes as its concern the analysis of the texts that form the canon of the management theory on which the discipline of management is built. It is a development that has supported critics who have taken initiatives in the deconstruction of management theory texts, and in the next section I describe and explore examples.

Deconstructions of management texts

The deconstruction of management theory is, as I write, still no more than a fledgling activity teetering from the nest. Stablein (1996) has pointed out that, 'Texts which are considered significant and influential in forming our knowledge of organization are the appropriate raw data [for the deconstructionist]' because 'It is "foundational" texts that constitute our well-accepted, comfortable empirical reality' (p. 512). And Kilduff (1993) too, has noted that many foundational texts 'give the appearance of straightforward objectivity' (p. 13) and this 'appearance' is perhaps one of the reasons why they should be challenged. Yet scholars who have worked with management theory texts in this way, viewing them as the raw data, ripe for text analysis, are still lonely and scattered voices.

Writing in 1999, Calás and Smircich note examples of deconstruction that range across accounting, information management, and marketing: from the field of organization theory they provide a very short list of eight papers, only four of which are deconstructions of management theory texts: Calás and Smircich (1991) have deconstructed organizational leadership literature, specifically the texts of Barnard, McGregor, Mintzberg and Peters and Waterman; Calás (1993) has deconstructed the literature of charismatic leadership; Martin and Knopoff (1997) have deconstructed passages from Weber's theory of bureaucracy; and Mumby and Putnam (1992) have deconstructed the concept of bounded rationality in management literature. Also of their company, but not cited by Calás and Smircich, are Kilduff (1993) with a frequently cited deconstruction of March and Simon's *Organizations*; Chia (1994) with a deconstructive analysis of the concept of decision; and the Bowring (2000) deconstruction of institutional theory that postdates their paper. Only two of these seven papers, Calás and Smircich (1991) and Kilduff (1993) are built around 'closer than close' analysis of a specific management theory text.

In their analysis and critical comment the authors of all seven papers recognize as key deconstructive strategies: the decentring of the subject, the recognition of binary oppositions in the text, and the reversal of this opposition when the privileged term is replaced by the submerged term. They also claim to recognize that deconstructive endings do not end in the overturning, or reversal, of the standard reading: that although they might well begin there, that they go on to show that there is no ending to the discovery of meaning in texts because displacing and disseminating standard interpretations creates undecidability.

Deconstructive practice does not, however, necessarily reflect espoused theory. Critical readers who argue 'against closure over what we – organizational scholars – could think and say as organizational theory and research' and who seek to 'deny . . . any claim of solid ground or final word' (Cálas and Smircich 1991: 597–8) may in practice simply replace one kind of closure with another, replace one subject or term with its opposite. They may seek out the binary oppositions of the text, but fail to show the restless displacement and dissemination of meaning; and talk of plurivocality, the many voices, whispering and calling in the spaces and margins of the text, but deny the ultimate elusiveness of meaning.

I see a reinstatement of definitive meaning (a quasimodernist approach to reading and interpretation) as the outcome of the 'deconstructive' readings of management theory that arrive at (unintended) closure because a politicized position has predetermined the role deconstruction is expected to play. Calás and Smircich, for example, tell us that they will use 'feminist deconstructive strategies' to 'expose' the rhetoric and culture of organizational research and theory (p. 567); and Mumby and Putnam subtitle their paper 'A feminist reading of bounded rationality'. Feldman (1998) writes of 'the assumption and implications of the notions of deconstruction as they are found in writers concerned with organization theory', that 'Deconstruction posits the oppositional nature of language and symbolism as a violent hierarchy and seeks to overturn this hierarchy to achieve human freedom', and that 'Stable structures of meaning are needed over time to find a traditional and thus legitimate base for business ethics' (p. 59). Such closed 'deconstructive' interpretations become easy targets for deconstruction's critics.

Where text analysis simply overturns standard meaning, and substitutes, for example, the object for the subject of the text, female for male gender, the disenfranchised for the enfranchised, then a 'reading' may be a rewriting of the original text as a concrete 'product', an 'effect' of the reader's imaginative response. That all readings are effectively reader rewritings is thoroughly argued in the literature of reception theory,[33] but in the literature of management this is, as yet, largely undiscovered territory. The 'deconstructions' on which I comment below tend to present reinterpretations of theory texts as 'truth' claims.

Because it was a pioneering work, Calás and Smircich's (1991) often cited feminist deconstruction of 'four classic texts of the organization literature' is significant. It is presented as a rereading of standard versions of these classics, and the authors explain that they selected these particular texts because they have two claims in common: they were 'written more for organizational practitioners than for the scholarly community', but were yet 'influential in both communities'; and though written in different periods of time, 'each text offers a definition and a prescription for effective leadership' (p. 568).

Along with the generalized claim that the deconstructive strategies they employ will help us to understand that any body of knowledge to which we might subscribe is 'linguistically constituted' (there is no referent external to language, but only 'the rhetorical and linguistic forms' which signify our assumptions about the way the world is) they say that their particular aim is to show that for every linguistic construct we employ, there is an 'oppositional term' hidden in the margins and spaces of the text: that meaning excluded by, or submerged in, this ambiguity is revealed in their deconstruction of the text. They describe their deconstructive strategies as 'intended to enhance the doubleness of every discourse' (p. 569) and somehow also go on to assume that this 'doubleness' is synonymous with polysemy, the multiple meaning of words. The assumption of 'doubleness' underpins their alternative rereading of the selected texts as they seek to expose 'some of the rhetorical and cultural conditions that have sustained the organizational leadership literature as a seductive game' (p. 567). It leads to their presenting their 'reinterpretations of each book's meaning based on feminist poststructuralist analyses of Freud's work' (p. 571) as if these readings claim some kind of authenticity, some kind of truth, beyond that of their subjective experience, beyond their individualistic 'writing' of their own text.

Confusion here is exacerbated by inconsistencies in the poststructuralist theory espoused and the demonstrated outcomes of their deconstructive practice. On the one hand they theorize the 'undecidability' of meaning, and on the other, in stressing the dichotomy, rather than the polysemy, of the words they play with, they claim that their poststructuralist approach differs from that of other organizational theorists with 'more typical interpretive approaches'. They charge the latter with *resorting* to 'subjective and inter-subjective understanding' which lead them to posit the possibility of '*real final understandings* [original italics] located in subjectivity'.

Yet ironically this surely is exactly what they, Calás and Smircich do: they allow their 'reading effects' (p. 570) to take on, in the intertextual context in which they choose to place them, a concretized, politicized role. In fact, they seek assistance from the dictionary to discover meanings to support their argument. They clearly conclude that the 'reality' in the 'leadership research/literature' they have 'reread' is of a 'homosocial libidinal economy of competitiveness and glory' (p. 593).

In their comments on deconstruction, Calás and Smircich espouse theory that returns always to Derrida's notion of 'différance', to the multiple layers, many spaces, and endless postponement of meaning, but in practice they present a provocative reading as if it represents a non-negotiable truth. It is exactly this delusion, this conclusive and provocative positioning, that leaves them open to Mintzberg's (1991) scathing response to their efforts: a wickedly undermining satire which he wrote in the guise of a complimentary letter.

Addressing the authors, Mintzberg says, 'What undermines the argument, however, is a methodology that in your hands proves impotent', and he then goes on to tell a 'sexual joke'.

> It's about this man who goes to a psychiatrist and responds to every Rorschach he is shown, with – 'that is two people (let us say) fornicating'. After several of these, the psychiatrist stops and says, 'You are the most sexually obsessed person I have ever come across!' 'Sexually obsessed? Me? It's you who keeps showing those dirty pictures!'
>
> (p. 602)

The point of the joke is, of course, that sexual obsession emanates from the imagination of the reader, not from the text read. Had Calás and Smircich taken responsibility for their own reading, self-consciously reflecting on the formative experience that Mintzberg accuses them of not sharing, rather than objectifying it out into a 'problem' of a 'homosocial libidinal economy' community, then they might have parried the most damaging impacts of his attack. Had they acknowledged that their reading (interpretation) is a 'writing' of their own text, an outcome of their own worldview, then Mintzberg's charge – that they have found, 'read into', his text an image of the 'homosocial libidinal economy' that they presuppose to exist there – could have been subverted. And it may also be that Mintzberg's stinging reply has left the management community disinclined to revisit this territory.

I would personally be more comfortable with their interpretation if, instead of arguing definitively that the text means as described above, they were to acknowledge that their reading, while valid for them, might not be so for others. Deconstruction based on dictionary meanings, as conducted by Calás and Smircich, assumes that texts are paralysed, that the meanings of words inscribed in a lexicon are, like the figures on Keats' Grecian urn, caught forever in a frozen moment of time. What is caught, moreover, is generally the denotation, the literal meaning of the word as interpreted by the lexicographer. But it can be argued that words without a context simply fail to mean. Given a context it can be argued that the connotations of the word, its emotive impact, carry more meaning than its conventional meaning, or semantic sense.

Perhaps as Fenollosa's comments, noted earlier, suggest, the poets intuitively understand texts in ways that critics, including postmodernists, struggle to accommodate. For me the poet John Keats best sums up the paradoxes of printed text – its frozen representations of passionate thought. Keats paints an image of a Grecian urn. Two figures are poised to kiss, a piper is piping an unheard note, people are sweetly caught in unexplained ritual. They are all forever telling and forever not telling.[34] They are forever engaging our intellect and our emotions, and forever denying answers. Keats' famous conclusion, that all we need to know is that truth is beauty and beauty truth may be a clichéd impasse, or it may be a challenge to the precocity of intellects that would be more than finite. To me it suggests that we should look to the 'how' of our 'sayings': that if our theorists' texts have aesthetic appeal, then this is in itself a kind of truth with which we would do well to engage.

Despite all of the above this is still a 'seminal' – Minzberg's words again! (1991: 602) – paper. It argues against closure; it employs deconstructive techniques previously unfamiliar in management scholarship; and notably, it proclaims *'the need to accept the temporality of our knowledge and the need to write and re-write organizations and organizational theory'* (Calás and Smircich 1991: 598, original italics). It speaks directly to my inquiry in that it presents a text analysis of foundational management theory texts with a focus on 'the social role played by organizational research and theory (writing)' (p. 568). Citing their own earlier paper, 1988, Calás and Smircich describe writing as 'another form of organizational practice; that of the academic community, whose purpose is the creation of knowledge for other members of society' (ibid.).

Two years after the fracas with Mintzberg, Calás (1993) published another deconstruction of the literature of leadership. In this paper she spells out the steps that she claims all deconstructive analyses follow: first the reader 'focuses on a suspected binary opposition where one term seems to be privileged while the other is ignored or submerged' (p. 310); second the reader reverses this order, replacing the privileged with the submerged term; and third the deconstructionist displaces the argument by trying to show that the hierarchical ordering of the text has not simply been reversed, but has been disseminated into other parts of the text. She claims to follow this 'textual strategy . . . a form of commentary over certain texts' (p. 307), and adds that her approach to textual analysis is mostly associated with that of Jacques Derrida.

To the extent that her reading of the leadership literature questions gaps in the text, and makes 'truth' undecidable (Calás 1993: 307), her reading has been influenced by French poststructuralism. In other ways it is very unlike the deconstructions of, for example, the perhaps best known and most often cited deconstruction, Barthes' (1974) reading of *S/Z*. It is unlike in that it does not linger over particular words and phrases. Calás' focus of interest is the argument of the text, the logic of what is said about whom. She does not explore the poetry of word and phrase. She does not, in short, engage in closer than close reading of the play, ambiguities, connections and ironies that so delighted the poststructuralists. She does not fully heed her own 'note' (1993: 325) on deconstruction where she describes it as 'a very close reading'.

It is in this same note that she records the most apt explanation of deconstruction in organization studies that I have encountered:

> It is important to notice that deconstruction is *productive* in the sense that the analyst must articulate, 'invent' as if were, the textual strategy in accordance to the text being analyzed. No deconstruction would end up being like any other. If it were like something else, it would not be deconstruction for its uniqueness hinges, precisely, on the productivity of language – that is the multiplicity of possible interpretations elicited in any one reading of the text. However this must not be confused with 'free-for-all' interpretation. In fact deconstruction is *very close* reading of how 'rational writing' betrays itself . . . [it is] a way to open up a space for questioning what might seem unproblematic otherwise. But that space is never settled . . .
>
> (ibid.)

Calás, in company with so many other critical readers, seems to be more *au fait* with the theory than she is comfortable with theory-based practice.

A very early example of deconstruction in organization studies, was provided by Joanne Martin (1990), who promised to introduce her readers to deconstruction by reconstructing a deconstructed story from a feminist perspective. She models much of her critical reading on that of the literary critic Terrence Eagleton, a Marxist critic who seeks out ideology, rather than elusive meaning, in texts and so sets about dismantling the dichotomy of the text. Working with the main narrative of the text, she effectively displaces the privileged (male) subject, but does not pursue the notion of dissemination that a closer analysis would entail.

Another early feminist deconstruction of organization theory, the work of Mumby and Putnam (1992) is described by its authors as 'a poststructuralist feminist reading of Herbert Simon's construct, bounded rationality' (p. 465). Yet again these authors note that the aim of deconstruction is not to reverse binary options but to problematize the idea of opposition, but they see this as creating a space for a middle voice, not as plurivocality. They are forthright in their recommendation that deconstruction be put to use as a political tool in order to enable feminists to expose oppressive hierarchies. Seeking to do this, they describe Simon's notion of bounded rationality as a text-created fiction, and from that point on explore the concept rather than the text.

Five years later Martin, with Knopff (1997) again set about uncovering gender implications in apparently gender-neutral language, this time through an analysis of key passages selected from Weber's writings. They declare their feminist perspective, describe their reading strategy as deconstruction, and claim that it enables them to study the way in which language and/or silence may be instrumental in suppressing subordinate groups. Their stated aim is to expose layers of 'theoretical obscuration' (p. 33) and present their own 'truths'. At the same time they join in with the chorus of voices endorsing multiple interpretations and the endless process in which they say their deconstruction engages. More knowingly, they also set out to disarm the critic who might challenge their own 'truth claims', the feminist interpretation of Weber that they promote, by inviting the deconstruction of their own text. This seems to me to acknowledge something of the endless process of interpretation in much the same way that a chain letter will continue to be passed on as long as the recipient is prompted to respond with a new version. What it does not do is suggest the provocative, playful, tantalizing, on-going exploration that opens out interpretive textual moments when the deconstructing reader engages intimately with them.

Martin Kilduff's (1993) deconstructive reading of March and Simon's (1958) *Organizations*, even though it too depends very much upon binary, polarized, meaning-making, effectively provides an 'other' reading of this classic and is a very substantial demonstration of previously unrecognized meaning in a foundational text. His paper highlights two aspects of the subject text to show that it both replicates the mores of the predecessors it criticizes, and arrives at conclusions that maintain the worldview of the theorists it challenges. March and Simon argue that organizational theory had, up until the time at which they were writing, accepted the classical, scientific view of organizations as machines, and that their alternative, a human-centred perspective of organizational functions, was revolutionary. Kilduff utilizes two deconstructive strategies to explain his alternative reading: he notes that the literature not cited by March and Simon would undermine their claim that organizational theory at the time of their writing had not then moved away from the mechanistic view of organizations; and that March and Simon have themselves continued to represent workers as machines.

Taylor linked the physical attributes and operations of workers to the parts and workings of machines: March and Simon, as read by Kilduff, link the functions of the human mind to the programming of a machine. Kilduff's reading reveals that in this text March and Simon's basic assumption is that the human mind functions like a computing machine, just as Taylor's assumption was that the human body functions like a labouring machine (Kilduff 1993: 21). Within the root metaphor of the machine we simply see a move from a focus on the body to a focus on the brain: from the mechanical to the computer-programmed machine.

March and Simon demonstrably rely on a root metaphor, the machine metaphor, to explain what they describe as a new perspective on organizations, yet Kilduff's analysis of the metaphor demonstrates that no such shift has taken place. As noted in the previous chapter, root metaphors have been little explored in management theory since Morgan's first foray into this territory, and picking up the challenge to address this, I intend that my analysis of management theory will discover something of the contribution they make to subtextual meaning.

With all of the above I have no quibble, and indeed Kilduff himself spells out his own qualification of 'this deconstruction': 'Different readers can potentially unlock different narratives from the same text. All of these narratives may be present in the text, especially if the text is complex' (p. 27),[35] and insists that 'the deconstructive process itself is not reducible to a set of techniques' (p. 6). Yet when he engages with the text Kilduff, in deconstructive mode, seems to peer through the same bifocals as those worn by Calás and Smircich: a dichotomous 'not this but that'; or the 'one' and the 'other' dominates his reading of March and Simon's foundational text. 'The text of *Organizations*' he blithely tells his readers at the outset, 'is organized around a structure of presence and absence' (p. 17).

Emphasis on dichotomy, rather than on plurivocality, still continues in Bowring's (2000) deconstruction of institutional theory when she stresses its use in the discovery of hidden political content (p. 264). On the other hand, and helpfully, she suggests that her deconstruction exposes the hidden meanings and subtext of positivist organization theory and therefore challenges taken-for-granted objectivity and impersonality (p. 269).

All of the deconstructive analyses commented on above challenge assumptions that are so comfortably familiar, they are not otherwise easily discerned. On the other hand, the fracturing of what these authors profess to be about, and the outcomes of deconstructive practices in management studies to date, are possibly an underlying reason for the more recent Calás and Smircich (1999) postulations. They say that although 'there is still much work to be done in organization studies through postmodern analytics . . . it is now too late', and that 'the major contribution of postmodernism is, precisely, that it has become partially exhausted, for this exhaustion has opened space for other theoretical approaches' (p. 658).

The latter comment may be no more than a nod to other commentators who have suggested that whether or not it has significantly impacted on management thinking, postmodernism has run its course.[36] Yet in the argument that leads into this conclusion they provide substantial support for the on-going exploration of management theory texts via deconstructive practices. They argue that:

The problematization of foundational theorizing posed by poststructural analyses offers pause and a good space for reflecting over the constitution of knowledge in any disciplinary field. In particular, poststructuralist analysis permits us to think 'the unthinkable,' to move, as it were 'outside the limits,' and to consider taken-for-granted knowledge-making operations under very different premises.

(p. 657)

Their conclusion, that 'deconstructions, as close reading for understanding the constitution of knowledge . . . demonstrate the 'great books' of the field to be complicit in exclusionary knowledge practices' (p. 658) immediately suggests the import of my inquiry: deconstruction of the 'great books' (foundational theory) of our field, management, has scarcely begun; and that if we are to 'think the unthinkable', to place our foundational 'knowledge-making operations' under the microscope of informed critical reading, then deconstructive readings must be enabled. In order to do this securely we need to be guided by a philosophically sound and functionally accessible method of text analysis.

Border crossings

While all of the pioneering voices described above ploughed gamely on, often groping through their own obfuscations, an interdisciplinary development in text analysis that questioned the assumptions embedded in the language of academic scholarship, was largely being ignored by management theorists. The Project on the Rhetoric of Inquiry (POROI)[37] has mapped a route that organizational researchers would do well to heed.[38]

Across the disciplines

A movement that rapidly gained momentum in North America in the 1980s, the POROI, seeks to question assumptions bedded in the language of academic disciplines. Scholars who have taken up the challenge to explore the constructed worlds of scholarship represent disciplines as diverse as economics, philosophy, mathematics and psychology, but to date management has been largely content with a spectator role. Although these critics work with diverse understandings of the role of rhetoric in research writings, and adopt a variety of rhetorical strategies as they investigate and debate the texts they question, their common purpose is the deconstruction and reinterpretation of the 'knowledge' represented in their scholarly texts. They share a common concern with questioning practices and assumptions in the communication of research. They question texts in which scholarly communities talk with each other and also with people outside their academies; and they foster self-awareness in all aspects of inquiry, acknowledging that dialogue across disciplines enables the capacity for self-criticism in each participating field. Generally they insist that if we focus critical attention upon rhetoric, how we write as well as what we write, we will begin to perceive the elusiveness of a final position. The rhetoric of inquiry insists that all inquiry, in its attempts to establish a position, is ultimately dependent upon the discursive practices of its discipline.[39]

To the extent that my inquiry is premised on the notion that all the texts of scholarship are rhetorical – a constructed view of texts – I place myself in this interdisciplinary community. The members of this community affirm that what have long been considered the abstruse issues and discussions of particular disciplines, for example in philosophy or science, might more profitably be addressed as rhetorical issues. It is from this stance that they engage in talk of 'decentring' and 'defamiliarizing' scholarly texts, so that critics might better practise what Ricoeur has called a 'hermeneutics of suspicion'. It is a project that undermines foundationalist notions, such as the correspondence theory of truth and of scientific language as a neutral mirror of reality, and has led to a call from interpretive scholars from across the disciplines for further text analysis of foundational texts. When we see all texts as rhetorical constructions, then familiar distinctions between fact and fiction become blurred.

My use of the term 'human sciences' is inclusive of the many and varied disciplines which are generally sited within the humanities and the social sciences (and in this sense it reflects a continental European tradition of thought that does not attempt to set up boundaries between these 'two' traditions), but even more widely, it is a term that suggests that all sciences, like the arts, are human constructions. Management's fit within this usage of the term is clear on both counts: commonly understood as both an art and a science the discipline of generic management derives its theories and methodologies from scholarly works which identify with the tradition of learning sourced from across the spectrum of the human sciences, but there is not yet a body of literature that addresses 'writing management'.[40] The work of the POROI affirms the central role that literary criticism should perform in moving us towards this interdisciplinary destination – rhetorical reading of foundational texts.

We should read our texts rhetorically because the texts of scholarship, from mathematical proofs to literary criticism are all rhetorical: they set out to persuade because acceptance of them brings reward in the form of power and/or resources. It is the relative rhetorical skills of the researchers that shape the field of knowledge. The tradition of argumentation in scholarship ensures that, regardless of field, all scholars, including scientists, rely on common rhetorical devices such as metaphors, invocations to authority, and appeals to audiences.

Klamer (1987), for example, begins his inquiry into the discursive aspects of economics, by calling attention to its rhetorical forms, particularly its persuasive arts, and argues in support of his belief that 'the language of rhetoric and literary criticism is more appropriate to economics than the language of methodology' (p. 164). As explained by Klamer, the rhetorical approach is about 'seeing through' or making transparent, or – in literary terminology – deconstructing, the superficial meanings of economists' expressions. Acknowledging the impact on economics of Deidre McCloskey's *Rhetoric of Economics*, Klamer claims a deeper purpose: where McCloskey and her followers critically examine the way that economists discuss what they do, Klamer, aims to 'see through' what they say.

But 'looking through' the text as well as 'looking at' the text as is precisely what Lanham (1993) sees McCloskey's critical reading of economics as having achieved. Writing in the context of a discussion of the 'professional self-consciousness coming upon American disciplinary inquiry,' Lanham concludes that 'the learned professions' are facing an 'identity crisis' (p. 63). Confronted, by an emergent pedagogy that stresses the rhetoric of disciplinary languages, they will perhaps learn to read, as Lanham claims McCloskey does, both rhetorically ('looking at' the text) and philosophically ('looking through' the text). McCloskey herself approves Lanham's assessment and explanation of her approach to reading when she echoes Lanham's comments on interpretation of economics texts:

> In his recent work Lanham contrasts the rhetorical looking *at* the words with the philosophical looking *through* . . . Lanham explains . . . To read economics as McCloskey suggests is always to be toggling between looking at the prose and through it, reading it 'rhetorically' and reading it 'philosophically'.
>
> (McCloskey 1998: 4)

She further explains philosophical and rhetorical readings as understanding what the passage says (looking through the text in a philosophical reading), as well as 'how it achieves its end, persuasion' (looking at the text in a rhetorical reading). In other words, we need to develop the ability to read the depth and surface of the text at the same time.

Furthermore each field or discipline has its own rhetoric and this entails a set of values that is also shared. Easton and Araujo (1997) remind us that in 1985 McCloskey was urging economists to adopt a literary approach to the analysis of economic argument not with the intention of establishing a definitive argument, but rather in order to see beyond the received view on content and to discover the means by which authors persuade their readers. They conclude that 'We could apply the same argument to management research' (p. 104).

And although the voice of management is seldom heard in this interdisciplinary exploration, much of the discussion taking place highlights the exclusive positioning noted in the debates on the role of metaphors in management theory that I described earlier in this chapter as being grounded in the opposing worldviews of those who wear lenses provided by Aristotle versus those on the ramparts of Plato's camp. McCloskey, for example, argues that the primary philosophical difference between methodologists and rhetoricians

> is what divided Plato from Aristotle and after them much of the intellectual world, namely, the transcendental absolute as against the social character of truth. For 2500 years the followers of Plato have been trying to find a way to vault out of human society into a higher realm of forms, to find a procedure for deciding whether a proposition is true or false in the eyes of God. Meanwhile the rest of us have been making decisions in human terms, sentencing people to death, resolving to mount an expedition to Syracuse, concluding that the multiplier on government spending is greater than 1.0.
>
> (McCloskey 1988: 292)

In its early phases, much of the impetus for the interdisciplinary movement that challenged the positivist research traditions came from initiatives taken by anthropologists. They were in the vanguard of researchers whose perceptions were that their research findings reflected more of their own worldview than that of the subject culture or society, and that their research findings were as much predetermined by their chosen research methodologies as they were representative of original discovery and outcomes. They understood that their representation of the 'other', when written up, emerged from a worldview bedded in the familiar discursive practices of the author. At a time when all codes and representations are contested, when the constructed nature of scholarship, the text-making of scholarship, is being rhetorically challenged, interdisciplinarity needs the traditions and expertise of literary knowledge if it is to engage in reflective research awareness.

As he introduces what was then an emergent interdisciplinary phenomenon, Clifford might well have placed the reflexive management theorist on this path:

> Interdisciplinary work, so much discussed these days is not about confronting already constituted disciplines (none of which, in fact, is willing to let itself go). To do something interdisciplinary it's not enough to choose a 'subject' (a theme) and gather around it two or three sciences. Interdisciplinarity consists in creating a new object that belongs to no one.
> (Roland Barthes, *Jeunes Chercheurs*, cited in Clifford 1986: 1)

This 'new object' could be the rhetoric of inquiry. Nietzsche, claiming that it is the problematic of rhetoric that enables criticism to position itself within the contemporary epistemological landscape, insisted on the rhetoricity of language, on the human 'drive to form metaphors', as the basis of our rendering of the world. It is also Nietzsche who most succinctly sums up the relationship between 'truth' and language:

> Every idea originates through equating the unequal . . . what therefore

is truth? A mobile army of metaphors, metonymies, anthropomorphisms [which] after long usage seem to a nation fixed, canonic and binding: truths are illusions of which one has forgotten that they are illusions.

(Nietzsche 1972: 5)

Hernadi (1987) too, has announced that, 'When human scientists begin to reflect on the master metaphors of their texts, the literary critic can welcome them as fellow students of figurative language' (p. 263), and the desirability of a 'literary turn' of this order, although it is as yet embryonic, is glimpsed in the initiatives of the POROI. Collectively they have imported the theories and methods of literary criticism into the analysis of the texts of their own distinct disciplines; and if asked, 'but what does literary criticism have to do with history, sociology, science, and, in our case, management studies?' their voices might well echo McCloskey's response:

The service that literature can do for economics is to offer literary criticism as a model for self-understanding.

(1998: xxi)

McCloskey goes on to point out that literary criticism does not achieve this through passing judgements, for it is not in the business of pronouncing on what is good and what is bad. Its concern is with making readers see how authors construct their texts, what meaning critics can reveal by deconstructing them, and how readers reconstruct them in the context of their own experiences and worldviews. She concludes:

An economic criticism . . . is not a way of attacking economics, showing it to be bad, because it is rhetorical . . . everyone is rhetorical, from the mathematician to the lawyer. A literary criticism of economics is just a way of showing how economics accomplishes its results.

(ibid.)

I think that it can just as certainly show how management writers accomplish their results, how texts can speak in many voices, and how readers fashion their own interpretive responses.

I therefore turned again to management scholarship searching for more examples of significant initiatives in the 'literary criticism of management theory'. There I met up with a small group of management scholars who have explained the literary theory and critical practice that their text analysis has called upon.

Calling literary criticism

Following hard on the heels of the 'linguistic turn' and then the 'interpretive turn' taken by the human sciences, and responding to a call from many prompts for a literary turn, the world of western scholarship has tweaked open a door to the more imaginative arts. In management, text analysis has appeared in many guises, but critical approaches to text analysis named as 'literary theory', have only very recently made a cautious entry into the theatre of management – much of the management literature that I reviewed in the section entitled 'Postmodernism' is based on readings of literary theory, but it is rarely denoted as such.

Ellen O'Connor has argued substantially the contribution that the literature- and language-based disciplines can make to organizational theory.[41] Her careful explication of each of three foundational texts on the profession of management, authored respectively by Taylor, Fayol and Follett, tends to operate within the epistemological reach of expressive realism and the New Criticism (both of which I briefly discuss in the next chapter), as she seeks out thematic parallels, logical argument and 'rhetorical posturing'. Her declared intention in conducting this analysis is to 'clearly locate ourselves both as products (of past) and producers (of future) history, in this case our history of management', and she concludes that the texts are based on self-authorized authority:

> Taylor does not discover his management science; rather he invents it himself by virtue of his own authority which he simply positions as scientifically derived. Fayol explicitly says his doctrine represents his personal opinion based on his business experience (although he never describes those experiences). Follett situates herself at an abstract, philosophical level in speaking about the compelling but elusive 'law of the situation'; so there is neither a way nor a possibility of grounding her view. Her position resembles more of a philosophy of management (and of life); Fayol's a system of order (even of aesthetics); Taylor's a 'variation on a theme' of science.
>
> (O'Connor 1996: 46)

It is a conclusion that is based, as advocated by the New Critics, on close reading of texts, and as would be expected of a critical reading working from this methodology, argues uncompromisingly that this particular interpretation – 'that all three authors work to legitimize management' – has been substantiated beyond dispute. Her readers are expected to concur with her interpretations. Clearly, it is a reading that builds a significant bridge between literary theory and the foundational texts of management theory, but because it ignores all of the contributions to literary theory made by deconstructionists and reader-response theorists, it fails to recognize the intriguing mystery of the plurivocal, infinitely layered, endlessly paradoxical text.

Martha Banta (1993), working from a theory base in literary criticism, has also made a particular study of some aspects of Taylor's rhetoric, concluding that he sets out a moral argument for a tightly contained, time-defined society with a brutal management edge. Her analysis sweeps across much of Taylor's writing, revealing some seminal elements of the persuasive devices that may draw readers into sharing his perspective of the world and workplace. Her comments range widely across much of Taylor's writings and across an extensive array of societal activities and beliefs. She comments with acuity on the power of story-telling and the authorial roles Taylor develops, as well as on the rhetoric which conveys his notions of a promised Utopia. Her approach to text analysis is more broad-brush and wide-ranging than it is close up, finely honed or deeply curious.

Easton and Araujo (1997) claiming that management researchers might learn from literary criticism, position the text, or as they describe it the 'work' between 'audience' (or reader) 'universe' (or context) and 'artist' (or author). They do not begin to deal with the profundity of the textual inquiry which has engaged the latter half of the twentieth century, and as it has been described earlier in this chapter, for the 'taxonomy' they describe places them firmly among what I will describe (Chapter 3) as the expressive realism critics. While I think that introducing post-war critical literary theory to management as if it were contemporary thinking does both disciplines a disservice, they do nevertheless demonstrate to management readers that literary criticism, because of its 'antiquity and urbanity' has developed diverse ways of reading texts, *modi operandi* which offer not only models of how to read (strategies of interpretation), but also philosophical arguments that address such questions as why we read in certain ways.

Basing their categorization of critical literary theories on distinctions literary criticism makes between the mimetic (attempts to represent the universe in the arts), the expressive (concerned with the emotions of the writer), the pragmatic (attention focused on the effect of the text on the audience) and the objective (a focus on the text as a self-sufficient entity) they provide a basic introduction to the theory that falls within these frames. They specifically advocate the text analysis of master tropes and styles of representation within the text that point to 'hidden relationships', and the deconstructive 'overturning' of the logocentric tendencies of the text. The latter activity, as they remind us, is an act of meaning-making that is imposed on the text by the reader who necessarily draws on a personal history of experience, knowledge, and cultural conventions in order to reconstruct textual meaning. Their final point, that we should read a small number of texts closely instead of skim-reading a great many is endorsed by Barbara Czarniawska.[42]

Czarniawska (1999) has long been championing a role for literature in the teaching and theorizing of management, particularly in *Writing Management: Organization Theory as a Literary Genre*, where she cites Eco *et al.* (1992) on the naive (semantic) reader and the critical (semiotic) reader. The former assumes that the text carries a message that can be paraphrased in a retelling of the original text, while the latter 'enjoys' discerning author strategies designed to lead him (*sic*) to identify with the author's intended meaning. The first reader is denoted a 'victim' and the second is perceived to be a textual connoisseur:

The former uses the work as semantic machinery and is the victim of the strategies of the author who would lead him a little by a little along the series of provisions of expectations. The latter evaluates the work as an aesthetic product and enjoys the strategies implemented in order to produce a Model Reader of the first level, a semantic reader.

(Eco 1990: 92)

Building on this distinction, Czarniawska affirms the role of both kinds of reader, but also warns that the 'aspiring semiotic reader' (characterized by Czarniawska as typically already having confidence in their 'natural' attitude) often asks for help: 'What should one look for? What do the clues look like? How does one establish connections between one text and all the others?' (1999: 25). Her unequivocal answer to these questions is that 'there are no interpretation rules'. She cites Ricoeur's 'there are no *rules* for *making* good guesses. But there are *methods* for *validating* guesses' (italics added).[43]

This citation, and Czarniawska's affirming of it, highlights a difficulty: to the extent that the management community seeks the security of methods that provide 'rules', models of methods that can be readily replicated, it is disconcerted by the notion of a method that is a non-method. That working with literary methodologies leads to interpretations of management texts that rely on demonstrations of interpretive processes, rather than explanation of them, is a challenge that the reading method I explain in Chapter 4 seeks to address.

Czarniawska also recognizes that 'reading and writing are inseparable', that 'to read is to write'. Introducing reader-response theory, originally ushered in by Iser, to a management audience, she both reminds readers that it 'subjectivizes' the act of reading (readers are understood to reconstruct textual meaning within the context of their personal experience and world-view), but at the same time 'neglects the institutional effect', the common understandings that are shared by semiotic readers. In drawing together these two interpretive stances, the personal (subjective) and the public (objective) Czarniawska presents her own preferred critical stance as relying on performative criteria as to what constitutes a text that will be positively received. These criteria are of two types, the pragmatic and the aesthetic: the first attach to a text that is well adapted to the purpose at hand; the second is admirable because it is beautiful, it moves the emotions.[44]

In order to demonstrate what all of this means to 'actual genre analysis', Czarniawska demonstrates that organizational texts employ textual strategies traditionally attributed to literature.

Constructing our way

As we farewelled the twentieth century, two publications marked out the management climate to which the community of authors described had contributed: the journal *Studies in Cultures, Organizations and Societies* produced a special issue (1999b), guest edited by Stephen Linstead, entitled 'The textuality of organizations'; and in its last issue of the millennium, the *Academy of Management Review* produced a special issue entitled 'Special topic forum on theory development: Evaluation, reflections and new directions' which included a paper, authored by Calás and Smircich (1999), entitled 'Past postmodernism? Reflections and tentative directions'. Together these two papers broadly sum up, in voices that purport to represent the discipline of management, its present, and its supposed future, the positioning of text analysis in management theory.

At a conceptual level, Linstead[45] notes that 'how the "truth" effects of accounts [are] achieved (e.g. rhetoric, narrativity)' is being questioned, and that 'One branch of this tendency has been the alleged "deconstruction" of the research accounts of others'. At the methodological level, Linstead notes as a 'significant area of study' that researchers are 'Paying particular attention to specific genres or tropes in use in meaning construction, such as metaphor, rhetoric and irony', in support of his claims. Third and finally, as Linstead sums up, management theorists are now asking 'What is the connection between how the organizational text is interpreted and how it is represented? What is the nature of authorship and readership? What are the power relations involved between subjects, authors and audiences?' and 'Can these be dissolved?' (p. 4).

Calás and Smircich (1999) attempt to establish some consensus as to understandings of the theory debates that have been occupying management scholars through the last two decades, and to indicate where debate, and exploration founded on these debates, might lead us in the opening years of the new millennium. The authors give a casual, generalized wave in the direction of postmodernism and poststructuralism in the social sciences, but suggest that so much has been written about this that they cannot review it all, and will instead:

> ... highlight those arguments and issues, such as the incredulity toward metanarratives, the undecidability of meaning, the crisis of represen-tation, and the problematization of the subject and the author, that were particularly influential in organizational theorising as it turned into more reflective knowledge making.
>
> (p. 650)

This is a very succinct summary of the elements of postmodernity as it has been understood (or to the extent that it has been understood) in the disci-pline of management in the closing years of the twentieth century, and as such serves very well as an image of the disciplinary environment into which I have placed another text.

They also attempt to sum up the shared concerns of the emerging theories and theorists. These they identify as: an emphasis on the relationship between power and knowledge (they articulate the relationship 'between those who do knowledge and the knowledge that gets made'); an ambivalence about the way that knowledge is represented in texts; ambivalence about the anti-essentialist tenets of poststructuralism and a preparedness to abandon these tenets and to seek out theory that supports theory that 'could engage the world "outside the text"'; and a recognition that because writers of theory actively participate in the knowledge-making enterprise they need to adopt an ethical position that questions this role.

The first two of the concerns listed here as those of the emerging theorists are shared with the postmodernists; the last two distinguish a moving on from the postmodern worldview. In that these latter two concerns determine to create bridges between 'the text' and 'the world', they are concerns that I share.

Commenting generally on the articles in this millennium issue of *AMR*, and on the Calás and Smircich contribution specifically, Karl Weick concludes that the authors:

> Help us to understand the last twenty years of theorising, dating back to Burrell and Morgan (1979) and the *Administrative Science Quarterly* (1979) special issue on qualitative methods edited by van Maanen. Both of these anchors in 1979 were marginal voices at a time when the center was defined by positivism and functionalism. What has changed since 1979 is the growth of reflexivity regarding the knowledge-making enterprise.
>
> (Weick 1999: 799)

Much of the story that emerges from all of this comment is told in the spaces and margins of the text I am presently writing. There is no story here of a concerted movement towards a literary inquiry into the foundational texts of our discipline, and I have not unearthed examples of text analysis that came 'closer than close' to the text; that engaged as intimately with our theory texts as a literary reader might do. The story that dominant metaphors, the root metaphors that shape organizations and organization theory, that reveal their linguistic constitution, that enable us to construct, convey and perceive profound meaning, could tell has not yet been heard.

Moves towards a postmodern consciousness in management studies have created a climate of inquiry which would support the telling of these stories. And to the extent that critical readings of the management theory texts to date have provided alternative interpretations to the 'common sense' understandings provided by traditional readings, they have helped to build an inquiry in the discipline of management that has, especially in very recent years, placed increasing emphasis on the need to explore texts in management studies. Specifically this development has destabilized traditional modernist approaches to establishing the meaning of management texts by moving the centre of critical interest from the author to the reader, from the subject to the margins of the texts, and from the supposedly determinant 'truth' conveyed by the text to the inconclusive, infinitely variable, multiplex interpretations of progressive readings. Perhaps as a result of this criticism, the focus of interest in management texts has very recently begun to shift towards the rhetorical and narrative theory that supports emerging modes of more pragmatic critical analysis.

There is little coherent discussion of the contribution that contemporary literary theory could make to the diverse approaches critical scholars have taken in their readings of management texts. Many have 'read' the spaces and the margins of their texts, they are used to 'decentring' and 'defamiliarizing' the textual subject, they assume the 'doubleness' of every discourse, and have discussed the plurivocality of texts. But the elusive, the endless postponement, of final meaning is still a notion – not a reading mode. Nor is there a profile of reader-response criticism in the literature reviewed, although Czarniawska makes mention of it. Analysts of the texts of management theory have not brought reader-response theory into their discussions of textual meaning. While a significant community of management theorists suppose that our texts construct our world, there is little overt debate about the extent to which it is writers who, through their texts, construct our world for us, or whether the individual readers who interpret the texts construct worlds of their own making. This issue, which I address in my discussion of critical literary theory in the next chapter, is an issue central to debates about approaches to text analysis in management theory.

Critical readers have not provided their own readers with a narrative that 'tracks' their method of reading. While there has been plenty of theoretical support for 'close critical reading' of our texts, few scholars seem to have acquired the practical expertise that would enable them to demonstrate and explain how this might be done. While all of the literature discussed has contributed to a more comprehensive understanding of the texts of management, it has not provided a methodological approach to analysis readily accessible to the management community. In the literature reviewed, I did not discover a method of text analysis that would both support reading closely enough to reveal the multilevels at which texts 'mean', and at the same time allow for interpretation that does not assume closure: that does not competitively argue for one 'truth' by attempting to annihilate another 'truth' in the process of textual reconstruction.

This final conclusion prompted me to return to the many theories of literary criticism familiar to me, in search of methodology that would support and progress my approach to reading management theory texts: my 'method' of text analysis. I planned a summary review of this reading that would describe my own evolutionary journey as at first a literary critic, and more latterly as a critical management theorist. My story would, I hoped, serve both as a microcosmic sample of the development of literary criticism in the latter half of the twentieth century, and would also bring an understanding of the role of the reader in creating textual meaning to the discipline of management. I expected as I completed my review of this literature that I would be equipped to trial my reading approach in preparation for sculpting the method on which I would base my reading of selected management theory texts.

3 Pre-scripts in literary theory

Sure he that made us with such large discourse,
Looking before and after, gave us not
That capability and godlike reason
To fust in us unus'd.

Hamlet, IV, iv, 36–9

I read and write all the texts with which I engage as conduits to my participation in diverse virtual communities. Like all social constructions, these communities are paradoxically both ahistorical, yet caught in moments of transitory time; and they are shared knowledge-making entities, yet uniquely experienced. So, in the previous chapter I explored readings of management theory texts, authored across several decades, as if in immediate conversation with them, and I also touched on the climate of the community, management scholarship, which has welcomed them. At the same time, as I described my own response to these texts, I assumed that you, my reader, would also be actively engaged in these discursive experiences.

The subject texts of which I wrote are denizens of management theory, and some of them are tied up in a web of intertextual linkings to literary theory – and since 'literary theory' is hugely explored and contested, in this chapter I intend to outline my particular understanding and experience of it. Like the field itself, my understandings of textual meaning-making will be seen as a restlessly on-going process; and my personal search for a more complete picture of my reading experience, will reflect the historical development of critical literary theory, especially in the latter half of the twentieth century.

Embarking on this stage of my research journey I carried with me a mixed bag of theories and lived narratives; baggage that perhaps contained a few smuggled nuggets of old wisdoms and partisan disciplinary stances, and a hasty collection of carry bags, spilling packages of disparate recent experience. The home from which I had long since departed, and to which I now planned a return, is literary criticism. The territory in which I had recently been delayed by my 'rough guide' to exploratory tours was management.

What I discovered on the route back is that there is no longer a clearly demarcated border crossing to negotiate. The landscape changes with each reading of a new text or rereading of an old text, but theory has colonized all the nation disciplines into one commonwealth of learning:

> . . . literary criticism has been drawn into the vortex of a powerful new field of study in which all these [linguistics, psychoanalysis, philosophy, Marxism] disciplines are merged and interfused, and which goes under the general name of 'theory'.
>
> (Lodge 1988b: x–xi)

Lodge had already explained that during the 1970s the Anglo-American world finally became aware of structuralism:

> . . . a movement in what Continental Europeans call 'the human sciences', which sought to explain and understand cultural phenomena (from poems to menus, from primitive myths to modern advertisements) as manifestations of underlying systems of signification, of which the exemplary model is verbal language itself, especially as elucidated by the Swiss linguist Ferdinand de Saussure.
>
> (ibid.)

The interest in theory that this movement was instrumental in generating bore, among literary critics, two kinds of fruit: initially a much greater interest in, and anxiety about, the theory of their own subject and, more recently, a role in the collective enterprise that as Lodge describes it, ambitiously attempts 'nothing less than a totalizing account of human consciousness and human culture (or else a tireless demonstration of the impossibility of such a project)' (ibid.).

For me, two important identifications rapidly evolved and fused. First, that literary criticism recognizes the interdisciplinary interest in texts that represent the generation, promulgation and interpretation of theory as I described it in the previous chapter; and second, that literary critics comfortably recognize that this pursuit, whatever one's disciplinary 'home', has a common base in a general concern with 'theory' as described above by Lodge.

But literary criticism is a huge, and hugely contested, field which speaks a (sometimes esoteric) language, a tongue perhaps foreign to many of my readers. My understanding of this theory, gleaned from reading that is as often literary as it is critical, is just one small story among countless others; so in this chapter I will outline only the critical literary theory that has been a formative influence on the development of my method of reading, but I hope it will be read as a micro-image of a macro-story.

Representation and the romantic: Expressive realism

The most traditional stance of contemporary literary critics, and one which is still widely subscribed to, is expressive realism (Belsey 1980). Under this label, Belsey places the merging of the mimetic mode of criticism (the literary work is seen as a representation or reflection of the world and human activity) and expressive criticism (the text is understood as the product of an author who gives voice to, and expresses, thoughts and feelings). Emerging as a distinct discipline in the latter half of the nineteenth century, literary criticism was at first dominated by the expressive realism perspective, and then later, despite challenges by formalists, structuralists and poststructuralists in the twentieth century, still retained loyal subscribers throughout a period that has seen the rise of industrial capitalism.[1]

Critics who take up this position assume that their task is to reveal to readers, readers perhaps less adequately equipped with interpretive skills than is the critic, more of the author's intended meaning. They assume that texts can represent an objective knowable reality: that the author's intended representation of external truths can be conveyed to, recognized by and internalized by, the knowing reader. Expressive realism is then, a position that reflects both the Aristotelian concept of art as mimesis, the imitation of reality, and as with the romantic movement, assumes that texts express the ideas and emotions of the author. It combines classical realism (the mimetic representation of the external world) with romantic expressionism (writing from the heart); and expects what Barthes (1974) has described as a *lisible* ('readable') text, one that follows the conventions of composition, and takes up what Belsey denotes a 'common sense position':

> Common sense assumes that . . . texts . . . tell truths – about the period which produced them, about the world in general or about human nature.
>
> (Belsey 1980: 2)

It is an 'obvious mode of reading',

> a way of explaining in theoretical terms what we already – and on the whole without encountering any difficulties – do when we read
>
> (ibid.)

and one which 'is widely taken for granted' (p. 7).

Because this is the position that most writers, readers and critics of management texts unquestioningly assume, recognition of it is important. Common-sense interpretation of the text, reflecting the expressive realism of this tradition is still the kind of reading which ubiquitously dominates discussions of management theory. Caputo (1997: 77) adopts Derrida's term, 'dominant reading' to denote it.

Caputo explains that the 'very idea of a deconstructive reading presupposes this more reproductive and classical reading' and that such a first reading, 'preparatory, preliminary, ground-laying, contextualizing' always precedes 'a more "productive", fine-grained distinctly deconstructive reading'. He also defends the meticulous, scholarly responsibility that Derrida assumed as a deconstructive critic by pointing out that the juxtaposition of the two readings, dominant and deconstructive, allowed the latter to expose the 'something in the text that tends to drop out of view' in the former.

But deconstruction is a late twentieth century development. Long before this European movement pervaded the western world, another seismic shift, the birth of semiotics in the writings of Saussure, and the European Structuralists who followed his lead, presented a major challenge to the expressive realism tradition. It merged into initiatives by the so-called New Critics on either side of the Atlantic which led to a radical shift in Anglo-American approaches to literary criticism.

The sovereign text: Structuralism and the New Critics

Saussure (1974) developed a science of signs, or semiotics, based on the way that they are perceived to function in all spheres of human activity and experience. Many of the concepts Saussure describes, and the terminology he developed, have permeated the language and practice of textual criticism to such an extent that all late twentieth century textual commentary seems to return to him. Saussure explained the relationship of the subject, the thing or concept referred to, and its textual representation, in terms of the signified (the thing or concept) and the signifier (its textual representation – the sound of the word, or the marks on a page that represent it). The word itself, the verbal sign, consists of both components, the signified and the signifier. This relationship is the essence of the word, and – Saussure's crucial point – the relationship that we ascribe to these two components is arbitrary. It is

> a convention accepted by all users of a given language, not the result of some existential link between word and thing.
>
> (p. 1)

If, for example, we consider the word (or sign) 'manager' then we see that we can distinguish the subject (or signified – in this case a person who manages) and its representation (or signifier – the print marks I have made on this page with my word processor). What we do not know is how I (the writer) or you (the reader) relate the signifier to the signified: we do not know what any number of writers or readers imagine this word 'manager' to mean. Do you, for example, as you read the word 'manager' image an efficient person, a power-hungry achiever, a servant of the workplace, a political manipulator? The possible range of constructed meanings is infinite.

Language, then, is made up of words: and though we recognize the conventions that attach certain meanings to particular words, in fact because the relationship between signified and signifier is arbitrary, there is scope for vast differences in the interpretation of this relationship.

Structuralist critics applied the analytical distinctions and concepts recognized in Saussure's semiotics to literary criticism, and explicitly challenged expressive realism and the supposition that a text is its author's communication with readers. They turned attention away from the author and towards the reader as a decoder of signs, but concentrated their energies on the text, the written artefact, composed and understood according to any number of accepted codes and conventions. Readers and their meaning-making, were then thought to be bound within the strictures of codes. With their attention firmly concentrated on the independent text, severed from any connection with its producer (author), structuralist critics endeavoured to scientifically unravel the conventions and codes that bind the text's component elements. By this means they sought to enable us to better see how textual constructions achieve determinant meaning. Ultimately this is not an approach to reading that I share. In my rhetorical analysis I respect the endless autonomy of the interpreting reader, and I will shortly return to the theories of deconstruction and reader-response that support this view.

Meanwhile, there were developments in Anglo-American thinking that both draw on the Paris-based structuralism, and also anticipate the methods of the poststructuralists. It is this theory that directly informs the second stage of the scriptive reading process which I describe in Chapter 4. It begins with the work of Ogden and Richards, and the so-called 'New Critics'[2] who followed them, and echoes the arguments of the European structuralists to the extent that they see the autonomous text as the primary focus of text analysis, and think that it is the critic's job to explain how various parts of the texts work together to construct meanings. But, whereas the structuralist pays more attention to the formal codes that bind words into meaningful patterns, the New Critics were more concerned with the network of symbolic associations that is set up by connotations and ambiguities discovered in particular words and phrases.

As they describe them, all words are symbols and, in step with the logic of semiotics and structuralism, they build their arguments on the perception that since a symbol is a representation of a thing rather than the thing itself, the connection that we make between the two, the signifier and the signified, may be as much the outcome of emotional experience as of rationality and logic. In texts, since we meet only, or first, with the word, not with that to which it refers, the connection that we make between the two (the word, the signifier, and the subject, the signified) is an act of the imagination: it demands the reader's participation in emotive, as well as rational acts of meaning-making. The New Critics approach to reading, based on these perceptions, changed reading practices in classrooms throughout the Anglo-American literary world after the Second World War, and their critical practice is still current in many classrooms today.

Long before Barthes announced the 'death of the author', this Anglo-American movement which developed independently of the European schools of thought, had declared that texts are autonomous: that once released into the public arena, their connection with an author becomes no more than tenuous, and often irrelevant. The New Critics encouraged readers to respond directly to the words on the page, and to make of them what they would without regard for what might be thought of as the author's intended meaning, as sought out in associated biographical, historical or author comment.

Text analysis under their guidance was based on close reading of the text: the closer the reading, the more meaning the text would yield up. Aesthetics, emotions and ideas were seen to be inextricably woven one into the other, and the aim of the critic was to tease out these relationships: to reveal the meaning that syntax, rhythm and sound patterns convey, while at the same time tracing the pattern of images and ideas which flesh out the architecture of the text. Close reading, or explication, as practised by the New Critics, entails looking into paradox and pun, irony and particularly metaphor in an attempt to uncover the human themes that, it is assumed, are of paramount importance in the text.

For these critics, text analysis resulted in comment that could mark out all the interweaving, interlacing networks of content and form within the boundaries of the text. The 'text was the thing'[3] and released from the pursuit of the author's intended meaning, readers revelled in the new-found freedom to relate directly to it. It was still assumed that 'truth' might be found there, and that the critics or readers who could most carefully, and it must be said cleverly, explicate the many layers and myriad mazes of meaning to be found in it, could then most cogently argue that they had 'found out' what the text was about.

In the Anglo-American world of the New Critics then, the text was the focal subject of critical theorizing and debate. Their critical theory and practice moved critical attention away from the author's work and intended meaning, on from attempts to decipher codes and conventions, and focused instead on interpretation of the autonomous text. Texts, when released for reading, were treated like found objects with no relationship to authorship, or the circumstance of authorship.

My method of reading retains much of what I learned about close reading from them, but it finally rejects the autonomy and boundedness of the text. Close reading encourages readers to engage fully with individual words and tropes, to explore an endless array of associated emotions and ideas, and all the while to delight in paradox, pun and all the possibilities of ambiguity and irony. I find this valuable and have incorporated it into the second stage of the reading process I have developed and describe in the next chapter.

But New Critical close reading, like structural analysis, also insists that exploration takes place within the confines of the text itself: it takes the reader in deep, delving down into a swirling underworld of the one text to a place which ultimately smothers itself in its own isolation. The reader who is moving on to poststructuralism, who strikes back up to the surface for air, discovers that texts move out from the confines of this boundedness: that they spin out into an infinity of possible connections with other texts, other readers and even, yes, the author.

A return to authorship is, at this point in my narrative, premature, but the poststructuralists have, like the structuralists and New Critics before them, irrevocably changed our understandings of texts and my methodology owes much to their theories.

Zapping the subject: Poststructuralism

In poststructuralist theory, the subject is decentred. Language is primary. All previous theory assumed that texts are produced by authors. As explained above, the structuralists and New Critics argued that, after production, texts become independent artefacts that speak directly to readers, but these critics never fully challenged the assumptions of expressive realists: that texts reflect individual consciousness and the external world. They assumed that humankind sits at the centre of the universe in all of its manifestations: that there is an external reality which is fixed and can be known. Their logocentric thinking also assumes the existence of an absolute, an essence or ground that may be elusive, but is nevertheless evidenced in foundational knowledge.

Poststructuralist theory reverses that order. Reality is seen as a social construction; one that is language dependent. If the self can only be known through the medium of language, then it is to language itself that we must look if we would discover how we come to create the identity of self. As Richardson (1994) sums up, 'poststructuralism links language, subjectivity, social organization, and power', but 'the centerpiece is language' (p. 518). When we understand that language does not 'reflect' social reality, but creates it, then we also see that 'understanding language as competing discourses, competing ways of giving meaning [to] and of organizing the world, makes language a site of exploration [and] struggle' (ibid.).

Antifoundationalism is often seen as a cataclysmic reversal of all previous theories about the production of perceptions of self, and of all of our understandings of the external environment, natural and man-made. Discovery of the process by which texts may be seen to hijack the primacy of the speaking subject is much too large a field for me to cover here, so the comments which follow are narrowly focused: my aim is simply to demonstrate the role that poststructuralist theory plays in my methodology.

Jacques Derrida in his early writings (1972, 1976, 1978) pushed poststructuralist theory to such extreme limits that finding meaning may seem to become an elusive, and perhaps ultimately an impossible, goal. Working from the premise that links between signifier and the signified are arbitrary, he suggested first that this arbitrariness offers an infinite variation of individual interpretation; and second that meaning is never static. Not only is every interpretation of every word different, each of these distinct interpretations wrestles with meaning which is never finally captured, is always 'deferred'. Just as the signifier cannot be said to represent any pre-eminent meaning, so too the signified does not have an essence that we can finally know. We can only approximate what it might be by distinguishing it from other essences that we perceive as different from it. Grint (1995) provides a useful illustration:

> the word 'management' gains its meaning not by reflecting the essence of the group of people who manage but in *relation to the difference between this* group and the group that is managed by them – the 'managed'; one cannot make sense of the word 'manager' without simultaneously understanding the word 'managed' or 'non-manager' or 'employee' . . . it is the differences not the essences that we should concentrate on.
>
> (p. 8)

Derrida's famous portmanteau word *différance* expresses these ideas succinctly: essence is expressed through the portrayal of 'difference'; but understanding is always 'deferred' because essence is finally unknowable. Since any and every word is differently, and never finally, interpreted by every reader, we cannot ultimately know what it means. Grint concludes that in his example, 'management' might mean, for example, 'a group of high-status individuals or a group of exploiters or a task or the butt of numerous jokes or the legitimation for one's rapid and ungracious exit from a nightclub' (ibid.). So, language is not a field of finite meanings, but of infinite 'play' of meaning. The school of criticism that is built on this notion, and was fathered by Derrida, is that of deconstruction.

Deconstructionists premise their approaches to text analysis on the notion that language does not reflect the world, but constitutes it. Furthermore, they disestablish the priority, in traditional views of language, of speech over writing, and instead privilege writing over speech. Derrida, very loosely translated, says that our ultimate recourse is 'to these black marks on paper' (Derrida 1972: 203). This too is a significant reversal of the old order of things, again taking the notion of the autonomy of the text, as understood in Structuralist and New Critical theory, to further extremes. For me, a visual image from Ted Hughes' *The Thought-Fox* analogizes the import of Derrida's isolation of the printed, finally unknowable text.

Hughes gives us, at midnight, the perfect silence of a virgin white, moonlight snowscape: and etched across the snowy silence we see the imprints of fox-paws. There is no fox. All is silence; and there is vastly more of the silence and the endless awesome whiteness than there is of print. So, alone in the midnight forest, pen poised over white page, 'this blank page where my fingers move', Hughes hesitates, aware that something is alive. It comes nearer, though yet deeper within the darkness, 'entering the loneliness': a fox, its nose as cold and delicate as the dark snow itself, touching a twig, a leaf; and with two eyes, eyes that serve a movement, for now: 'And again now, and now, and now [it]'

Sets neat prints into the snow

. . . . . .

Till, with a sudden sharp hot stink of fox
It enters the dark hole of the head.
The window is starless still; and the clock ticks,
The page is printed.

(Hughes 1995: 3)

Marks (words) inked on paper or fox-paw prints? Essentially unknowable, what we see around these (prints) marks, separated by blanks and surrounded by (whiteness) spaces and margins, are repetitions and differences. Just as the snowy emptiness is visually 'read' because it is not paw-marked, so too the spaces and margins of the printed word are 'readable'. The white, marked landscape, like the written text, 'consists of what we find when we look at it', for *'un texte déjà écrit, noir sur blanc'*: black marks on white paper are the sole things that are actually present in reading.

'The only givens are the existing marks', for *déjà écrit* – 'we are denied recourse to a speaking or writing subject'. Even syntax is given no role in determining the meanings of component words; and all the while the spaces that are not written into, the texts (in the original French 'text' connotes 'textiles', a cloth within which we find 'folds' of meaning) that are not visible on the page, carry their own meanings.[4]

Deconstructive reading then, begins with the written words on the page and moves out into the connections that the reader associates with these textual symbols. It pauses to note the play [*jeu*] of meaning which glances from word to word and from text to text: sometimes the dance is lit like a mocking twinkle; sometimes it seems to agonize under strobe lighting, but always the play of meaning, like the play of light is shifting, shaping and reassembling, but never still.

There are no boundaries around the text here. On the contrary, deconstruction places all texts into the context of everything that was ever written, and suggests an infinity of 'not-knowing'. J. Hillis Miller, an American follower of Derrida, who authored numerous books on the application of the French philosopher's deconstructive theories and methods[5] describes his own, and Derrida's procedure as follows:

Deconstruction as a mode of interpretation works by careful and circumspect entering of each textual labyrinth . . . The deconstructive critic seeks to find, by this process of retracing, the element in the system studied which is alogical, the thread in the text in question which will unravel it all, or the loose stone which will pull down the whole building. The deconstruction, rather, annihilates the ground on which the building stands by showing that the text has already annihilated that ground, knowingly or unknowingly. Deconstruction is not a dismantling of the structure of a text but a demonstration that it has already dismantled itself.

(Miller 1976a: 341)

Barthes too played with images of a thread as he sought to explain the complexities of texts: 'In the multiplicity of writing, everything is to be disentangled, nothing deciphered; the structure can be followed, "run" (like the thread of a stocking) at every point and at every level . . .', and again, 'Text analysis requires us to represent the text as a tissue (this is moreover the etymological sense), as a skein of different voices and multiple codes which are at once interwoven and unfinished'.[6]

The threads of meaning that the deconstructive reader follows weave patterns of meaning that criss-cross and whirl in many directions simulta-neously. As classical or dominant readers, we have been used, for example, to a dependence on what Barthes describes as a horizontal logic that drives a text towards its end. Based on the logic of argument, action, description and the chronology of time, this horizontal function has dominated the 'readable' experience of over-determined texts.

If, following Barthes, we recognize the 'integrational' (vertical) levels of meaning that can be discovered in any one unit of discourse within the larger system, and pause to explore this axis before moving further along the 'distributional' (horizontal) level, then we begin to see that the 'aporia' (the unresolved moment of doubt or impasse), the explosion of connotation and connection, and the space that also 'means', spins the reader from one level to another, and engages the reader in a production of the text which may result in endless stop-overs in verticality, delaying the horizontal journey indefinitely.

To embark on the reading of a text is thus to begin a process without end: the reader does not set out with the over-riding intention of reaching 'the end' of the text: 'having described the flower, the botanist is not to get involved in describing the bouquet'.

Images of texts as the spinnings and weavings of webs of meaning-making, of the reader attempting to explore a way through a vast labyrinth, while clinging to a delicate wisp of silk, always aware that at any moment a gentle tug may undo the maze itself, seem to me to suggest the role of the decon-structive reader more adequately than much of the heavy theorizing that usually accompanies the process. But following Ariadne's thread does not lead out of the maze, the labyrinth, but rather to more threads, connected to ever more threads. It may even lead to the noose with which, in one version of the myth, Ariadne is said to have hung herself when she realized that there was no way out, that she had been deceived by all the hints, the suggestions, and the moves towards a phantom 'real world' escape route.

So then, in a deconstruction only the marks on the page are of concern. The author is dead. The language of the text exists in its own right and its spaces, margins and omissions are integral to the play of meaning. There is no determinate meaning to be discovered, only the endless moving, melding, transitory moments of perceived linguistic pattern. The analysis of the historic relationships between texts is abandoned (in so far as this implies an attempt to specify particular chronological and biographical textual dependencies) and is replaced by recognitions of intertextuality: 'a text is made of multiple writings, drawn from many cultures and entering into mutual relations of dialogue, parody, contestation . . .'. The intertextuality also enables every text to speak to any other. Taylor's *The Principles of Scientific Management* might for example be as much illuminated by juxta-position with the Bible, as with a manual on operating a machine, or a ledger of accounts.

While my method of reading draws on some of the interpretive strategies that are integral to a deconstructive reading as outlined here, philosophically I do not identify with the worldview to which it ultimately leads. Derrida, for example, in his own unique and inimitable way, is an absolutist: 'Derrida is an absolutist without absolutes' (Abrams 1989c: 273–4); he believes in his own theory (absolute) that there are no absolutes, 'Absolutes though necessary, are dead, therefore free play is permitted'; and I do not share his absolutism:

> What Derrida's conclusion comes to is that no sign or chain of signs can have determinate meaning . . . his origin and ground are his grapho-centric premises, the closed chamber of texts for which he invites us to abandon our ordinary realm of experience in speaking, hearing, reading and understanding language . . . Derrida's chamber of texts is a sealed echo-chamber in which meanings are reduced to a ceaseless echolalia, a vertical and lateral reverberation from sign to sign of ghostly non-presences emanating from no voice, intended by no one, referring to nothing, bominating in a void.
>
> (Abrams 1989b: 244)

It is this final position in deconstructive theory and practice which my method of reading veers away from, the *mise en abyme* – the paradox of the word that both opens up a chasm of meaning, but simultaneously covers it over by naming it, 'fills' it with nothingness, leaves us vertiginously close to the edge, and yet provides a vista of a bottomless ground that is only a glimpse[7] – which presents 'a Nietzschean affirmation . . . of a world of signs without error [*faute*], without truth, without origin', and which Derrida himself visions as a yet unnamable something which cannot announce itself except . . . under the species of a non-species, under the formless form, mute, infant, and terrifying, of monstrosity.

(Abrams 1989b: 244–5)

Instead, with Abrams, I find that

those of us who stubbornly refuse to substitute the rules of the deconstructive enterprise for our ordinary skill and tact at language will find that we are able to understand the text very well.

(p. 252)

For this reason I turned for further guidance, as I developed my reading method, to the critics who have developed approaches to reading that are supported by the theories of reader-response on which I will comment in the next section.

In sum, although like many other critics of the late twentieth century,[8] I do not finally identify with the postmodern philosophies of the Derridean school of criticism, in company with these critics I have learned much from the arguments and analytic strategies of the deconstructionists. Graphocentrism has taught textual critics to question the place of the subject; listen for voices that have been subdued or excluded, and to dig below surface meanings for embedded texts and assumed ideologies.

As I understand them, deconstructive readings are not destructive. On the contrary, they affirm and expand texts by opening them up to more and ever more understanding. In popular (mis)conceptions, deconstruction is often described as a process which pulls (textual) constructions apart, scatters fragments all about the place, and leaves in its wake, the debris of (non)understandings. My image of a deconstructive reader reflects not the demolition worker, but an architect: not the architect responsible for the original design, but visitor architects, visitors with intimate knowledge of many constructions, and with skills and aesthetic sensibilities which enable them to appreciate how these lines and spaces, came into being, and how choices were made which selected these angles and not others, suggested this emotion and not the other – in short is able to appreciate and describe some of the aesthetics and ideas, as well as the materials they theoretically take apart, fragment by fragment.

At the end of such an exercise, the house is understood only in the intellectual pursuit of its endlessly morphing and diffusing and finally unknown parts and possibilities. In the context in which I am now writing – that of the discipline of management – I suggest that communities of readers do discover finite meaning in texts, and that deconstruction might well be understood in the context of the familiar root metaphor of 'framing'.

Working with multiple perspectives is now commonly understood as framing:[9] each different perspective of the same situation is seen as offering varied, but valid understanding. 'Frame' suggests a window. If, in our intellectual voyaging we arrive at a particular house, one with many windows, then we see that the angle of vision, and therefore the interior image that is glimpsed, alters, perhaps dramatically, as we move from window to window; and yet we are all the while looking into the same house, perhaps, or the same room, seeing the same things. So the one text, in a dominant reading, may mean different things to different readers as each gazing into the room's interior from a different window, brings to their reading the lens, the frame of their own experience through which to view it.

The deconstructive reader (and I am now thinking and writing within the 'frame' of the larger root metaphor of construction, of building) who arrives at a locked door, instead of just peering through a window, prizes it open, and tries to go inside that room or building, in endless pursuit of a knowledge of every last nail, every whiff of glue, every tiny space, even of the absent inhabitants of that room, that house, that place. The construction of each room consists of a myriad of smaller and larger constructions, all supporting, in tension with, perhaps threatening the existence of all other parts of the construction, and simultaneously denying that which was not constructed.

As a reader, I am interested in both the construction itself, the physical artifact, the black marks on the white page, and the syntax which makes sense of these, but I am also much intrigued by the spaces the building has enclosed, and the great spaces outside that it has excluded. I want to explore every nook and cranny of this construction, this building, this room, this fleeting moment beneath my hand of tiny, intimate whorl in wood, or print on the pane or page, as I return again and again to the same scene for never-ending discovery.

But as I understand it, deconstruction is an abstract, imaginative idea of an ideal understanding of text. It is not, of its very nature, achievable. In deconstruction there is always more meaning still undiscovered, for *différance* suggests an infinity of suggestion rippling out beyond the text, and of ripples not yet even shimmering to life. So in the end I abandon the quest by pausing for a moment, to try to capture what I am exploring at that moment in that place. This is the moment I write and try to share with readers: I write 'my exceedingly close, fine-grained, meticulous, scholarly, serious, and, above all, "responsible"' discovery. It is a responsible approach to reading. It is responsible both in the sense of 'responding' to something in the text that tends to drop out of view, and in the sense of being able to 'give an account of itself in scholarly terms' (Caputo 1997: 77).

Thus the close reading advocated by the New Critics is expanded and deepened by incorporating into it some of the deconstructive approaches to reading that the theory outlined above supports. Close reading of texts becomes closer than close. And yet although by the 1970s Anglo-American critics were importing the theory of the European poststructuralists, the challenge that this presented to the practice of textual criticism based on the – now well-entrenched – New Critics approach, was seemingly limited by two factors. The first discomfort that may account for rejection is that deconstruction, the interpretive strategy of poststructual criticism, is revolutionary – it overturns standard meaning – and is often perceived to be deeply upsetting, even subversive. The second discomfort is that deconstruction is a reading strategy that is necessarily based on familiarity with complex and difficult theory – impatient readers may, even though they identify with what they know of the theory, be tempted to abandon efforts to employ practices based on it, dropping it instead into the 'too hard' basket. For these reasons perhaps, poststructuralist approaches to text analysis have never achieved the popular uptake that was accorded the New Critics.

This then was the critical world of literary scholarship until it was challenged by reader-response theorists. This later movement listened to the debates engendered by the deconstructionist, engaged in them, absorbed a great deal of critical theory from them, and then began to move attention on from the text to the scriptor, the reader. These theorists argued that texts do not 'mean' until readers interpret them, and theirs is the theory that my next section covers.

The reign of the reader: Reader-response theory(s)

The evolution of classical theories of text interpretation and analysis into the epistemologies of poststructuralism, and even more latterly into reader-response theories is, I think, illuminated by Barthes' theorizing of the evolution of perceptions of the creation and control of textual meaning.

In classical traditions writing is understood to be a function of authors. Their role has priestly attributes in that their 'work', their texts, convey nonnegotiable meaning: when a work is written by an author, the verb 'to write' is intransitive. As Barthes describes them, authors' texts are works that are *lisible* (readable) because they follow recognized conventions of, for example, logic or plot, and syntax, and are therefore comfortably interpreted by the literary establishment. The reader assumes the role of the consumer, consuming the product produced by the author – and this is the dominant mode of capital. The reader-as-consumer is assumed to be dependent upon the recognizable, overdetermined, development of a lisible text.

When written by a writer, the verb 'to write' is understood to be an activity, and the writer's role is that of the clerk. Writers engaged in the activity of putting black marks on white paper, make texts of many genres, and collectively this *écriture* (body of texts) is understood as a social institution. It exists for all readers to make of it what they will. They are not bound by a creed that demands obeisance to an author. These texts may be perceived as illisible (unreadable) when the scriptor (reader) is understood to be the successor to the author. When the scriptor is the producer of the text, it is always in the process of production, for meaning is discovered in the aporia, rather than the development, of the text.[10]

In general then, critical theories which can be loosely designated as 'reader-response',[11] tend to replace the graphocentrism of the structuralist and poststructuralist movements by insisting that we should focus not on the text, but on the reader of the text. Their theorizing replaces 'an aesthetics of production by an aesthetics of reception'.[12] Even as the traditional focus of criticism, elucidation of the intention of the author, was displaced by the movements which placed the text itself centre-stage, so too the centrality of the text was displaced by theory which argued that readers 'write' (create) their own meanings.

This shift of perspective, emphasizing the act of reading, and taking into account all of the experiences, expectations, worldview and responses of readers as they engage with the text, leads to the conclusion that because meaning is the 'production' of the reader, there can be no one primary or right reading. There will be as many productions, as many interpretations, of the text as there are readers, and each reading will have its own validity. Because from this position it may follow that it is impossible to establish 'well-grounded distinctions between fact and interpretation, between what can be read in the text and what can be read into it',[13] through much of the theorizing of the act of reading, the question of authoritative meaning remains contentious. Two literary theorists, Wofgang Iser and Stanley Fish, address this challenge: Iser seeks to explain an author–reader complicity that involves us all in shared textual meaning-making; and Fish introduces his notion of 'interpretive communities' in order to explain why individual interpretations may, or may not, find wide currency.

Iser's theory seeks out the delicate balance of textual determinancies and readable interpretations. He suggests that the reader becomes creatively involved in meaning-making when authors suggest more than their texts actually say: when the 'unwritten' part of a text stimulates the reader's imagination to supply what is not there. In fact, the text is not completed until it is fully 'realized' in the mind of the reader. It is this collaboration of writer and reader in the art of what Fish has called text-making (1980: 172), that Iser describes in detail, and it is a theory that is particularly supportive of my approach to text analysis.

Iser (1972, 1980) describes the act of reading as finding a place between two poles: the artistic (the text) and the aesthetic (the reader). If we think of the act of reading being dominated by proximity to one pole or the other, or taking place somewhere along a continuum established between these two poles, then it is clear that some readings are more aesthetically realized than others. If the artistic (text) only comes alive when it is realized (read) in the reader's mind, then we see that some readers will contribute more to the meaning-making process (realize the text more completely) than others. The reader who reads a great deal 'into' the text (inputs more of their own understandings and emotional experiences) moves closer to the aesthetic pole and further from the artistic pole.

In later comment on this argument, Iser elaborates:

> In view of this polarity, it is clear that the work itself [the realized text] cannot be identical with the text or with its actualization but must be situated somewhere between the two. It must inevitably be virtual in character, as it cannot be reduced to the reality of the text or to the subjectivity of the reader.
>
> (Iser 1980: 106)

In other words, texts come to life, can be *konkretisiert* (realized) (Iser 1978) when responses are awakened in the reader that bring the words on the page to life: when the reader's imagination actively engages with the text and the 'gaps' in it, and fills them.

As already noted, to its critics, reader-response theories seem to suggest a cacophony of 'reader-written' texts, providing no common territory in which to explore meaning. How then can there be any common understandings among readers if the reader's imaginative meaning-making roves freely beyond conventional textual boundaries? Stanley Fish both acknowledges this seeming impasse and meets the challenge it presents by describing the concept of 'interpretive communities'. He first highlights the paradoxical notion that any one reading is both unique to a particular reader, and yet at the same time is produced by a common set of interpretive assumptions. As he tells it, this understanding led him to 'the problem of accounting for the agreement readers often reach and for the principled ways in which they disagree' (1980: 148). He addressed the 'problem' by developing 'the notion of interpretive communities as an explanation both for the differences we see – and, by seeing, make – and for the fact that those differences are not random or idiosyncratic but systematic and conventional' (ibid.).

Fish reminds us of two facts of reading: that the same reader will respond differently when reading two different texts; and that different readers will respond similarly when reading the same text, and then provides an explanation for these facts based on his notion of 'interpretive communities':

> Interpretive communities are made up of those who share interpretive strategies not for reading (in the conventional sense) but for writing texts, for constituting their properties and assigning their intentions. In other words these strategies exist prior to the act of reading and therefore determine the shape of what is read rather than, as is usually assumed, the other way around.
>
> (p. 171)

Fish insists here that what he has described as an 'interpretive community' is not a 'collective of individuals', but a bundle of strategies or norms of interpretation that we hold in common and which regulate the way we think and perceive. His statement encapsulates a seminal point in his theory position that I will shortly rely on when explaining my method of reading in Chapter 4, for Fish elaborates on his definition of interpretive communities as follows:

If it is an article of faith in a particular community that there are a variety
of texts, its members will boast a repertoire of strategies for making them.
And if a community believes in the existence of only one text, then the
single strategy its members employ will be forever writing it. The first
community will accuse the members of the second of being reductive,
and they in turn will call their accusers superficial.

(ibid.)

If the claim that Fish makes here is applied to the interpretation of management theory texts, then it is clear that those who belong to the first
community, and 'boast a repertoire of [reading] strategies', will produce
multiple readings of the same text. Members of the second community, those
who assume that there is one generally agreed strategy for interpretation of
these texts, 'forever' rewrite them according to this agreed script. Because
members of this second community are inclined to accuse members of the
first community of being 'superficial', of finding meaning that, even though
justified according to their strategies, is of no relevance to other readers, there
cannot be dialogue between such different communities until their different
strategies of interpretation are acknowledged and understood.

As I write, I am sometimes intrigued, more often bemused, by the interpretive communities of management theorists: the many chasms deeply
scarred through our diverse reading strategies deny a dialogue that could leap
the voids. An anonymous reviewer of a paper[14] I submitted to the *Academy
of Management Review* illustrates the point:

> Postmodernism (PM), [is] a school which asserts there is no such thing
> as objective knowledge or objective interpretation, that definitions are
> arbitrary, that there is no way to know reality, that reason cannot
> discover the truth, that everything is subjective, that all standard [*sic*]
> reflect the biases of one's reference group, that all moral standards are
> just personal preferences. This fact [*sic*] alone is enough to disqualify all
> post-modernist writings from serious consideration.

(Anonymous *AMR* reviewer,
personal communication, 11 October 2000)

Stanley Fish (1980) both generalized this problem of 'communities' and
summed up the barrier to dialogue when he wrote that 'the assumption in
each community will be that the other is not correctly perceiving the "true
text"', whereas of course 'the truth will be that each perceives the text
(or texts) its interpretive strategies call into being' (p. 171). This being so,
dialogue will only begin when different communities can discuss their
'interpretive strategies', an initiative that I am taking by detailing my reading
method in my next chapter. Then those who believe, as I do, that an infinity
of 'texts' (interpretations) may be discovered in any one text by different
readers, may still debate the 'true text' that any one reader finds there, on

the grounds that the particular interpretive strategies employed should be challenged.

But Fish makes one further point that highlights the legitimacy of a unique interpretation: while there is, as demonstrated by the concepts noted above, a stability of interpretation in any distinct community of readers, this stability, unlike the timeless stability of the physical text, is temporary. It is subject to 'shift and slippage':

> The notion of interpretive communities thus stands between an impossible ideal, and the fear which leads so many to maintain it. The ideal is of perfect agreement and it would require texts to have a status independent of interpretation. The fear is of interpretive anarchy, but it would only be realized if interpretation (text making) were completely random . . . In other words interpretive communities are no more stable than texts because interpretive strategies are not natural or universal, but learned.
> (p. 172)

Reader-response theory provides epistemological support for what many members of the community of management scholarship might well designate an idiosyncratic reading of management texts. If idiosyncratic is understood as individual, unique, special, then yes – I think that every reading act, including each rereading of the same text by the same reader, is a 'one-off'. The input of the reader cannot be circumscribed, but a reading that earns a place in an interpretive community will be one that is able to demonstrate the critical process from which it emerges. Text analysis, interpretation or text-making, is not random when readers declare themselves, give away all pretence of objectivity, do not hide behind an illusory presence, voice their interpretive strategies, and make transparent the cues that have directed their readings.

It is in the company of critics, such as Susan Suleiman,[15] critics who recognize this turn to the reader, this heterogeneous field of interests, this plurality of voices and approaches, theoretical and methodological, that the approach to reading that I have termed 'scriptive', finds a home. Suleiman, writing in the metaphor of the journey

> Not a single widely trodden path but a multiplicity of criss-crossing, often divergent tracks that cover a vast area of the critical landscape whose complexity dismays the brave and confounds the faint of heart.
> (Suleiman 1980a: 6)

that I too have built into the narrative of my text, calls up again for me, my interpretation of *The Thought Fox*, and my merging image of an awesome, empty winter landscape with print marks on the blankness of the snow-white page. But the tracks I see, the spaces I wonder at, are yet not those that Suleiman, or any other reader exactly shares.

Freund (1987) explains: 'In its variegated forms, reader-response criticism undertakes to narrativize, characterize and personify or otherwise objectify the reading experience and its conditions. It undertakes in short, to make explicit *features* of the reading experience' (p. 6, italics added). In a trend which is liberating the reader from 'enforced anonymity and silence' and amidst a 'labyrinth of converging and sometimes contradictory approaches' there is yet a general affirmation of the necessity to acknowledge the subjective, the unique, the possibly idiosyncratic voice of the always individual, always inevitably personal reading.

This swerve to the reader insists not only on reality as a hermeneutic construct, but also that until criticism re-recognized the role of the reader in the reading process, scholarly norms demanded that criticism be cognitive, not emotive: the 'rule of impersonality . . . pretends that the critic is as free of quirks and oddities, and of linguistic mischief, as he is of ideological and psychological motives' (p. 5). In the 'turn' loosely described as reader-response criticism, the supposed impersonality of critical reading and writing is unmasked:

> Reader-response criticism attempts to make the imperceptible process of reading perceptible by seeking to reopen to scrutiny that which has been declared inscrutable, illegitimate or trivial. It braves the ghost with a challenge to stand and unfold itself. . . .
>
> (ibid.)

Like Horatio, challenging the ghost of Hamlet's father, reader-response theory challenges the illusory reader to reveal herself, to voice her presence: for 'the swerve to the reader assumes that . . . all perception is an act of interpretation, that the notion of a "text-in-itself" is empty, that a [text] cannot be understood in isolation from its results, and that subject and object are indivisibly bound' (ibid.). Reflexive knowledge-making is well-served by reader-response theories.

It is under the rubric of this catholic embrace of the collectivity of individual readers that I discovered epistemological support for all that I perceive to be peculiar to my own reading. Because each and every reader may bring something 'counter, original, spare, strange'[16] to their textual interpretations, they may also find there, in the spaces, in the connections, in the drama of the text, meaning that moves from the communal to the unique and vice versa. Although reader-response theories continue to struggle with the tension generated by textual constraints on the one hand, and the enfranchisement of reader sensibilities and history on the other, 'the primacy of the reader as the founding term for a critical theory or practice' (Freund 1987: 154) though it may be challenged, will not again be easily ignored.

Performance, perspective and persuasion: Pragmatic criticism

At this point, recognizing myself as a reader-response critic, intimately and meticulously reading my way through texts as if watching a film, shown in super-slow motion, being analysed by an imaginative film critic; and attempting at the same time to keep my balance on Iser's artistic–aesthetic pole, I began to recognize a return to life of the relationship between not just text and reader, but also between author and reader, a relationship which it seems to me is facilitated by the text.

As I read, as I pulled on the loose threads of text that all too easily unravelled, and travelled along the interweaving strands of tangled skeins on the undersides of what had long been viewed as artful tapestry, or pushed miniscule filaments apart to discover meaning in hidden spaces, I made a surprising discovery. My 'closer than close', sometimes deconstructive, reading was ironically leading me not just further into, and further out from the text, but seemingly also towards a closer engagement with the author of the text. I was rediscovering authors who, far from being 'dead', seemed to live on as very vital presences in their texts.

On the one hand, the deconstructive and reader-response theories I was absorbed in seemed to be coherent, intelligent and fun; on the other my own reading practices seemed, as ever, to revolve around the old familiar text-mediated author-reader relationship. My experience is reflected in Freund's concluding remarks as she completes her survey of reader-response criticism and notes 'the existence of an insurmountable rift between theory and practice'. Although theory cannot maintain the distinction between the objective (the author's text) and the subjective (the reader's reconstruction) of it, in practice the distinction always returns. It returns in order that acts of interpretation can continue to be produced. Freund's final point is that 'reader-response criticisms are at once generated and undone by this unresolved tension' (1987: 152).

From this impasse there seems to be no way forward other than to acknowledge the following contradiction: although reading acts are always undertaken in the context of a unique situation, and texts are joint author-reader productions where we find the reader in the author's text and the author in the reader's text, there is, simultaneously, a conventional perception of the separation of the author's, or the autonomous, text from the subordinate reader that enables the interpretive act. I suggest that while much reading practice is dependent upon the maintenance of the 'fiction' of separation, the reading strategies employed by the readers who have wrestled with this fiction have been refined by the demands of the engagement.

As noted above, in my own reading practice, I have found myself moving back along the author–text–reader continuum. This direction was surprisingly enabled by my simultaneous progress through the theory debates that seemed to tug against this current. I was rediscovering authors, as well as exploring texts. I sensed that my theory explorations were about to return to pragmatic criticism, to the voices of critics who focus on what texts 'do'. In theories of rhetoric, ancient and 'new', critical attention is focused on the author–text–reader relationship and the textual strategies that build this. I seemed to be travelling a circular route in my quest for the theories on which I might base my reading method.

So at this juncture, I noted that while the theory I have already discussed supports my reflective approach to text interpretation (for I aim to acknowledge the uniquely personal experiences and proclivities – intellectual and emotional – which determine my reading outcomes) I also saw that my reading-response is, at least initially in the dominant reading, geared to the effects of certain textual strategies employed by authors in order to effect aesthetic, instructional and emotive responses in the reader.

The critical practices of New Rhetoric[17] undertake to identify and analyse these textual elements. They explore the rhetorical resources available to authors as they try, consciously or unconsciously, to impose their fictional worlds upon the reader. Because I had noted the diversity of theoretical persuasions among reader-response critics and the contended premises of their debates, it seemed that I might add one more theory strand to the fabric of my methodology, one that offers the insights provided by pragmatic criticism.

Under the rubric of 'New Rhetoric', Kenneth Burke (1989) best sums up my understanding of persuasive rhetoric when he suggests that it is all of the semantic and syntactic elements of a text that may be instrumental in bringing about the identification of the reader with the writer and/or text. If we see this as 'the art of discovering warrantable beliefs and improving those beliefs in shared discourse' (Booth 1974: xiii), then we may conclude that while we are back in the vicinity of Aristotle's 'famous, sweeping definition . . . an ability in each particular case, to see the available means of persuasion' (Covino 1994: 17), the distinct point of difference is that Burke's notion of 'identification' is much more all-embracing than Aristotle's notion of persuasion: it includes elements of perspective and performance.

When Burke argued that we should think of 'persuasion' in rhetoric as 'identification', he understood that readers actively participate in acts of persuasion, for 'you persuade a man only in so far as you can talk his language . . . identifying your ways with his' (ibid.). He linked this insight to classical rhetoric when he also cited Augustine:

> A man is persuaded if he likes what you promise, fears what you say is imminent, hates what you censure, embraces what you commend, regrets whatever you built up as regrettable . . .
> (St Augustine, *De Doctrine Christiana*, cited in Burke 1969: 50)

but also expanded traditional views of rhetorical theory when he noted that rhetoric persuades 'to attitude' rather than to 'out-and-out action'; and that persuasion 'involves choice, will; it is directed to a man only in so far as he is free'.[18] Classical notions of persuasion depict 'persuaded' persons as passive: Burke's explanation of identification allows that while the reader's thoughts and feelings may be directed by a text, perhaps by an author's voice speaking from within the text, readers who 'identify' with the text, choose to see in it messages that are in tune with what they are disposed to believe in and/or act on.

Persuasion then, as explained by Burke, is the first aspect of the identification achieved by rhetoric that I intend to work with. Foss *et al.* (1991) in their carefully honed definition of rhetoric, comment on two more aspects of the identification that effective rhetoric achieves: it is both 'an action human beings perform', and 'a perspective humans take' (p. 14). Construing rhetoric as perspective and performance, as well as persuasion, ensures that we do not lose sight of authors who, as performers in their own texts, set out to persuade readers to take up an attitude, to identify with the perspective, the worldview presented.

The second aspect of rhetoric that I have identified for comment, 'performance', is often interpreted as 'playacting or pretence – something divorced from reality' but Foss *et al.* return to the original meaning of the term, 'to furnish or carry through to completion' as they explain their understanding of it in a rhetorical context:

> This latter sense – of 'making not faking' – is what is meant when we talk of rhetoric as performance. To study rhetoric as performance is to examine any of the enabling and energizing forms of action through which humans and cultures constitute and reconstitute themselves. Performance is the act of bringing to completion a sense of reality – of bringing out the significance of meaning of some cultural form.
>
> (p. 329)

My interest in performance follows this line of thinking, but I do not dismiss the more popular understanding: that rhetors can be seen in the 'who' of the text, in the privileged voices of authors or the personas that seem to speak for them. Wherever I sense an author's presence in the text, spontaneous or staged I pull on the thread of my response to see if an unravelling begins to appear.

Classical rhetoric assumed that the orator who was known to be of good character was the one whose words were thought to be most powerful: we are more inclined to believe fair-minded people, more quickly than we do others. Credibility, and emanating from this, persuasive power, was discovered in the 'who' rather than the 'what' of the message. In classical rhetoric, the man most respected represented the moral virtues of loyalty, truth, steadfastness and generosity.

In the contemporary social and political environment, where expertise and wealth are respected more than virtue, we revere rhetors who present as experts and whose expertise is seen to have made them wealthy. We identify with business gurus or research scientists who can convince us that they know more than the rest of us, who are leaders among their own elite, but who yet seem to speak on behalf of all, not just for their own inner coterie of experts. It is perhaps when the rhetor presents as one who invites the reader into an intimate relationship, while delicately balancing this coziness against the security of distant authority, that we are most readily convinced.

It is through the author's voice, the author as a performer in the text, that readers are enabled to relate to the projection of this persona.

Authors who present as omniscient, remain outside their material, always in control, above or outside looking in. Able to come at their material from many diverse angles, they need never personally engage with the reader. They may remain unknowable and the reader may interpret this 'presence' as authoritarian, and may well admire or fear this seeming control of power over the text. If authors choose to write in the third person, from a particular point of view, the reader may be led to identify with this position, but they also run the risk of alienating those who feel excluded. When the author speaks to us directly, in the first person, sharing thoughts and personal experience, we may warm to these disclosures, and feel the author to be honest and accessible. If at the same time these authors convince us of the authority with which they speak, as readers we may feel complimented by our inclusion, while we are simultaneously impressed by gravitas, by the tradition, dignity and the authority of the text. We may become willing converts to the content of the message thus conveyed.

The third aspect of rhetoric that I have recognized as an element in reader/writer identification is described by Foss *et al.* (1991)[19] as a perspective that humans take:

> To say that someone takes a 'perspective' on something is to say that person has a particular way of viewing that object or concept. A perspective is a conceptual lens through which a person views the world. Just as a set of lenses can color our world, a set of conceptual lenses can color the way we interpret phenomena.
>
> (p. 17)

In rhetorical analysis, this notion of perspective may be searched out from either end of Iser's continuum: it applies to analysis that is directed at the artistic pole, the author's text, and may also be a reflexive examination of the aesthetic pole, the reader's reconstruction of the text. In the case of the former, rhetorical analysts probing both what the text seems to say and how it seems to say it, surface the values, assumptions, hierarchies and exclusions that they discern playing about the structures of plot or argument. This is a search of perspective situated at Iser's artistic pole. At the same time 'perspective' as situated towards Iser's aesthetic pole acknowledges that individual readers bring to their reading a worldview, a set of values, assumptions, ideas, emotions and lived or vicarious experience which, overtly or covertly, determine their response to the text.

Management theory texts are often purposive to the extent that they are intended to persuade readers of the substantiveness of a logical, researched argument. At the same time they assume a perspective that is dependent upon the worldview of the writer, and this may well be primarily carried by the root metaphors in the text. If rhetoric is understood as language that persuades the reader to identify with the worldview of the writer, then the root metaphors that both create and circumscribe this worldview are arguably rhetoric's most powerful device.

So, even while readers are discovering the character of the writer (*ethos*) through his or her performance in the text, and establishing the progress of the argument or the story or the creed around which it is built (*logos*), they may also be responding to the emotive impact of strategies designed to persuade (*pathos*): 'For we do not give the same judgement when grieved and rejoicing or when being friendly or hostile'.[20] The means by which this identification of reader, text and author are achieved are as infinite as the authors, texts and readers engaged in rhetorical text-making.

We now have an overview of rhetoric that recognizes reader identification with the text as containing the three elements of persuasion, performance and perspective. I see New Rhetoric as having evolved from its classical origins in each of these areas, and linking back also to much that I have discussed in the theory of literary criticism, where strands of persuasion, performance and perspective are plaited so closely together the text becomes just one fabric. Any or all aspects of the text may persuade readers to identify with the performance and perspective conveyed by it.

All rhetors, to a greater or lesser extent, engage through their texts with the emotions, as well as the mind of the reader. Readers who understand the skills of the rhetor, and the role of these skills in melding an identification of author, text and reader, control this three-dimensional relationship. Thus recognition of an author–reader relationship is the fourth and final step of my progress through literary theory. Ironically it is also a return to classical beginnings in 'old rhetoric', and perhaps the direction in which textual inquiry in the third millennium will proceed.

As I see it: My methodological position

Tracing my journey through the recent (twentieth century) history of literary theory has allowed me to disclose the development of my evolving critical understandings and to place my present critical position within this broad context. It has also provided me with the theory base on which I have built my approach to reading and which I describe in the next chapter. A summary of my understanding of the critical literary theory I have reviewed, and my responses to it, follows.

Traditional literary criticism focuses attention on the intention of the author. It aims to explain the standard or dominant meaning of the text. Common sense or standard interpretations of texts assume that language represents an external, knowable reality, and that the job of the interpretive critic is to reveal more of the author's intended meaning. Because standard readings dominate most discussions of text, any reading otherwise with which we engage cannot escape the conversations that take place across competing critical perspectives, and these dialogues will be constructive to the extent that diverse perspectives are understood and respected. I recognize this stance as the first phase of the reading process and incorporate it into my approach to reading. Derrida describes these standard readings as 'dominant' and this is the term that I too will utilize.

Structuralism and New Criticism focus attention on the text disassociated with authorship, and their close reading explicates more of the text's meaning. I am comfortable with critical approaches that find meaning in the patterns of imagery, wordplay, thematic idea and connotations that play in, through and about the text. But even as I work with structure on this level, identifying 'principles of unity' within the text, I understand why the New Critics were moved aside by the deconstructionists: their 'close readings' were not close enough, for as servants of the text they were still, unwittingly, in thrall to the author. The author's intended meaning is still served by their approach to reading, even though the New Critics acknowledged that their reading strategies reveal more than the author is consciously aware of having created. New Critical reading confirms the artistry of the text, as well as the message of the author.

Deconstruction, in stark contrast to the reading approaches described above, is sometimes imaged as seeming to blow the text apart. All the careful connections and constructions discovered by structuralist reading are laid out in little bits, the flotsam and jetsam of *différance*, of contraries and deferment. Meaning is understood to be endlessly elusive. It cannot even be approximated with assurance let alone definitively established.

Although I do not see my reading as finally deconstructive in that it does seek out meaning that is 'more or less justified, more or less free' (Barthes 1974: 5) I have assimilated a great deal about meaning-making from these theorists, and have adopted two other leanings in my approach to text analysis that demonstrate this. My reading is effectively 'closer than close reading' (de Man 1986: 116–17) and I also identify with Caputo's (1997: 77–9) description of the Derridean critic who, in particular reading moments, pauses before a chink, 'a little crack' in the text and searches for that which is going on in the text behind the author's back; for that which is omitted, forgotten, excluded, expelled, marginalized, dismissed, ignored, scorned, slighted, taken too lightly, waved off in other readings of the same text. There is in every 'nutshell' of the text, an infinite expanse of meaning to be explored.

I also keep company with the deconstructive critic who, accepting that deconstruction cannot ultimately be understood or explained because all explanations deconstruct themselves in the process of attempting an explanation, recognizes that deconstruction is best understood through reading examples of it. Hence there cannot be rules to guide deconstruction. The process of reading can be described and strategies of interpretation explained, but reading outcomes are ultimately imaginative acts and cannot therefore be controlled by the logic of systems and codes.

But although my method of reading has been very much influenced by the insights provided by deconstructive critics, I have found that to walk too far along the road they have mapped is to arrive at a nihilistic position which, in an organizational world of action and affairs, no longer makes any sense. We parted company when I met up with a party of reader-response theorists. As an autonomous reader, I see my role as that of a 'scriptor' the writer of my own text. Despite the final 'undecidability' of textual meaning, reading as a process-without-end, yet results in the production of reader-made-texts.

As a reader-response critic I recognize the autonomy of the reader, the scriptor. Endless variety and infinite possibility is the outcome of every reading, and potential reading, by every reader and all readers. Derrida's 'ghost of undecidability' does not image a 'pathetic state of apathy'. Instead it continually reminds us that there is something to decide, even though when a decision, an interpretation, has been made, undecidability hovers before, during and after the decision – for undecidability is a structural given in narrative. The possibility of reading otherwise must always be kept alive, for we must be serious about the elements of text 'delegitimated' in any one reading.

In the environment of an 'interpretive community' we must theoretically maintain a distinction that allows for the autonomy of the objective fact, a textual artefact, and for the autonomy of the subjective reconstruction of it, the reader's interpretation. For although both autonomies cannot theoretically be simultaneously maintained, and although attempts have been made to modify each 'autonomy' by placing readings on a continuum that runs from the artistic pole (the text) to the aesthetic pole (the reader's experience of text), my reading of critical theory as outlined above suggests that the jury is still out: the indeterminancy of textual interpretation and the inconclusiveness of critical debate are intrinsic components of the theory debate.

Despite these theory problematics, critical practice continues as always to thrive: readers interpret and reinterpret texts, sometimes on the basis of an attempted justification of the theory base from which they work; sometimes, particularly in management scholarship, with cavalier disregard for it. Given this mountainous fissure between theory and practice, it seems to me that the most enabling route to the accommodation of plurivocal commentaries is one that makes transparent the individual, perhaps highly personalized, epistemological understandings that have informed a particular critical practice. If I, for example, an interpreting reader-turned-writer, share my experience of this theory debate with my readers, then at least my text analysis may be understood in the context of these described perceptions.

In summary then, in my review of literary critical theory, I found critics who set out to discover the author's intention; critics who claimed 'the text's the thing' and the author irrelevant; and critics who claimed that it is the reader who is the 'maker' of the text. All of this was provocative and useful, but even taken altogether in one generous banquet, it still left me with a hunger for something more: despite the intellectual play and profound philosophy I discovered and explored in the many libraries of books on theories of literary criticism, I was dissatisfied with the theory base I was building until I came upon what I now see as the keystone to my own theory-building. In the world of management, texts are performances, author-acts in a world constructed by language, and New Rhetoric restores the writer–reader relationship denied by Barthes (1977a).

I found the final ingredient of the methodology that I have developed in the ancient, but recently revived, study of rhetoric. In the realms of comment on rhetoric I found that if understood not as the 'harlot of the arts' (the empty but emotive hype of add-on imagery), but as the dignified procurer of an author–reader relationship, rhetorical theory could close the loop of the circuitous epistemological route that I had taken. Rhetoric allows for the recognition of strategies that the author has utilized in bringing about reader identification with the text, and through the text-as-mediator, also with the perspective, the worldview, overt and covert, of the author.

Recognition of this role of the text does not in any sense 'compete' with the poststructuralist notion of the 'undecidability' of texts. Rhetoric is concerned with essentially contestable meaning, so there are no rules, no given procedures for discovering what or how a text means. As an art, rhetoric offers no guaranteed procedures because the essentially contestable can always be otherwise. While the author may be a performer, a privileged voice in the text, the extent to which the reader identifies with any textual strategy, perceived content, or particular voice, is an interpretive outcome ultimately dependent on the meaning-making of the reader-as-writer.

Rhetoric also brought me back to metaphor theory, not to the notion of the trope as descriptive analogue with which I began this romp through theory, but to metaphor as the 'master trope' Aristotle identified and admired for its powers of realization and persuasion. In the root metaphors of texts I might find embedded meaning, in the voice of the author and the interpretations of the reader I might find the dynamics of a writer–reader relationship, and, utilizing the tools of the deconstructionist, I might find in the text itself, the messages that readers may be persuaded of without their conscious recognition of them.

I saw that when rhetoric has achieved a reader–writer identification, the root metaphors embedded in the text may be absorbed into the worldview of readers without their being consciously aware of this osmosis; where the surface level meanings are logically argued and the rhetoric in which the argument is constructed is subtle yet seductive, the reader may 'buy-in' to positions and postures which are not consciously noted or discussed.

Conversely, and of equivalent import, rhetorically naive authors may also be captive to a root metaphor which circumscribes their worldview and into which they unwittingly draw their readers.

In sum then, I have distinguished the various elements drawn from a variety of approaches to literary criticism, with which I identify. The synthesis of them that I have described above forms the basis of my methodology. This methodology is designed to establish the means by which readers may recognize: the projected character of the writer; the logic of the stories, covert and overt, told and not told in the multilayered, infinitely expanding text; and the play of emotion into which they may have been drawn.

Following Abrams,[21] who calls his approach to reading 'newreading', I saw my approach to reading as relying on 'a principled procedure for replacing standard meanings by new meanings'. It would not be 'new' in that it would rest on precedents that reach back as far as ancient Greek and Roman attempts to 'uncover deep truths hidden within Homer's surface myths', and to reinterpretations of the Bible by Jewish Kabbalists; but it would be new in the discipline of management to the extent that my particular blend of interpretive strategies might lead me to assert that a passage means something radically different from what it had formerly been taken to mean.

At this point then, and drawing on more than 2000 years of textual inquiry, I felt that I had identified the ingredients of my approach to reading, of my methodology. An initial common-sense reading would establish the surface level or standard meaning of the text and the author's seeming intention; a second close reading, following some of the practices of the New Critics and the Deconstructionists would discover some of the multilayered, plurivocal possibilities of the text; and in a third stage, my reading would consider the origins and vagaries of my individual interpretation. In summary then, as I recalled the routes I had taken on my journey through the theory of literary criticism, and the picnic spots of rest and reflection, at which I have paused while reviewing my responses to this reading, I found that I had reached a point in my understanding of texts where I regard all texts as co-productions, an enterprise in which both author and reader are actors.

4 Scriptive reading

A method of text analysis

Horizontal equates with delusive,
When only the vertical
Remains open to my use,
And influence.
But I am unleashed by language . . .
    Ruth Fainlight, 'Definition', 1985

In order to context my method of text analysis in literary theory, in the previous chapter I described diverse literary theories which variously prioritize: the intention of the author; the multiple voices to be heard playing through the deconstructed text; the emphasis placed upon individual interpretation by reader-response theorists, and the renaissance of rhetoric in recognition of the text-as-mediator in reader–author identifications.

In management studies, as described in Chapter 2, there are textual analysts whose strategies of interpretation reflect a diversity of literary theory. These critical theorists are similarly encouraging readers to recognize both the autonomy of the text and the validity of multilayered, multidimensional interpretations of it. In recent years this field has now developed to a point where I see it as being ready both to consider seriously the development of interdisciplinary links with literary criticism, and to adopt interpretive approaches to reading based on methodologies borrowed from it, including this newly minted approach that I have termed 'scriptive reading'.

An approach to reading

My 'method' of text analysis progresses through a three-tiered critical reading process, culminating in a representation imaged by the 5Ps model (see Figure 4.2) presented below. While it floats upon torsive eddies of perpetually merging and dispersing theory, it is nevertheless consistently supported by the several readily identifiable epistemological currents summarized in the previous chapter.

Because I am both indebted to this diverse theory, and also conscious that I am transporting it across a disciplinary divide into a reading community for whom it may be largely unfamiliar, I suggest that my 'method', as explained below, is best understood as an approach to reading:

> How does one deconstruct a text? . . . As for critical method, there is none. Not really. Rather, the critic operates creatively, teasing out themes, inconsistencies, and pontifications in a text, starting down one path and then another, looking for semantic uncertainty until it is time to stop. A deconstructionist never *concludes*.
>
> (Hart 1997: 319)

As I noted in Chapter 2, deconstructive reading is better understood as a text analysis strategy, a form of commentary over the read text, a commentary that produces, as the reading progresses, another text. It is a productive reading in two senses: the reader both writes a new text, and at the same time invents and articulates the textual strategy appropriate to the text being analysed and the reading angle from which the deconstructionist reads and writes.

So while the 'method' that I will adopt will follow a described process, it will also employ whatever reading strategies spontaneously serve my questioning of the texts as I read. This approach to reading and text analysis is further supported by the theory of the deconstructionists who have pointed out that any attempt to systematize a critical approach immediately threatens the very nature of the enterprise:

> To present deconstruction as if it were a method, a system or a settled body of ideas would be to falsify its nature and lay oneself open to charges of reductive misunderstanding.
>
> (Norris 1987: 1)

I think that to most readers the word 'method' suggests replication and validation. It assumes outcomes that can be agreed upon; that there is a finite, final position that is comfortingly assured, resting as it does in some accepted logic of activity and interpretation. The approach that I will follow assumes that individual readers will arrive at different reading outcomes; that there can never finally be an agreed outcome; that an interpretation may include the exploration of an aporia,[1] or a space, or an intertextual link, or any kind of bafflement (De Man 1986: 23); that in itself any single interpretation is ultimately no more, nor less, than a recognition that simply offers itself up as yet another collection of marks and margins, and more spaces, for further exploration.

While I expect that my community of readers, my 'interpretive community', will recognize the road I have followed as I make meaning from the texts I read, perhaps even identify with the interpretive outcomes of my reading practice, I also allow that every described position in my discoveries is perhaps another reader's aporia or irruption, yet another moment in which the text disintegrates in the very act of being read, into further possibilities of deconstruction and reconstruction. So I present my conclusions as moments in my reading in which the infinity of possibilities that they represent simply becomes a little more visible.

To lay down rules of interpretation that could be followed by another researcher (as opposed to outlining the steps that have been taken in following a method) would be to deny the role of the individual reader, the writer of her own text, the scriptor, that my argument supports. It would be to circumscribe the interpretive process in precisely the manner that my scriptive reading aims to eschew.

My approach to reading then provides not a method, as it has traditionally been understood, particularly in the positivist traditions, but a reading process, one that allows individual readers who follow a similar process to arrive at dramatically different interpretations. I have identified with Gareth Morgan's generalized approach to research to the extent that he sees it as, 'the process of reflective conversation . . . a conversation that is exploratory rather than evaluative' and one that he illuminates in an image of 'crafting' that seems to me to arise directly from the image of both readers and writers as 'makers' or 'creators' of their texts, text-makers:

> The image that I have in mind is akin to what happens when a group of craftspeople come together and exchange views. They do not necessarily end up agreeing with each other, and certainly do not leave the gathering to produce an identical product. Rather, they use the opportunity to make better sense of their own way of doing things and to learn how they may do their own thing better.
>
> (Morgan 1983a: 406)

My craft of reading is based on a unique blend of critical theories described in earlier chapters, and formed from a similarly unique blend of the critical approaches and strategies promoted by these theories. In describing my reading objectives and reading process, I aim to provide generalized, but nevertheless clear, guidelines to my approach to reading, for my intention here is to make my approach to reading sufficiently transparent to enable other researchers to engage with texts in this way.

The method which I outline below is a guide to the stages of my interpretive journey: it is a map of a well-worn path that has repeatedly led me to the moment, the pause in the text, in which possibility is kept alive by my reading otherwise. As I pass through what I will be describing as the dominant reading, and without abandoning this traditional understanding – indeed working within it, in the second phase, to enlarge on the meanings arrived at as I explore what it excludes, expels or marginalizes, belittles, exaggerates or contorts – I will endeavour to capture my impressions in text that will, in the third stage of my scriptive reading become the object of my comment. I am aware of the irony of my attempt to 'capture' meaning, embedded or overt, in the face of claims that meaning is endlessly elusive, but I understand every momentary capture as no more nor less than one more resting post in a journey without end. Following Derrida I will both 'play' (*jouer*) with meaning and will yet be 'scrupulous, gravely in earnest, deadly serious' about all 'omitted – "de-legitimated" – elements'.

Mindful of the confusion and debate that sometimes threatens to drown out serious philosophical discussion of text analysis,[2] and mindful too that I am choosing to import this contentious approach into regions where some have as yet given it only a tenuous welcome, and where others may be beginning to fear the colonizing grab of text-based approaches to their discipline, I have chosen to explain my approach to text analysis in as methodical a fashion as I can devise. It is for this reason that I have incorporated into my explanations of my reading strategies as much of a recognizable, explicable method of text analysis as a (fundamentally) postmodern 'non-method' of reading can absorb.

It is because I intend my own, my particular, critical readings here to be taken seriously, to be the inauguration of new approaches to thoughtful rereadings of foundational texts in management, that I have designated what I am about here as 'scriptive reading', and have set out to explain it methodically.

I have also summarized my interpretations of the texts that I have analysed on three matrices (Chapter 6). I see my readings as 'new texts'. They are not intended to represent final positions or conclusive meaning, but simply suggest some patterns of interpretation that may stimulate more new readings and further discussion of the texts themselves.

Reader as 'writer'

'Scriptive' is the descriptor that I have coined to denote my approach to the reading of texts, because as a reader, I perceive myself to be the maker, the 'writer' of my own text. When, in his *Poetics* Aristotle illuminated understanding of the creative act of writing by explaining it simply as 'making' (House 1956) – the meaning-maker, the poet, is simply a 'maker' – he might well have been describing the interpreting reader, for it is in this sense that I see the reader as ποιητής, the meaning-maker, the creative writer, a text-maker.

It is also his perception of this reader role that led Barthes to declare the death of the author, for it is 'language which speaks, not the author' and 'the modern scriptor [reader-as-writer] is born simultaneously with the text' (1977a: 143–5). Whereas in a traditional environment it is assumed that the reader is the consumer of a product, the *lisible* (readable) text, Barthes argues that readers should see themselves as scriptors, as the producers of a process without end:

What can be written (rewritten) today: the writerly. Why is the writerly our value? Because the goal of the literary work (of literature as work) is to make the reader no longer a consumer, but the producer of the text.

(Barthes 1974: 4)

It is this writerly activity, this scriptor productivity, that I have termed scriptive reading.

Etymologically, 'scriptive' is a word that reaches back to Latin roots in the verb *scribere*, meaning 'to write', but the root word from which both the Latin word, *scribere*, and the Greek equivalent, γραφειν, are sourced is *skrabh*, meaning 'to dig', 'to scratch', to engrave with a sharp point, and from Latin we also have *scrobis* meaning a ditch or a trench. These associated meanings enable 'scriptive' to conjure up a number of connotations that have immediate bearing on my method of reading.

Scratching the surface of an artefact may damage what had seemed to be intact, complete and finished, but it may also reveal previously hidden layers beneath that surface. Scratching the surface of a text may open up the little chink, perhaps a chasm, for further exploration. It suggests that my reading may become archaeological as I dig for root metaphors, for buried ideologies, for the constructed worldviews that are exposed in the deconstructed text. As I sit with my computerized notebook, reconstructing my interpretation of the text, a script of my own, I also understand 'scriptive' in the ageless text-making tradition of 'scratching or 'engraving' through the use of a sharp point. In this sense, words may be both physically inscribed and indelibly marked into the mind, and the markings made may be those of the picture-maker, for the Greek word, γραφειν, to draw with a pencil, to write, to paint, suggests the wordsmith as image-maker in the ancient sense of a pictorial text.

As I understand it then, the act of reading and interpreting a text is creative. It is an action outcome that is achieved via the imagination of each individual, and the product that emerges from this process mimics the act of the original author. Scriptive, in so far as it conveys the idea that readers are the authors of their own texts, is paradoxical, for it suggests that to read is to 'write', and it only 'makes sense' if it is also read metaphorically: the reader, like the writer, is a maker of meaning. Just as a *lisible* (readable and, from a post-structuralist perspective, overdetermined) text is formed in the crucible of its author's ideas, emotions and life experiences, before being transcribed into the literary conventions that enable its genesis on the page; so too the scriptive version of it emerges from a synthesizing of the reader's life experiences and formed worldviews with the ideas, values and emotions evoked by the text. Each reading act is unique. The meaning discovered in the text by any one reader will never be completely identical to that found by any other reader, though it may, with infinite variations, be more or less shared by other readers.

It is Barthes' recognition of the reader as scriptor, after the pronounced death of the author, introducing the reader as the author of her own text, producing scriptible (writerly) texts that enables me to slot the descriptor 'scriptive' comfortably into the lexicon of rhetorical theory.

Scriptive reading is inclusive of diverse perspectives in that it seeks to discover the play of previously unrecognized meaning in the subject texts, rather than to argue the validity of one meaning in place of another. It does not, for example, attempt to discount a dominant interpretation, but rather to supplement such a view by positing alternative, but equally valid, readings. It follows, of course, that the interpretation that a scriptive reading leads to is again no more than one of the many interpretations possible, and I aim to demonstrate this through an analysis of my own interpretation that suggests some recognition of the ways in which I have 'written my own text'.

A descriptive outline of the three distinct phases of the reading process that I employ follows.

The three readings

To contextualize my reading in both the conventional readings of management theory by students and practising managers, and in the manifold interdisciplinary rhetorics of qualitative research, I have constructed a method that progresses through a three-tiered reading process: the three phases of scriptive reading are illustrated in Figure 4.1.

First reading: Dominant reading

The first reading, phase one, is based on a summative paraphrase of the argument of the text. It may be understood as an example of a 'common-sense' response in the expressive realist tradition, is the response that might

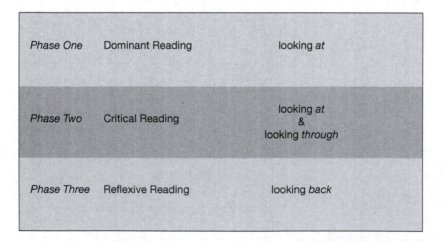

Figure 4.1 The three phases of reading

be typical of the ordinary reader, and is described as 'naive (semantic)' by Eco. I am more comfortable with Derrida's description of this kind of reading as 'dominant', for as in the classical tradition, it is a reading that follows what Caputo calls the 'dominant tendencies of the text, the smooth super-highways with numbered exits'. Moving easily along the highway, it passes by side-roads, walkways, rest areas and picnic spots, the aporias, the moments, the impasses, of doubt and difficulty that are discovered in the critical reading which immediately follows it.[3]

The dominant reading summarizes the argument, the *logos*, of the text, and attempts to reflect the intention of the author in so far as this can be assumed in line with standard interpretations. Although this reading is very restricted by the boundaries that I have placed on it, and therefore seems to me to be unsatisfactory as a 'stand-alone' response to the text, it is nevertheless presented as part of my own response to the text. In common with many other readers, and as a member of the interpretive community of management scholars and practitioners for whom the text has been written, this first reading represents both my own first response to it, and the response on which I have been accustomed to base dialogue about it with other readers. Indeed, it is a reading that I see as 'representative' in that I suppose it to reflect the many versions of the work that appear in student texts and management seminars. It is also a response which continues to provide a counterpoint to subsequent readings – one image of the revealed landscape in which I delve and twist and sift as I read again.

I describe this reading as paraphrasis because it is essentially a rewording of the original text. Because it is a free rendering, it is also a reading which will be guilty of what Cleanth Brooks has described as the 'heresy of para-phrase' (1947: 157–75) because an attempt to extract the main 'truths' of a passage, is immediately to subvert its 'truth'. It is discovered by looking at the text, at the surface level meaning conveyed in the argument or story of the text, the *logos*, of the text.

Second reading: Critical reading

Reading as a 'critical' (semiotic) reader, my second reading, the second phase of my scriptive reading, is my interpretation of previously unrecognized meaning in the text analysed. This is an idiosyncratic reading to the extent that the particular tropes, the turns, twists, tussles and tensions that I discuss are those in which I have a particular interest. A different reader would read these texts differently and this is acknowledged in the third stage of my scriptive reading process. But this second stage is the most detailed and the most extensive, and will capture the main thrust of my analysis. It is based on another set of three Ps: performance, perspective and persuasion. As illustrated (Figure 4.2) these three Ps suggest the complexity and depth of the second, critical phase of reading. They give it more weight and prominence than the simple paraphrasis of phase one and perpension of phase three.

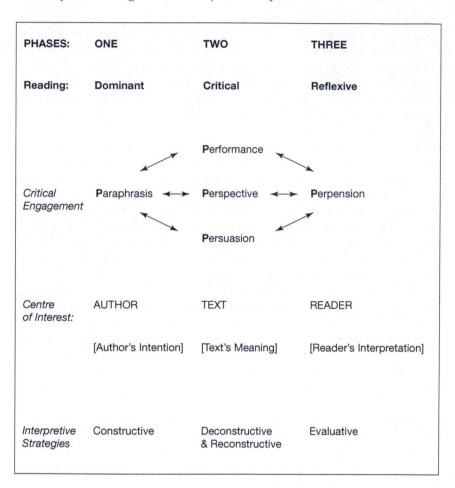

Figure 4.2 Scriptive reading: Interpretive phases

Performance

I identify the voice of the author as a performer in the text. This may not be the presence as seemingly intended by the author, or indeed as perceived by other readers, but support for my reading is provided through recognition of some of the semantic and syntactical strategies that seem to me to construct this presence.

Perspective

I also uncover, trace and connect the metaphorical meanings which work together to both construct perspective, or worldviews in the text, and also to attract reader identification with this meaning, overt and covert, in the text. In this second stage of the scriptive reading process I focus particularly on the role of metaphors in sense-making, because of the contribution they make to subliminal textual meaning-making. I search out the root metaphors that both 'assemble subordinate images together', and also 'scatter concepts at a higher level' (Ricoeur 1976: 64).

In Chapter 2 I described Lanham's notion of critical reading as 'toggling':

> This introspective quest for self knowledge, represents a broad-based willingness, if not a proclivity, to look AT what we are doing, at its stylistic surface and rhetorical strategy, as well as THROUGH it, to the Eternal Truth which we all, at the end of the day, hope somehow to have served. The characteristic schizophrenia dwells here too.
>
> (Lanham 1993: 170)

It is my attempts to look 'through' the text, to images of the 'Eternal Truth' that may, or may not exist, that my critical reading ultimately addresses and gathers together here under the generalized heading 'Perspective'. The discovery of perspective entails the seeking out of root metaphors, for these often provide a key to the 'other side' of Alice's mirror (Carroll 1960). In this phase of my reading, my focus of interest is not the images, in the mirror of the text. The representations of war, health, games, biology and mechanization that play in these texts are word pictures of a familiar world. They convey myriad aspects of organizations and work, people and society, managers and the managed and are fascinating to look at; but beyond these recognitions, below the surface of the text and behind Alice's mirror, there are more abstract notions – competition, conflict, motive, morality and justice – waiting to be discovered when we look through the text.

The distinction that I have made between looking at the text and looking through the text is illustrated in Figure 4.1.

Persuasion

This last aspect of my analysis is recognized in traditional rhetoric as persuasion and as an element of identification in New Rhetoric. I have opted for persuasion because identification – as understood and described by Burke, and on which I have commented in Chapter 3 – is more complex that persuasion. Persuasion works more overtly, suggesting a more immediate and intentional relationship between reader and writer, than does iden-tification. So in this closer than close rhetorical reading the selection of strategies followed and devices explored varies from text to text but always seeks to discover the means through which authors may set out to 'win over' the reader; to uncover the strategies that bring about reader 'buy-in' to the worldviews presented.

Third reading: Reflexive reading

My third and final reading phase is reflexive. Gareth Morgan has advocated viewing the process of inquiry through the lens of 'reflective conversation' for it is, he says, in conversation that we meet ourselves. This is conversation seen as a constructively critical way of attempting 'to confront and understand the nature and significance of what we do and how we might do it differently' (1983a: 406). In this sense, it is as much an exploratory, as it is an evaluative, step in the research process.

My interpretation of each text emerges from my own immediate experience of it. I do not attempt to historicize it, to read it in the reinvented context of the historical period of its inception. An attempt to do so would, I believe, involve me in layers of conjecture. Instead I respond to it as I would to any found document; I regard it as an artifact with a physical presence in the contemporary world and I read it as a living document.

Nor do I search out interpretive or critical comment on the texts before reading and responding to them myself. As a 'naive reader' with some, but limited, experience of both the text and comment on it, I see myself as a 'typical' management theory reader.

As this reading develops I may draw attention to my agenda in conducting the analysis, to my reader-based relationship to both author and text, and I acknowledge the interpretive community with whom I assume I am identifying. This latter is, significantly, one in which critic and theory are inclined to take precedence over text, and this is fully acknowledged. In analysing and describing my responses to the text I pay particular attention to my emotive reactions to the ideas and images it conveys to me, to the feelings engendered by these perceptions and to the synthesis of all this in my evaluation of it. I also comment on any contextual, environmental or other factors external to the text itself that may have influenced my reading of it. I describe this third approach to reading as perpension, my fifth P, because it is a process of apprehending, considering and evaluating and 'weighing up' the outcomes of my reading to this point.

The five P model

In Figure 4.2, I have provided a summary outline of the most significant elements in each of the three phases of the reading method described above. It illustrates the shifting emphases that move from perceptions of the author's intentions and analyses of what seem to be the constructions that reflect this; to a focus on the deconstructed text as an independent artefact, in which may be found a worldview, an authorial voice and suasive rhetorical devices, to an interest in the interpreting reader as a maker of meaning. What it does not show is that all of these elemental textual considerations cannot actually be separated out in, what appears to be, diagrammatically illustrated, a controlled fashion. Performance and perspective, for example, are aspects of persuasion, and perpension too could be seen as persuasive in so far as it seems to convey an objectivity that contributes to the 'reasonableness' of the deconstruction completed. In every text every element is concurrently present and part of every aspect of it as described above.

Caveat

In earlier chapters I described the literature reviews that led to the recognition that I should blend all I had learned from the review, merge this with my experience of text analysis and arrive at a method that would both guide my own interpretations, and provide a method that would enable other management scholars to follow the routes I have chosen.

I have described, and strive to work with, a reading process that might also be described as a method because, writing with my readers in mind, I am aware that my approach to reading is new in the discipline of management, and my intention is to make what I am about here as accessible as possible. But in strict counterpoint to this aim, I am placing a caveat on the method: on its seeming boundedness. Scriptive reading is boundaryless: in so far as I have described it as a method, I intend it to portray just what is discernibly happening in the reading process at certain given points along the way. Always there is hovering, somewhere within and just beyond the process I have described, and the *lisible* text itself, an imminent aporia, an entanglement of potential meaning that leads the scriptive reader, teasing out its knotty strands, further and further away from, and deeper and deeper into, the multilayered, multifaceted and plurivocal text, to a point where reading could both permeate and sop up like a soft blotter, the hypnotic pull of infinite possibility – to meaning-making that could become endlessly elusive.

My reading process

In conducting my text analysis, and basing this on the intensive method that I have described as scriptive reading, I have followed a reading process that entails reading the selected texts, and my analysis of them, several times. Step one in this process is a skim reading of the selected work before selecting a passage from it for analysis; step two is the three phases of scriptive reading of each of the selected passages; and step three is a review of the outcomes of my readings, and of my reading method, scriptive reading.

Step one, an overview, is included in the conduct of this particular inquiry because the texts chosen for analysis were lifted from the context of larger works: it is designed as a skim reading that allows me to place the selected passage in the context of the text from which it was lifted. While this contextualized overview of the passage selected for analysis may well impact on my interpretation of it, I see it as simply one of the many other cultural, biographical and professional factors that inform my unique readings.

Step three, a review, is included here because my inquiry ranges across five texts: it allows me to surface intertextual linkings that anticipate my discussion of key elements of the subtexts of management theory as they emerge from my readings.

Scriptive reading in action

Step two consists of the three phases of scriptive reading. Phases one and three of the scriptive reading process, the dominant reading and the reflexive reading, are familiar to qualitative management researchers. Phase two, the critical reading, is relatively unfamiliar to most management researchers and yet in scriptive reading, it is the most important of the three reading phases. I therefore describe the process of critical reading in more detail below.

As discussed in Chapter 3, deconstructive and reader-response theorists see no one fragment of text as ever being completely read, but as always in the process of being produced, so even a life-time of reading would not result in the complete reading of any text of whatever length: deconstruction is a process without end. Nevertheless, as I set out upon each scriptive reading, my interpretive excursions were generally shaped as follows.

As a scriptive reader, I begin at the beginning of each selected text and I search out meaning both horizontally ('distributional') and vertically ('integrational') for:

> To read . . . a narrative is not merely to move from one word to the next, it is also to move from one level to the next. . . . meaning is not 'at the end' of the narrative, it runs across it.
>
> (Barthes 1982: 259)

My dominant reading is primarily horizontal. Dominant reading assumes that the development of the text drives the reader, at varying speeds but more or less without hesitation, towards its conclusion. It also assumes that the text is coherent, and seeks to discover this coherency.

My critical reading moves along two axes as I explore vertically, as well as horizontally; on both axes I move spontaneously back and forth, jumping ahead and sometimes returning to a textual moment, perhaps an aporia, or a space, a submerged voice or a metaphor, pursuing wherever I sense them, more and more of the dispersing threads and fragments of textual meaning.

Reading in this way, I sometimes linger so long, in one continually fragmenting textual moment, teasing out elusive significations, that much of the text is left undiscovered. This is of no consequence as there will always be more undiscovered text on both axes, and I sometimes find it more illuminating to extensively explore up and down the vertical levels than to aim to get to the horizontal 'end' of the texts. Recalling the advice of Barthes, as explained earlier, I am content to have described the flower, and do not therefore fret about not having described the bouquet.

As described by Eagleton, this is the approach of the deconstructionist who

> seize[s] on some apparently peripheral fragment in the work – a footnote, a recurrent minor term or image, a casual allusion – and work[s] it tenaciously through to the point where it threatens to dismantle the oppositions which govern the text as a whole. The tactic of the deconstructive critic . . . is to show how texts come to embarrass their own ruling systems of logic.
>
> (Eagleton 1983: 133)

With this end in mind – an exposition of what the author seems to intend for the text, set in apposition to other intentions that I, as a critic, found in it – I set out 'to exhaust' some aspects of the text so that its multiple meanings became clearer. It is ironic that, as explained above, scriptive reading can be both exhaustive and yet never complete: it tugs at and shreds a fragment, a word, a phrase, a few pages, finding in these the particular thread that when played with first loosens and may finally unravel the fabric of the whole text. As a scriptive reader my pace is leisurely. I read my way through the text pausing wherever, and for however long I choose, at any given moment in my reading. I do not read my way sequentially through the selected text. Meaning is multilayered and widely distributed throughout the texts so that a network of connections and evaporations may find the reader diving back and forth, above and below, the sequential text. Text analysis is not 'a matter of recording a structure, but rather of producing a mobile structuration of the text' (Barthes 1988: 172).

In his text analysis, Barthes aimed to open up the significance of the text, to 'live the plurality of the text' (p. 173) and in order to do this laid out the four procedural measures that guided his reading. Although I do not follow his careful cutting up and numbering of the fragments of text on which he comments, I note and incorporate or adopt, some aspects of his four procedures into my own scriptive reading.

'We shall cut up the text'

Barthes describes these 'units of reading' as 'lexias' and he references them by number, but in order to maintain more readability and flexibility than Barthes allowed himself I do not do this: I have found that identifying the words or phrases I comment on makes the analysis more readable, and enables me to more readily focus attention on them. I do follow Barthes in seeing the word or phrase or sentence, the 'unit of reading', as 'an arbitrary product, it is simply a segment within which distribution of meanings is observed' (p. 173): and share his view that 'what the surgeons call an operating field' can be as short or long as the critic chooses:

... structurally the narrative shares the characteristics of the sentence without ever being reducible to the simple sum of its sentences: a narrative is a long sentence, just as every constative sentence is in a way the rough outline of a short narrative.

(Barthes 1982: 256)

'We shall observe the meanings to which the lexia gives rise'

Barthes writes here of the connotations, the secondary meanings, of his lexias, and describes them as 'the finest possible sieves, thanks to which we shall "cream off" meanings, connotations' (Barthes 1988: 174).

My critical reading sifts as finely as I am able the multilayered, endlessly connoting text.

'Our analysis will be progressive'

Barthes states his intention of covering 'the length of the text step by step, at least in theory'. He explains that 'reasons of space' do not allow him to provide more than fragments. It is this aspect of Barthes' analysis that provides comprehensive epistemological support for my decision to cut the selected texts back to a given number of pages, and I therefore quote it in full:

> ... for reasons of space we can only give ... fragments of analysis here. This means that we shan't be aiming to pick out the large (rhetorical) blocks of the text; we shan't construct a plan of the text and we shan't be seeking its thematics; in short, we shan't be carrying out an explication of the text, unless we give the word 'explication' its etymological sense, in so far as we shall be unfolding the text, the foliation of the text. Our analysis will retain the procedure of reading; only this reading will be, in some measure, filmed in slow-motion. This method of proceeding is theoretically important; it means that we are not aiming to reconstitute the structure of the text, but to follow its structuration, and that we consider the structuration of reading to be more important than that of composition (a rhetorical, classical notion).
>
> (ibid.)

My analysis moves in slow motion through the text, exploring structuration: both the web and the dispersal of meaning that weaves and eddies through integrational levels, even as it also leaps forward and back and forward again to varying stopovers along the distributional axis.

'We shan't [worry if] . . . we "forget" some meanings'

As Barthes explains this, 'forgetting meanings' is important: it is important to 'show departures of meaning, not arrivals; and he extrapolates further on this as he insists that what 'founds' the text is not some 'internal, closed, accountable structure' but, on the contrary, 'the outlet of the texts on to other texts, other signs; what makes the text intertextual' (ibid.).

Barthes, in his 'methodological conclusions' as he completes his analysis of the Poe text, states categorically:

> We have not carried out an explication of the text: we have simply tried to grasp the narrative as it was in the process of self-construction (which implies at once structure and movement, system and infinity). Or structuration does not go beyond that spontaneously accomplished by reading. In conclusion then, it is not a case of delivering the 'structure' . . . of . . . narratives, but simply of returning more freely, and with less attachment to the progressive unfolding of the text . . .
>
> (p. 191)

Barthes' explanation of his method of textual analysis in 'Textual analysis of a tale by Poe' has thus provided me with both supporting theory and a useful example of his method in action. I have described it in some detail as above in order to explain two aspects of my method: my selection of texts for analysis, and my approach to reading. The selected texts are not complete 'works' as classically understood, but 'blocks' lifted from their contextual bed. These blocks are read through varying levels, in varying concentrations, and are distributionally scattered.

All aspects of textual inquiry as represented by the five Ps are focused on this one short passage of text. Sometimes meaning-making seems to spin far out beyond, or delve far into the depths of the words on the page, but essentially this is a conversation that takes place about an isolated piece of text.

Selecting the texts

In order to select the texts for analysis, I first addressed two questions: 'What would be most useful to do?' and 'What would be most interesting to do?' As I saw it, these are quite distinct questions because whereas the first might, for example, involve a consideration of the classical theory texts that are most widely taught in business schools, the second might, for example, revolve around a personal choice of texts that I would be most interested in becoming intimately acquainted with. Pondering on these two questions I wondered if I should determine through a comparison of citations the scholarly impact of various texts; look at all-time bestseller lists; or perhaps attempt to synthesize the categorizations and conclusions of authors who have published collections of 'the most important' foundational writers.

All of these exercises appeared fraught. Foundational texts are often the source of the basic tenets of management that are presented in academic text books, but they are just as often introduced to students as the interpretation of every other classroom teacher: the authors are seldom read in the original. Bestseller lists may be the outcome of marketing chicanery; and published collections are usually put together on the basis of personal choice rather than empirical research.[4]

Having problematized the field of inquiry I searched for a third, and what was ultimately to be a much more useful, question: 'What analyses of theory texts do we currently have, and where might there be gaps (or gaping holes), the filling (or at least temporary inhabitation) of which would be useful to other researchers engaged in text analysis?' To some extent all three questions seemed to merge in the recognition that we have a few examples of the deconstruction of classical management theory,[5] and a few examples of rhetorical approaches to guru texts,[6] but while there are some attempts to classify both gurus and classical theorists on the basis of the kind of expertise that they bring to their writing,[7] there are also academic theorists who vehemently reject the 'guru' label, perceiving it to have pejorative connotations[8] even as others seem to welcome it. Given that it has not been established that the two genres of theory are distinct anyway, I decided not to exclude texts with guru characteristics.

I decided that if my selection were to start by including in my list only those texts that have been accorded academic recognition, then I could further refine it by focusing on texts that have also been appreciated by management practitioners. On this I followed the lead of Calás and Smircich (1991) when they 're-read four classic texts of the organizational literature': Barnard's *The Functions of the Executive*, McGregor's *The Human Side of Enterprise*, Mintzberg's *The Nature of Managerial Work* and Peters and Waterman's *In Search of Excellence*. They state that 'these texts have a common claim of being written more for organizational practitioners than for the scholarly community, but *they have influence in both communities*' (p. 568, italics added). This suggested to me the route I would travel.

Following Huczynski[9] in his search for the most popular management ideas of the twentieth century, I particularly noted his list of the eight most influential contributors to management theory (Fayol, McGregor, Drucker, Herzberg, Peters, Taylor, Likert and Argyris), and from it I selected two authors, Frederick Taylor and Peter Drucker. Huczynski's categorization of guru writers of the 1980s as academic gurus, consultant gurus and hero-managers further suggested to me that choosing from authors he lists as 'academic gurus' (business school professors or gurus with educational institution affiliation) would ensure that theory admired by both academics and business practitioners would be represented in my reading. So I added Rosabeth Moss Kanter's *The Change Masters* to my list.

Looking for some historical balance in my growing list, I decided to analyse two examples of influential texts dating from the foundational years of the discipline of management in the first decades of the twentieth century; two examples of 'classical' texts – that is, texts that (having been written from the 1950s to the 1970s) have withstood the first challenges of time and are still regarded as very influential by both academic and business practitioners; and an example of a very recent academic text (published in the 1980s and 1990s). I therefore added Henry Mintzberg's *The Nature of Managerial Work* from Huczynski's list of eight academic gurus.

Balancing my list as described above required the addition of one more foundational text. I chose Mary Follett because she also provided some gender balance, and because although she has recently been described as a 'prophet', and a 'management guru ahead of her time',[10] and was both a popular speaker at practitioner functions and also highly respected in the academic circles within which she moved in both the UK and USA, after her death her written texts though sometimes read were mostly ignored.

Because all of Follett's texts, her contribution to management theory, were originally written in preparation for their delivery as lectures, all of the theory authored by her that we read today is a written version of spoken discourse. But these texts are what management scholarship has been reading for more than half a century. Whatever the original audience, and however Follett might have geared her writing to that contemporary context, what the discipline now has is text, artefacts, black marks on white paper, and my definition of text (see note 1 in Chapter 1) is inclusive of written texts and written versions of texts designed for oral presentation.

Profile of texts selected

My final selection became the list illustrated in Table 4.1. This selection encompasses the following reflections and diversity. All the texts are individually representative of academic management theory: Taylor and Follett are classical theorists from the first foundational period of management; Drucker and Mintzberg are also foundational from the middle management period, are most often described as 'classical', but are also increasingly denoted 'gurus', and both are still writing and speaking; Kanter, one of the highest earning academic gurus currently consulting, writing and teaching, represents the final decades of the twentieth century.

Table 4.1 Texts as data

Theorist	Text	Date first published	Pages
Frederick Taylor	*Principles of Scientific Management*	1911	5–29
Mary Follett	*Freedom and Co-ordination*	1933	30–49
Peter Drucker	*The Practice of Management*	1955	1–13
Henry Mintzberg	*The Nature of Managerial Work*	1973	1–6
Rosabeth Moss Kanter	*The Change Masters*	1984	17–23

Further to these distinctions, I made my selection with four further 'repre-sentations' in mind. The first consideration was that there are very few women theorists from whom to choose. Mary Follett though not well known in her own time was hugely respected by the business and academic com-munities with whom she engaged, and has, in the last decades of the twentieth century, been widely reassessed and endorsed; Rosabeth Moss Kanter is one of the most successful (in terms of international profile and earnings) of a current handful of academic gurus.

Kanter shares her international profile and high earning capacity with Drucker and Mintzberg, both of whom also enjoy huge recognition by the academic communities. Thus a second consideration, that the selection includes authors who are highly regarded by both management practitioners and academics, is covered.

Third, although all of these authors are North American, three of them have close links with Europe. Mary Follett, although American, established deep empathies with and affections for the English way of life – she spent a year at Cambridge, the lectures from which I have selected text for analysis were delivered to London business audiences, and she lived the last years of her life in London. Henry Mintzberg, a Canadian, has been described as having a 'contrary' view of mainstream American management theory (Merriden 1998: 105–6), and spends much of his time teaching and working outside North America; and Peter Drucker, though enthusiastically American, is an Austrian who emigrated there, via Britain, in the 1930s.

Finally, two of the five theorists, Drucker and Taylor, are represented in Huczynski's list of the eight most popular management writers – the 'hard core' of really influential writers about whom there is consensus as to their contribution.

Because of my intention to discover patternings of differences and simi-larities across all texts after completing the analysis of each individual text, the criteria of selection as outlined above reflect my intention to arrive at a grouping of texts which would provide me with some broad suggestions as to what both their unique and their representative voices might highlight. Generally then, the criteria that guided my selection of texts were designed to ensure that all of the texts analysed have enjoyed academic acclaim: that is that they have all been written by research-orientated academics and/or consultant academics; that they are all particularly well-known, widely read and influential in the world of business practice, and that they are represen-tative of at least some historical, trans-Atlantic and gender differences of authorship.

Many months after making the decisions outlined above I was interested to read, under the subheading 'A research agenda: Taking a gendered look at the classics', Joanne Martin's (2000) suggested strategies for 'operationalizing' a selection of 'foundational or important' management scholarship texts to be 'targeted' for text analysis as they generally follow my own as outlined above. She follows up these suggestions by providing examples of what analyses of texts by three 'classic' theorists – Mintzberg, Taylor and Follett – might reveal, thus choosing three of the five theorists whose texts I had already analysed.

One outcome of the decision-making process that I have followed is that all of the texts selected are major works: books authored by five significant management theorists. Since the five books consist, on average, of 277 pages, even a dominant reading of each would become an overweighted exercise in my inquiry, and the critical readings would loom in even more unwieldy bulk. I therefore selected a section of text from each book for analysis.

Texts, whatever their length, offer the critical reader endless discovery, and I therefore had to decide how much text to analyse. Aware that the critical reader who gives away something of the 'scope' of the text in exchange for an in-depth study of some small part of it is rewarded by the 'power of the insight made available', I was also reassured by Hart's analogy of the anthropologist:

> The critic therefore operates like the anthropologist who sometimes finds in the smallest ritual the most complete depiction of tribal history and culture. The good critic never studies a particular text simply because it exists but because it promises to tell a story larger than itself.
>
> (Hart 1997: 25)

Hart also compares rhetorical analysis with case study methodology, for insights and understandings are gained via an in-depth study, with the critic as 'sampler'. Because the critic's focus is tight, the critic's challenge is to tell the largest story possible given the necessarily limited evidence available.

While discussing the critic as 'sampler', Hart also provides one warning:

> So the critic is a sampler, and samplers must be both modest and cautious and modesty and caution are not altogether bad. But modesty and caution do not ensure unimportance. What the critic gives up in scope is offset by the power of the insight made available. What ensures this power? Choosing a provocative text for study, asking important questions of that text, and drawing intriguing conclusions.
>
> (ibid.)

As I considered which part of the selected text might 'promise to tell a story larger than itself', and how, in choosing that part, I might provide for a measure of consistency and comparison across all of the original texts, I turned to Kenneth Burke's critical method. One of his favourite techniques is to extract from just a bit of text some intricate conceptual design. He looks at a piece of discourse for its representative anecdote, perhaps a scene/act imbalance, a narrative habit, a pattern of imagery, or a telling example, that sums up its rhetorical tone. According to Burke, such an anecdote will be representative if it contains the basic agon or master metaphor of the discourse system in general.[11]

In search of just such a representative anecdote I chose to focus on the introductory pages of each selected book. The final selection of pages is given in Table 4.1.

Each of the five authors has, in these introductory pages, provided generalized comment on their concerns and their ideas, as well as some kind of overview of the work on which they have embarked. They have, collectively, also chosen to use these pages as attention grabbers, seeking to draw readers on into the chapters ahead by making dramatic statements, and by giving readers a taste of what is to come. For these reasons, I surmised that the selected pages, when analysed, might, to this extent, be both representative of the works from which they have been drawn: and also that the patternings of similarity and distinction that my analysis would reveal, would relate to microtexts performing similar functions in the environment of the work as it has traditionally been understood.

The selected passage from the introductory chapter of each of the selected texts is then the 'data' that I analysed: and, in each case, the selected passage with which I intimately engage is just a few pages of text. I nevertheless also briefly indicate the structural fit of these pages into the context both of the chapter as a whole, and beyond that, of the chapter into the whole work, the book from which it has been lifted.

Interpretive community and dialogue

Having selected my texts, and mapped my approach to reading, I chose to read them as a 'naive' critic: one who reads the words on the page and responds directly to and intimately with them, eschewing reference to a historical or disciplinary context. As explained in Chapter 3, I do not see my interpretation of these texts as being in competition with other readings. On the contrary, I think that all critical readings that make transparent the strategies that have enabled the reading, that can demonstrate a grounding that supports their engagement with the text, deserve to be heard.

In Chapter 3, I also explained that I expect critical readings to be as multifarious as the readers who 'write' them, that the more readings we have of any one text, the more fully we may understand it. Rather than argue about what a text means, I would like to add my reading to other extant readings. At the same time, while not seeking closure, or attempting to win some imaginary argument about what these texts mean, I do also hope to initiate and stimulate more interpretation of, and comment on, these texts. In pursuit of this goal, as I complete the analyses of individual texts I turn to the bigger worldview to which they contribute. I sketch an outline of a generalized management-theory constructed world: the world that management theory assumes we live in, and the world that we are expected to want to inhabit.

To this end I complete each of the five analyses with a brief consideration of the outcomes of my scriptive reading. I look back over the sequenced readings and comment on aspects of my text-making that the scriptive reading process has stimulated and highlight developing concerns as they emerge from the promptings of dialogue that the juxtapositioned readings suggest. I reflect on my own text-making and hope that readers of my texts will read them scriptively.

Summing up

In a scriptive reading, all of the five Ps should be understood as a guide to the various stances I have adopted as I interpret the texts which are the subject of my critical analysis. They are not intended to provide a set of rules dictating set interpretive strategies: they do though provide a guide to my approach to reading, an approach that others might choose to adopt. To me these guidelines suggest a holistic reading rather than a fragmented one; a reading that gives the reader scope to dive and float, splash, stir and sail through the eddying currents of meaning that any text throws up as an infinite array of possible explorations. Because every individual reader has an infinite array of reading strategies to choose from, as well as the galaxy of possible interpretive routes to map, the reader is as much the maker of meaning as is the author.

5 Scriptive readings

There are some words . . .
Smooth-trodden, abstract, slippery vocables.
They beckon like a path of stepping stones;
But lift them up and watch what writhes or scurries!
Robert Graves, 'Forbidden Words', 1959

This chapter consists of five sections. In each I record my scriptive reading of one of the five selected texts. As already explained in the previous chapter, I have chosen to read and reconstruct the introductory pages of each text. Each scriptive reading is preceded by an overview of the selected passage, and concludes with a brief review of reading outcomes as enabled by my approach to reading.

The five texts that I selected for analysis range across a time span of eight decades. I read each text as an independent artefact, with a contemporary status in the environment of management theory.

Text one: Frederick Taylor

Overview

The text that is the subject of my inquiry here is selected pages from *The Principles of Scientific Management* (Taylor 1967). First published in 1911, the complete text of 138 pages is divided into two chapters of dissimilar length, preceded by an Introduction of just three and a half pages. Chapter 1, 'Fundamentals of Scientific Management', is 21 pages long, while Chapter 2, 'The Principles of Scientific Management', makes up the remaining 113 pages. Because the Introduction is particularly short, I have forayed out into Chapter 1 in order to extend the scope of my analysis.

The complete text is a work the author, Frederick Winslow Taylor, hoped would provide readers with principles of management that would be as applicable to the management of all social activities, as to the managers of the industrial and manufacturing establishments for whom it was more immediately written (p. 8).[1] Certainly the author of and 'the father' of management theory has remained, whatever the vagaries of academic fashion, somewhere near the centre of management thinking and debate for more than eight decades

Dominant reading

Taylor clearly sets out his own terms of reference, as he overtly sees them, in the opening line of his Introduction:

> President Roosevelt, in his address to the Governors at the White House, prophetically remarked that 'The conservation of our national resources is only preliminary to the larger question of national efficiency'.
>
> (p. 5)

'National efficiency' is his over-riding concern and goal and he immediately insists that 'competent' men will achieve it; and competent men will be trained when a scientific system is prioritized. Each of the following five paragraphs is built around his notion of efficiency and its inverse, inefficiency. The phrase 'national efficiency' is repeated in four of the five paragraphs. In paragraph six, Taylor moves to his notion of competence, repeats the word 'competence' twice in both this paragraph and the next, and in paragraph seven also returns to the now very familiar phrase, 'national efficiency'. With this connection between competence and efficiency forged by the iteration, he moves to his advocacy of 'right' training (training which will enable 'ordinary men' to co-operate efficiently) and the system that will provide such training: 'systematic management'.

Lest we should be in any doubt as to his intentions and beliefs, he summarizes for us the three main tenets of his argument (p. 7), listing them under italicized headings: the whole nation is 'suffering through inefficiency'; this situation could be righted by 'systematic management', and this management rests upon fundamental, scientific principles. So fundamental are these 'principles' that Taylor prepares to promote them with 'equal force to all social activities' (p. 8).

In Chapter 1, Taylor introduces maximum prosperity as the overriding, the 'principal object', of scientific management, and goes on to link it first with profit, and then with production. In the first eleven paragraphs he sets out his 'prosperity' argument: prosperity for all results from the increase in profit which is directly proportionate to the increase in production which results from the training of competent men in a scientific system of management. The goal, maximum prosperity, is dependent upon the efficiency of the worker.

Taylor illustrates the need for management to hear his argument by drawing a comparison between the achieving sportsmen of England and America to the nations' underworking workmen. He lists as the cause of this 'condition' three factors: worker belief that increasing output will lead to unemployment; defective management systems, and rule of thumb methods of working. He elaborates on each of these factors in illustrative anecdotes and analogous extensions of his argument.

He concludes by asserting that if work tasks are done according to scientific laws and under the active guidance of management, all obstacles to obtaining maximum output will be 'swept away' (p. 27), and all people will be more prosperous and happier.

While I do not assume that Taylor consciously structured either his argument or the rhetoric in which it is conveyed as described above, I do assume that he would more or less concur with the general tenor of the comments I have made here. I also see my dominant reading as representative of most standard textbook accounts of Taylor's ideas, in that it reflects much of the traditional and popular reading of his text across the decades. It highlights the voice of Taylor, the scientific management theorist.

Critical reading

A critical reading of Taylor's text calls out other voices: Taylor the moralist; Taylor the preacher, and ultimately, Taylor the Utopian. These are voices that sing solo only when the interpreting reader mutes the more strident tones of surface level meaning, as described above, and also hushes down some of the more decorative tropes that a traditional reading comfortably acknowledges – tropes that ornament the text. These are tropes that dress ideas, making overt connections as they highlight certain attributes of the subject in illustrative analogies, and Taylor makes effective use of them.

Conspicuous examples, already familiar to most of his readers, are metaphors such as those of war, 'a large part of the organization is for war rather than for peace' (p. 10); sport and war, 'Whenever an American workman plays baseball . . . he strains every nerve to secure victory for his side' (p. 13), and health, 'The elimination of "soldiering" . . . would have a more permanent . . . effect . . . than any of the curative remedies' (p. 15). Even as I focused on the dominant reading, rhetorical images of competition were trying to creep into my comments.

Competition in the employee–employer relationship 'is war' (p. 10), says this text, but as the emphasis changes first to profit (pp. 10–11) and then to production (pp. 11–12), so too 'competition' (from outside the company) is legitimized as the motivator which will persuade workers and managers to be 'for peace' (p. 10). Concluding his 'reasoning' (p. 12) Taylor reminds us again of the 'object' (p. 12) sought: competent workers, producing with maximum efficiency, and bowing to the 'self-evidence' (p. 13) of his 'principles' (p. 13).

He illustrates his argument with anecdotes and folk-wisdom. 'Soldiering' (p. 13), the deliberate slowing down of production by workers who choose not to work to their potential, is described in some detail. That the attitude that inspires this practice is not the natural disposition of workers is promoted through the juxtaposition of sport and industry. On the sports field of cricket, in England, and baseball, in America, any workman who 'fails to give out all that there is in him' (p. 13), so goes this analogy, is 'branded as a "quitter," and treated with contempt'. Back in the workplace, any worker who attempted to achieve his best output would bring out the same opprobrium as the 'quitter' in sport. Thus 'underworking' or 'soldiering' must be explained, confronted by the scientific principles of management, and ultimately trained out of the worker's *modus operandi*.

As he makes the shift to explanation and advocated direction, Taylor's metaphors of sport and war make way for the 'curative remedies' (p. 15) his science prescribes. Picking up on the notion of the 'suffering' (p. 14) of the nation, and the implied illness which a 'remedy' would cure (p. 7), he later describes soldiering as that which has 'afflicted' (p. 14) working people, suggests that 'curative remedies' currently being prescribed are not coping effectively with this 'condition' (p. 15), and generally links the 'alleviation of suffering' with the 'diminution of poverty'. Metaphor moves into narrative when he tells us that, far from resulting in the injustice of unemployment, increased production will lead to more comforts for workers and their families – they will wear shoes every day – and narrative melts back into metaphor when we are told that the speed of mechanized production provides an object lesson.

Men were first bracketed with machines two pages back, 'the output of each man or machine in the trade' (p. 15) and the machine metaphor for which Taylor is justly famed begins now to frame his arguments. Organic, 'rule-of-thumb' (p. 16) methods are denigrated and the 'sciences' of measurement (p. 20) and 'true facts' (p. 18) promoted. Seemingly unaware of contradicting his earlier sporting anecdote and accolade, he goes on to tell us that it is the nature of man to be lazy: 'the natural laziness of men is serious' (p. 20) and restricts even the 'product of the machine' (p. 24). Only the discovery and adoption of the 'one method and one implement which is quicker and better than any of the rest' (p. 25) will correct this inherited flaw. As revealed by science, this saviour will be the 'accurate, minute, motion and time study' which will involve 'the gradual substitution of science for rule of thumb throughout the mechanic arts' (p. 25).

In the concluding section of the chapter, Taylor sets up yet another vast platform for the reign of managerialism: 'the workman who is best suited to actually doing the work is incapable of fully understanding' the scientific system, the one best way, and must therefore rely on 'the guidance and help of those . . . over him' (p. 26). Certainly his mentor, from whom he will receive daily help, and who will enable him to do his work 'better and quicker' (p. 26) will be friendly, even 'close' and 'intimate', (p. 26) but the 'co-operation' (p. 26) will be imposed, and the routines discovered, 'the essence of scientific management' will be 'mechanized' (p. 26).

Complementing metaphor analysis as above, more meaning may be discovered in the text if we 'forget' the overt message conveyed primarily by the nouns in Taylor's text, such as the endlessly iterated calls for 'efficiency' (p. 1) and 'prosperity' (pp. 9–12). Instead I have noted the qualifiers, the adjectives, what emerges as 'right' (p. 6), 'better' (p. 6), and 'best' (p. 7), or 'evil' (pp. 14, 18, 20), 'lazy' (p. 20), 'greedy' (p. 22), 'selfish' (p. 22); and the verbs, what should not be 'suffered' (p. 7), or should be 'believed' (p. 8), by those who 'mislead' (p. 23) and 'deceive' (p. 23) and the message that emerges is a moral message. It is also is a moral message that finds its clearest expression in the root metaphors of the text, and it is the root metaphors in the text, metaphors that play about below the surface of the dominant reading that, dug up, primarily reveal the other voices in Taylor's text.

One of the root metaphors upon which Taylor has built his text is that of an ideal moral order which seems to emerge from the received wisdom of a seemingly Christian Taylor. It is held in place by notions of good and evil, of right and wrong, and of a better way of being. It assumes a morality that necessitates endeavour to realize an ideal world and laments the fallen state of an ignorant humankind. It images a barbaric 'now' of sin and suffering and visions a future time of civilized order and virtue. Even the materiality of this vision echoes the physicality of Christian teaching and belief. Much of the rhetoric of the text reinforces this bold contrast: present evil, poverty and suffering are set against future virtue, riches and peace.

In the everyday world, the 'nation' is despoiled, 'wasted' and 'suffering' (pp. 5–14). Its citizens are 'ignorant' (pp. 17, 21), 'evil' (pp. 14, 20), 'hypocritical' (p. 23), 'lazy' (p. 20), and led by the 'devil' (p. 20). They live in a 'hunting' (p. 6) ground beyond the bounds of civilization where 'truth' (p. 29) and the 'profound' (p. 29) could be the birthright of virtuous citizens. In Taylor's ideal world, happiness is equated to prosperity: 'under scientific management . . . [people] will be far more prosperous, far happier' (p. 29). It seems that he has no notion of virtue other than hard and efficient work habits, and on the inculcation of this 'certain philosophy' (p. 28) he is 'profoundly convinced' (p. 29) that 'the civilized world' will 'sooner or later' provide a 'better' life 'for all the people':

> That these principles are certain to come into general use practically throughout the civilized world, sooner or later, the writer is profoundly convinced, and the sooner they come the better for all the people.
>
> (p. 29)

In the ideal world that Taylor would have workers and employers alike strive to achieve. Where the 'right' (p. 6) and the 'best' (p. 7) reign, there would be order, 'rules and laws' (p. 25), and security, because all would share total commitment to belief in Taylor's system – 'there is always one best method and best implement' (p. 25); the securing of 'maximum prosperity' (p. 9), the 'highest state of excellence' (p. 9), maximizing material gain (pp. 9–11) would guarantee 'happiness' (p. 29) to all, because all would be 'first-class men' (p. 7) trained right (p. 6), and therefore the 'best' (p. 14).

A second root metaphor to emerge from my reading is that of 'money as a God substitute' (Gusfield 1989: 168–76). It has been argued that Christianity's great fear of the devil-as-Mammon recognizes the threat of a powerfully attractive alternative to the Christian God as a moral motive, and critical reading suggests this is a position which Taylor has taken up: 'better men' (p. 6), 'first-class men' (p. 7) the 'best men' (p. 7) must believe with Taylor that making more money is the 'highest' (p. 9) goal. Striving, the need and will to progress individual and societal goals (itself a western, capitalistic assumption), here becomes identified with a Christian focus on good works, or an action-based moral path, as the only, the 'one best' way (p. 25) to virtue. Those who do not recognize the call, Taylor's call, are 'evil' (pp. 14, 18, 20): they have fallen prey to the lazy, slothful habits of the ignorant.

Extracted from the text in this crude way, Taylor's vision loses much of its charm. Yet in context, the voices of the root metaphors that are submerged in the tide of his scientific reasoning may engulf the reader in an overwhelming swell of rhetoric. Initially Taylor utilizes the words of a secular prophet, President Roosevelt, to establish a sense of national identity: 'the conservation of our natural resources . . .' (p. 5). His Introduction opens with a direct quotation from the President's prophetical address ('President Roosevelt prophetically remarked that . . .' (p. 5) to the White House Governors, and he follows through with an insistence that Roosevelt is the voice of the nation, 'the whole country' (p. 5), the voice of all the people, 'no one can deny' (p. 11). Taylor also assumes that he speaks (in the first person plural) for all his readers; 'We can see and feel' (p. 5), 'What we are all looking for' (p. 6). Later in the text, with this assumed common identity, problem and search in place, Taylor disguises his personal views in the anonymity of the third person singular, 'It is hoped' (p. 10), the passive, 'This paper has been written' (p. 7), and the passive combined with third person singular, 'The illustrations chosen are such as, it is believed' (p. 8). A few pages further on he generalizes, 'no one can be found who will deny' (p. 11), and as if confident that he speaks for all, briefly reminds his readers of the perspective he assumes they share with him, 'let us now turn to the facts' (p. 13). He addresses them directly in the rhetorical question he poses, 'Why is it, then . . . ?' (p. 15) before answering in the even more remote guise of 'the writer' (pp. 17, 18, 20, 21, 25, 27). In the role of the omniscient author, speaking anonymously, his words take on an air of assumed objectivity and authority.

Lest readers should have been somewhat alienated by the opening harangue, Taylor is also quick to remind them that 'the English and American peoples are the greatest sportsmen in the world' (p. 13), so that with national and personal pride restored, readers are expected to still be on his side as the bombast builds through pages 17–21. Workmen and their fathers before them are all 'ignorant' (p. 17); the workmen, labour agitators and sentimental philanthropists all actively spread fallacies (pp. 17–18); laziness is a natural instinct (pp. 19–20); 'soldiering' is evil (p. 20) and the whole present situation 'ludicrous and pitiable' (p. 20). As his argument gathers emotive pace, 'soldiering', described as the 'greatest evil' with which working people are afflicted (p. 14), becomes an 'evil' against which 'hardly a single voice is raised' (p. 18). Men who 'loaf' are following a 'natural instinct' (p. 19) for 'the natural laziness of men is serious' (p. 20). It is the 'greatest evil' (p. 20) from which both workmen and employers suffer. In the interim, intimacy with the reader is furthered by the homely anecdotes of sports, 'soldiering' and shoes. Taylor's rhetoric draws us from the grand picture of a suffering, impoverished nation, back to the life and plights of the individual worker and his family.

His opening appeal to secular authority (President Roosevelt) has already been noted. Through this page of text peppered with the word 'efficiency', the image which emerges is one of a vast wasteland in the making: forests, soils and mineral wealth squandered in the flood-waters which sweep down to the sea. In the midst of all this desolation, profligate human-kind is 'blundering', 'ill-directed', 'awkward' and 'inefficient' (p. 5). What is needed, says the author, in the dominant reading, is 'greater national effi-ciency' and 'competent men' (p. 6). What is needed, says the text, as I have interpreted it in this critical reading, is 'better' men, men who realize 'duty' (p. 6), men who are 'right', who are 'born right' (p. 6) as well as 'trained right' (p. 6), who are 'first-class' (p. 7) and will 'rise to the top' (p. 7) because they are 'best' (p. 7).

Perhaps this should be read as signifying no more than the Victorian hierarchy of class and birthright, of duty to King and country, but here, Taylor is building immediately into the first of his three statements of aims: he intends to point out the great loss which the whole country is suffering through inefficiency in almost all of our daily acts. Suffering, righteousness, right and wrong actions, the import of morality in even the slightest of daily endeavour, begin to suggest a text that has a biblical voice.

Suffering, in a biblical context, is the natural condition of fallen man and must be atoned for by good works. In Taylor's text it is the state in which the 'ordinary' (p. 7), and 'the average man' (p. 19) must exist, until shown the one best way to happiness and taught to believe in it. This same biblical voice echoes in the vocabulary: the repetition of 'daily' (pp. 6–7) and comment on 'the fruits of their labor' (p. 7), as well as the already noted references to good and evil. It is captured too, in the paratactic style of, for example, paragraphs 3 and 4 (pp. 5–6) so phrases within sentences and complete sequences of sentences, are placed one after another with few connectives other than a noncommittal 'and'. It is a lean, dramatic and action-implied style that echoes the phrasing of the Bible. Paragraphs throughout the first chapter of the book of Genesis begin, for example, 'And God said . . .' or 'Then God said . . .' (Genesis 1: 1–31). Sentences in paragraphs 4 and 5 begin: 'And for this reason . . . As yet there has been no . . . And still there are . . .' (p. 6).

All of these intertextual links with the Bible play through the illustrative anecdotes that, like the parables, provide moral teaching in the form of small, friendly stories.

In the sporting analogy of cricket and baseball (p. 13), Taylor adopts a self-righteous tone of 'contempt' for the 'quitter' who does not 'give out all there is in him', and the 'golf caddy boy' is presented as the potential victim of the 'licking' awaiting workers who do not learn 'soldiering' quickly enough (p. 21).

Much of the tenor of this intertextual play dances also through a reading of the parable of the workers in the vineyard. The biblical version tells of a landowner who hired workers for his vineyard, and paid them unequally, but in accord with both their contract and his generosity. That narrative concludes, 'so the last will be first and the first will be last' (Matthew 20: 16). Taylor concludes, 'in the past the man has been first: in the future the system must be first' (p. 7).

Showing the way, creating the vision, is the role of the prophet and the priest and is the moral voice of the text. This new world, this Utopia, will be one where poverty is banished – the workers and their families will not only wear shoes all the time, they will have, if they want, two pairs per year! (p. 16); where 'afflictions' (p. 14) are cured with 'remedies' (pp. 7, 15), and where men will live free from 'discord and dissension' (p. 29). It is a 'civilized world' (p. 29) built upon a moral order that is visionary; and which calls upon readers to envision in 'an act of the imagination' (p. 6).

Recognition of Taylor's principles will inspire a new order which is premised on what is right, 'the right man . . . trained right as well as born right' (p. 6). and what is good, 'better . . . more competent men . . . [who] realize . . . duty' (p. 6), and will be realized when endeavour raises men from their natural fallen state of 'ignorance' (p. 18), 'laziness' (pp. 19, 20) and 'apathy' (p. 6). His principles are to be applied not just to industry and manufacturing, but to all social activities (pp. 8, 29). If we would enter into this ideal order, then we should premise the way we live in all social spheres, from home and farm to church, university and government, on his teachings: his 'principles' (p. 8), his 'theory' (p. 27), his 'philosophy' (p. 28), or, in sum, his 'scientific management' (p. 28).

Set against this vision, as is the wont of the redemptive priest, the voice of Taylor the preacher paints a despairing picture of the reign of 'evil' (pp. 14, 18, 20) over human creatures who are enthralled to the 'devil' (p. 20). He insists that men are 'lazy' (iterated three times on p. 20), and 'loafing' (p. 19) and that this 'natural laziness' is serious. Men are also 'ignorant' (pp. 17, 18, 21, 26); 'greedy and selfish' (p. 21); deceitful and 'hypocritical' (p. 23); 'suspicious' (p. 24), and stupid: of 'insufficient mental capacity' (p. 26). Later in the text these men are classified as animals: men 'of the type of the ox' (p. 62); they are 'so stupid, and so phlegmatic that [they] more nearly resemble in . . . mental make-up the ox than any other type' (p. 59). These are the 'awkward', 'ill-directed' and 'blundering' (p. 5) men of the opening paragraphs who inhabit a land of waste and destruction, and whose 'ill-directed' actions continue the process of despoliation.

Silhouettes such as these, when etched against the backdrop of the surface narrative of the text might seem to be so alienating that the aware reader might question how it is that other readers have so readily subscribed to a worldview that incorporates materialism, inequality of birth, distinctions based on class and a Hobbesian view of human nature, all wrapped up as a moralistic vision of a better world. Readers who imagine that they have simply concurred with a rational, scientific argument, might well reassess their imaginative identification with the total package when they consider the emotive suasion in which the argument has been couched.

The voice of Taylor the preacher employs the rhetoric of the orator and the pulpit to win his readers' identification. He assumes that author and readers speak with one voice in his use of the first person plural: in the first four paragraphs (p. 5) 'we' 'appreciate', 'see' and 'feel' the sad plight of 'our' nation. We are at one as 'the whole country' shares the problem and the challenge he depicts. In the constant appeal to our visual perception, in repetition of the 'we can see', he insists that while the visible problem is familiar to, and accepted by all, the 'less visible, less tangible' is an equally shared, though only 'vaguely appreciated' common problem and challenge.

To ensure that readers are moved by his argument, the impact of all of these opening paragraphs is strengthened by antithetical images and ideas. Antithesis is a powerful rhetorical device because the setting of any one thing against its other radically defines the element 'victimized': it brings 'dramatic saliency and at least apparent clarity to any issue' (Gusfield 1989: 73). In the first four pages of the Introduction, Taylor writes that a 'large movement' (p. 5) is working for conservation, but there is 'no public agitation' (p. 6) for 'greater national efficiency' (p. 6); and 'our daily loss . . . has stirred us deeply' but 'our waste . . . has moved us but little' (p. 6). Within a short sentence we move from 'the presidents of our great companies down to our household servants' (p. 6). Instead of 'hunting' for men we should 'train' them (p. 6). 'Captains of industry are born, not made' and 'great men' are placed along-side 'ordinary men' in the next sentence. Where 'in the past men have been first; in the future the system must be first' (p. 7), and within this system the 'best' men will 'rise to the top' (p. 7) just as in the old system, the 'hunt' for competent men moved 'down' to our 'household servants' (p. 6).

As he compares and contrasts, Taylor's rhetoric also reassures: 'our' people and 'our' country are our shared concern, and we are all there, captains and servants, engaged in activities that range from 'our simplest individual acts to the work of our great corporations' (p. 7). Through the classical rhythm of 'the one . . . the other', 'the one has stirred us deeply, while the other has moved us but little' (p. 6), confidence in a seemingly balanced argument is maintained. As the rhetoric swings us from one side to the other, it is easy to assume that all the territory in between has been surveyed, accounted for and the conclusions justified. Taylor's confidence in his own rhetorical success is palpable: within three pages he is assuring the reader of his ability to 'convince the reader' of 'results . . . which are truly astounding' (p. 7).

Counterpointing the angry, threatening voice of the 'preacher from hell' is the (comparatively) unemotive voice of the rational teacher. All of this evil, this waste, and this ignorance can be countered by an understanding of and acceptance of, Taylor's principles. That workers must be 'trained' (p. 6), 'developed' (p. 7), 'guided' (p. 26), and 'taught' (p. 26) is displayed in carefully structured italicized headings and in paragraphs constructed around a clear line of argument. In sharp contrast, he introduces anecdotes in colloquial style 'Take the case of shoes for instance' (p. 16); quotes popular maxims 'Captains of industry are born, not made'; (p. 6) and his sometimes spontaneous enthusiasm for a subject, such as 'soldiering' (p. 13) conveyed in broken syntax.

Taylor describes his principles as 'scientific', yet also insists that we must believe in them, and couches their virtues in a breathless series of superlatives. These 'fundamentals' of which we must be 'convinced' (p. 7), and in which we must 'believe' (p. 10), are the 'highest', the 'largest' and the 'greatest' (pp. 9–11) . . . compared with what? He does not say.

But rational acceptance of his principles will not satisfy. His rhetoric invites us to share his 'firm conviction' (p. 100), his 'truth' (p. 11), his 'profound conviction' (p. 29). For Taylor, truths are self-evident: a good man is one who is trained to work with maximum efficiency; an evil man is one who does not do so. Moral order in an ideal world would be determined by the unchallenged control of scientific managers, who would eliminate material waste from the processes of the scientific system. Taylor himself, as he concludes his treatise, declares that he expects to devote the rest of his life chiefly to trying to help those who wish to take up this work as their profession.

To me it seems that a morality with a recognizable Christian genealogy is discoverable in a root metaphor in this text, even though the secular western world has comfortably accepted it as Taylor's presentation of his argument as a scientific treatise. I suspect that dominant readers of this text may have been 'colonized' by a metaphor which, dug up and laid out above ground level in a critical reading, they might have chosen to reject as alienating.

Reflexive reading

I have divided this third reading into two sections – generic and specific – because although I am commenting here on my reading of Taylor's text, I intend to read five texts, and some of my comment will be common to all five readings. The generic section of my reflexive reading places my interpretation of the analysed text in the context of my personal heritage, experience and worldview: it is therefore common to all of the readings that

I have completed for this inquiry. It should therefore be assumed as I complete each subsequent analysis.

The second, specific reading, notes aspects of the context that frame my reading of this particular text. It is unique to Taylor's text. In the reflexive reading that completes my analysis of each of the five selected texts the specific section will be unique to the particular interpretative context.

Generic

In common with all readers I bring various life experiences, some that I was born into, and some acquired in the life I have lived, to my interpretation of texts.

I am female, an academic and a New Zealander, and I began my scriptive reading of these texts in 1999, an intense *fin de siècle*: the last year of the twentieth century, and the last year of the second millennium.

There is some evidence that response to management theory is culturally dependent (Huczynski 1993b), so it may be significant that I am a fifth-generation New Zealander, of English and Celtic descent, reading mainly British and American texts which have been published and widely read across four continents (Europe, Asia, the Americas and Australasia). My convent schooling (Dominican), early education in the humanities, and my life-long reading of English and European literatures, has fostered a leaning towards Europe rather than the USA; but like most New Zealanders I am also at home in the popular culture of a Pacific Rim community saturated in North American mores. Pragmatic, egalitarian and understated (sometimes irreverent), Kiwi perception of cant and pomposity may well tinge my interpretations with an impatience that seems to belittle the texts.

As a female reader I find myself constantly being reminded that the discipline of management is built on texts, contemporary as well as foundational, that are potentially fraught with contested gender perceptions, but in my analysis I have chosen not to become involved with gender issues as such. Feminist methodology[2] is one of a number of different approaches to text analysis, for example Marxist, Black African, that are premised on political stances and therefore lie outside the literary theory I have chosen to draw on as I developed my method.

Specific

My interpretation of Taylor's text highlights its moralistic elements. In focusing on values, moral values and assumptions, I have consequently played down the many other voices that resonate in it, voices that speak for 'science', which speak of class and race, and of capitalism and gender. Bit part or protagonist, these actors, as well as a multiplicity of author roles murmuring in the margins, are voices that other readers might well choose to explore further.

Yet I think that some of the distaste I feel for Taylor's hierarchical, system-dominated worldview, colours my interpretation of his text. My own metaphors are carried by verbs that 'dance' and 'sing' and 'decorate' and 'etch' the texts I discuss, suggesting a playful 'other' that seeks to escape the mechanized, material environment of Taylor's Utopia. There is an ironic edge to my comment on the vision he idealizes, a disparaging of missionary zeal that is not 'in tune' with the preferred emotive climate that I am setting up in competition with his, and that pays no dues to the sinewy vigour of his rhetoric.

Review

In this, my first review of my experience of scriptive reading, a number of conclusions pertinent to my inquiry emerge. First, and importantly, I am comfortable with the balance of justice, perception and honesty that it has allowed. The dominant reading creates space for interpretation I assume I share with other readers. It acknowledges Taylor's status as the 'father of scientific management' (Boone and Bowen 1987: 32), and subverts a potential challenge: that my critical reading is a mis-reading of his text. It also establishes grounds for a dialogue with other dominant readings, taking its place among numerous textbook paraphrases of his theory.

Taylor's foundational theory of scientific management has made an enormous impact on management practice throughout the western and westernized world; and as Guillen (1997) has already pointed out, it has come to be accepted that all of our main theories, including scientific management, convey ideological as well as technological messages. In recognition of this awareness, Frederick Taylor's theory has always, even in his own lifetime, been subjected to energetic and often harsh, criticism.[3] My critical reading opens up space for new dialogue about this already much discussed and criticized text. I have maintained a particular focus on the moral message that my reading highlights, suggesting that Taylor's simplistic, hierarchical splitting of good and evil 'men' (*sic*) on the basis of their efficiency, competence and hard work, is portrayed in persuasive rhetoric. His insistence on material reward as the highest and overriding goal of our endeavours suggests the total materiality of his moral vision. My critical reading has exposed a moral message in Taylor's text that has not previously been recognized.

As I completed my scriptive reading with reflexive comment I discovered that because I had already planned this reading phase before beginning my analysis, I had allowed myself more reign in the critical reading than I might perhaps otherwise have done. Because I knew, even as I was writing my critical responses, that I would shortly comment on my emotional involvement in, and response to, my reading – that if my critical reading seemed to be as much a response to my own preoccupations as to Taylor's text I would later say so – I felt my sense of the need for some kind of scholarly justice while writing critically to be tempered by the freedom to express my spontaneous response to the text.

Text two: Mary Follett

Overview

The text by Mary Parker Follett that I have selected for analysis has been published as Chapter 1, 'Constructive conflict' in *Dynamic Administration: The Collected Papers of Mary Parker Follett* (Metcalf and Urwick 1941). Although it was not published in this form until many years after her death in 1933, I believe that its place in the corpus of the author's work makes it a choice that is consistent with the selection of the other five texts (all of which are lifted from the introductory pages of major works by their authors).

Not widely known or appreciated in the latter half of the twentieth century until Pauline Graham's landmark publication of a compendium of her writings (Graham 1995b), Follett's contribution to management theory was, in her own lifetime, primarily presented in lecture series on both sides of the Atlantic. The published version of the series of twelve lectures organized by the Bureau of Personnel Administration, New York, which she gave to executives at various times between 1925 and 1932, is contained in *Dynamic Administration* (Metcalf and Urwick 1941) and is still her best-known work.

Chapter 1, 'Constructive conflict', opens with the words:

> The subject I have been given for these lectures is 'The psychological foundations of business', but as it is obvious we cannot in four papers consider all the contributions which contemporary psychology is making to business . . .
>
> (p. 30)

clearly indicating that by the time Follett came to deliver this lecture, she had planned the whole of the series, saw it as an entity, and wrote this lecture as the introduction to it.

Furthermore, in a note in their 1941 edited publication of this lecture, Metcalf and Urwick explain that this, the first of the four papers reprinted in *Scientific Foundations of Business Administration* (Metcalf 1926) was also the first of the four papers presented to a Bureau of Personnel Administration conference group in January 1925.

As the first lecture, in the first series of lectures delivered by Miss Follett 1925–32, my selection of it for analysis therefore follows the pattern of my choice of the introductory sections of the books by the other five authors.

Dominant reading

In this text Mary Follett discusses the nature of conflict and how we best understand and handle it. She builds her argument around her suggestion that conflict should be understood as difference, that we should learn to put it to constructive use, and that the three main ways of dealing with conflict are domination, compromise and integration. She notes that we are familiar with the first of these two ways of dealing with conflict: domination, which is the easiest method and results in a victory of one side over the other, and compromise, the most popular and approved method, which means that each side must give up something. Further describing compromise as 'the basis of trade union tactics', she first illustrates this with an anecdote of union negotiation, and then later notes that compromise is always only a temporary solution because neither side is entirely satisfied with the outcome.

Follett advocates resolving conflict through a third way, integration. To achieve this, she says, invention must find a position that accommodates the desires of both parties, and she gives examples of how this has been done that range across disputes over the opening of a window, the unloading of cans at a creamery factory, the location of the meetings of works committees, jury service in a murder trial and the decision-making processes of the League of Nations.

All of this builds into her definition of conflict as 'a moment in the interacting of desires' (p. 34); a moment that we should 'use' to make conflict 'do' something to constructively progress what already exists towards a goal that is possible. Whereas a compromise solution allows conflict to resurface in another form, as the parties to it pursue what they did not initially achieve, integration stabilizes: it allows future conflict to occur at a 'higher level' (p. 35).

Such progression of differences is, she says, social progress, for we become spiritually more developed as the nature of our conflicts matures allowing new values to emerge; but before concluding this section on methods of dealing with conflict, she adds a rider. Integration is not always possible – it is just more often possible than is commonly recognized.

In the next section, 'Bases of integration', Follett sets out the steps that must be taken in order to achieve it. The first step is 'to bring the differences into the open' (p. 36). In three examples of wage negotiation she describes where this was not done. She imputes the competitive mindsets of the negotiating parties as the cause of suppression, obscurity and evasion, because the real aim was 'not agreement but domination' (p. 38). Like the psychiatric patient whose conflict cannot be solved unless he (*sic*) is prepared to be honest about his situation, so too in business it is necessary to distinguish between real and declared motive.

This recognition of desire will enable evaluation that may lead to revaluation, and if both sides engage in it then unity often 'precipitates itself' (p. 39). In fact, says Follett, a business should be organized so that the whole field of desire can be viewed, and it is when one whole field is compared with another that this view may be estimated differently, that motives may be weighed one against another. It is important because the 'revaluation of interests' may alter the confronting desires and therefore bring about, in itself, the realignment of the groups.

Further to all of this she reminds readers that because difference is complex it is not always the dramatic moments in conflict that are the most significant, so finding 'the significant rather than the dramatic features' (p. 40) of industrial controversy involves breaking it up into its constituent parts, and this is the second step in integration. As an example of the need to break up the whole she quotes Shaw's six steps in solving business problems (p. 41), and points out that the process 'involves the examination of symbols', and she quotes as an example of this a friend who reinterpreted her declared desire to travel to Europe as the desire to meet people.

Pursuing this theme, the interpretation of symbols, a little further, Follett recalls the Loeb–Leopold case, and comments on the language of marketing co-operatives as she reminds us that all language is symbolic and that we should 'be always on our guard as to what is symbolized' (p. 42).

Still considering the theme of recognizing the constituent parts of the whole, she next neatly inverts all of the above with a reminder that the 'whole-demand, the real-demand' may become 'obscured by miscellaneous minor claims' (p. 42), and that it is the leader's job to articulate this. Moreover, the leader must anticipate response, and in this way will successfully integrate different interests by determining the moves to be made. Two examples, a domestic relationship controlled by the husband, and a business relationship where middlemen attempt to control farmers, serve her point. As she comfortably notes, her theory of the anticipation of response has been likened to playing chess: because good chess players recognize a 'conflict of possibilities' (p. 44) they do not necessarily have to play them all out.

Follett turns to another game, tennis, to analogize another, deeper aspect of response. If we have so far been thinking of response as 'linear' we must now also understand it as 'circular' (p. 44): every act in part determines the response that is made to it just as the return of a ball in tennis partly depends upon the way it was served. Although this seems to her to be a simple, everyday matter, yet she says we continually try to avoid taking responsibility for the responses we receive, and so in conflict, we are in effect partly in conflict with ourselves. Response includes response to a relationship.

Finally, Follett includes a section of 'obstacles to integration'. In a series of paragraphs running through the next two and a half pages, she lists and describes, with examples, the actions and responses that get in the way of integration by comparing it with domination. First, domination, based on the urge to fight, is easier than the intelligence and inventiveness required by integration; and second it is more enjoyable, more thrilling than 'tame' integration.

Her third point – that integration tends to be theorized instead of being enacted: that in contrast, a proposed action tends to focus the mind – is illustrated in a detailed analogy of a union meeting, and she then moves on to her fourth point. Language, when it is not used with care, is a serious obstacle to integration (p. 47) and she describes a mix of several business and domestic examples. The fifth obstacle to integration that she notes, but does not elaborate on is, she says, the undue influence of leaders, a very important factor, but one that she does not have the space to cover. Instead she moves on to the sixth and final consideration: that we are not trained to work towards integration.

Our education teaches us to debate, not to confer. College courses and public speaking classes enable us to strenuously argue our preconceived ideas, but we are not taught 'the "art" of co-operative thinking' (p. 48). It is in genuine conference that we test our ideas and change them if convinced of a different view.

In her two concluding paragraphs, Follett emphasizes personal responsibility. She reminds us of 'circular response' (p. 48) and that individual behaviour both partly accounts for, and at the same time shapes, the situation. In this perception we may see a 'map of the future' that we each participate in forming even as we are ourselves shaped by the evolving map. As she looks towards a later paper, she also concludes with an exhortation to her readers that directly rests on her arguments to this point: never, she proclaims, 'be bullied by an "either–or"'. There is always, she believes, 'the possibility of something better'.

Critical reading

Follett introduces herself to us as the passive recipient of an instruction – she has 'been given' the subject of the lectures she is here embarking upon – yet before completing the sentence, she both draws her readers alongside her, in her decision that 'we cannot in four papers consider all', and then quietly takes control of the situation in her concluding 'I have chosen' (p. 30). She moves from presenting her role as that of a pawn in some unknown player's hand, to that of a bustling familiar conspirator 'it is obvious we cannot . . .' (and she begins to list in parentheses the multifarious contributions of psychology, but stops breathless with an 'etc.'), to that of pedagogic director; but before she leaves her introductory sentence she also softens the momentary assurance of 'I have chosen' into the blurred, round sound of 'seem to me to go to', and arrives in the emotive metaphor at 'the heart' of the people-problems of industry. In this way then she introduces her series of lectures and herself, and then promptly addresses the issue she will consider in this particular paper.

And consider she does, repeating the word four times in the first two introductory paragraphs. 'Consider', to think on, contemplate, take into account, etymologically from Latin *considerare* to examine [the stars (*sidus*)], sums up the stance she takes, and repeatedly invites her readers to share. And 'invites' does aptly describe her tone throughout this text, for even when her opinions are sinewy and the expression of them uncompromising – she still graciously asks readers to 'consider'. Her verbs are a little hesitant, 'I wish to consider'; dependent, as in the subjunctive 'I should like to ask'; placatory, 'ask you to agree'; and hypothetical, as in the infinitives 'to consider', to ask', to think', for it always seems that final positions have not yet been taken, will not be taken, until we, author and reader, have thought together on the issues raised. She asks us to reserve judgement, conflict is 'neither good nor bad', to avoid 'pre-judgement', and to consider, to think – in fact, to imagine – in an abstract, not a material realm: to imagine 'conflict' as 'difference' not 'warfare'.

Conflict, by the time we reach the end of the first paragraph, has emerged as the subject that we are to think on together, and is mentioned for the fifth time as paragraph two opens, but by now Follett has subtly, but assuredly, instated 'difference' in its place. At first, conflict is just the 'appearance of difference', but Follett insistently taps home her message in the staccato iteration of the word 'conflict' as the first paragraph closes and the second opens. Within these few lines we first hear that conflict has the 'appearance' of difference, then that it 'means' difference, and finally that it 'is' difference, 'As – conflict – difference – is here'. By this time, conflict has become synonymous with difference (iteration of both words has occurred five times) and is also so emphatically driving the text that the personification into which it gracefully forms, is unobtrusive. Follett's verbs suggest the actions that should dictate our relationship to it: we cannot 'avoid' it, should 'use' it, should not 'condemn' it, and finally, we should set it to 'work' for us. From being something unpleasant from which we might step aside if we could, conflict/difference (they are one and the same here) evolves into some kind of object or instrument designed with a purpose; metamorphosizes again into some kind of person ('condemn' has a dimension of moral meaning), and finally becomes metaphorically fully realized in the text as we imagine setting it 'to work for us'. Called to account, facing our judgement (ironically, if we recall Follett's careful admonition against moral judgement a few lines further back) conflict/difference is not to be condemned (killed off or interminably incarcerated) but sentenced to hard labour. We, reader and author, sit in judgement, and our role is to assign a role to an abstract concept, conflict/difference, to find some kind of useful employment for it. It has, in a sense, become the employee.

In summary then, as paragraph two opens, conflict/difference has taken on roles in two metaphors: one is legalistic and the other work-related. It is both the defendant on trial before author/reader as judge, and the employee, perhaps slave or tamed beast, 'set to work' for author and reader and all the humankind they represent. 'Set to work' suggests to me a master/mistress relationship to servant, slave or animal, for there is also a suggestion of power, of one will in the absolute control of another, in this phrase. 'Use it' also suggests the role of tool or instrument, but this suggestion is immediately negated in the sentence that follows it: 'Instead of condemning it we should set it to work for us' (p. 30).

Follett seems almost a little taken aback by her own temerity in making such a firm recommendation. She follows up instantly with a quick retort – to a hovering, unspoken question – in the form of a direct question to her readers, her own rhetorical question: 'Why not?' And, in a second rapid question, turns just as promptly to the sensible, pragmatic world of the mechanical engineer: 'What does the mechanical engineer do with friction?' Conflict, which we had just learned to identify with difference is now, without further explanation, to be thought of as 'friction', and in the remainder of the paragraph, to ensure that the new identification is hammered home, 'friction' is iterated not just five, but ten times.

In the rapidly cumulated examples of friction that immediately follow this new identification, Follett presents friction as instrumental in achieving power, polish, music and civilization itself before returning to its role in business. In images of factory, 'the belt and pulley' and transport, 'the locomotive and the track' friction powers industry, but then too, 'All polishing is done be friction' (p. 31). The deafening noise, brute force and black smoke of industry are juxtaposed with the quiet gleam of an aesthetic as ready to suggest the achievement of the domestic and the artisan as it is industry, and as suggestive of wood, leather or precious stones as it is of manufacturing. It is an easy step to the music of the violin, to the friction witnessed in the elegant sweep of the bow across strings, but also heard in the music that resonates out from the polished wooden instrument.

Just as that sentence seemingly leaves the violin mid-note, so too with Follett 'We [leave] the savage state . . .' as the next begins but drop, on a note of bathos, to 'when we discovered fire by friction'. It's a fun note that Follett strikes here, for 'fire' immediately recalls the locomotive we thought to have left two sentences back, the 'friction' of the two sticks required to produce it mimics the action of the violin bow and strings, and yet ironically, in this primitive action, she images for us the beginning of all the industrial power (the locomotive) and the musical aesthetic (the violin) that represent the civilized state we have arrived at as we left behind the 'savage'. The path to the 'friction of mind on mind as a good thing' has been so well laid it seems natural to assume that the kinds of 'friction' in the images of the text that we have just shared with her symbolize the intellectual dimension of the material (industrial) and aesthetic (musical) civilization that she now presents as a moral (good thing) *fait accompli*.

In a few short sentences we have traversed human history, from the stone age to the industrial era, but return in a moment to business: 'So in business' introduces the penultimate sentence of the paragraph, and as we make this move with Follett, eased back from flights of analogous fancy to the subject of our 'consideration' by the conversational 'so in', we are first encouraged to distinguish what 'we have to know' by the sharp antithesis of 'eliminate' set against 'capitalize', and at the same time reminded of the seriousness of this necessary distinction by the heavy Latinate pace of these two words. Simultaneously we are returned to the notion that friction is something that we cannot only use as we would any other resource – to work for us, to make money, 'capitalize', for us – and also returned to the earlier metaphorical notion that friction is an entity that we should assume mastery of, should 'make' work for us.

In the concluding declaration of the paragraph, Follett sums up what she wants to do in the lecture, 'I wish to consider here', and the outcome she intends 'for us': conflict is to be mastered, 'set to work', with an intended action-based outcome, to 'make it do'.

Yet with all of this, the irony of the engineer's role is ever present for just as Follett reminds us as she begins her analogous history of the role of friction, that although the engineer must 'use' friction, his 'chief' role is to eliminate it, so too, as she concludes, she seems to be suggesting that perhaps his chief role is really that of discrimination: this potentially useful worker (physical friction has become synonymous with the metaphor of conflict as 'worker'), may sometimes be even more useful if wiped out, 'eliminated'.

Throughout the first two paragraphs, Follett has been comfortably present in her text, she has consistently written in the first person, and has also often assumed identification with her readers in her use of the first person plural 'we' in her 'considerations'. She is inclusive as she takes the reader into her confidence, 'I have been given' (p. 1) and shares her reservations about her brief, 'we cannot'; definitive as she clearly delineates her own role in determining the subject of the lecture, 'I have chosen' and 'I wish to consider'; and polite as she asks for the reader's co-operation, 'I should like to ask you', draws the reader alongside as she suggests, 'We shall not consider', and advises 'we should'. She also speaks directly to readers, strengthening the immediacy of the relationship, in the form of the rhetorical questions already noted. She maintains this presence in the text and her relationship to the reader through to the end of the second paragraph, concluding in the tone with which she began, 'I wish to consider here'.

When the third paragraph opens we find that she has momentarily disappeared. She becomes, temporarily, the omniscient author, as the text pronounces on the 'three main ways of dealing with conflict: domination, compromise and integration'. The succinct balance of a sentence built around a colon, the Latinate naming of the 'three ways', and the triple statement all add weight to the authoritative tone she commands here, but, interestingly, Follett remains absent from the text for three more lines while she quickly deals with, and deals to, 'domination'. Picking up the root metaphor of conflict as war – first introduced in paragraph one where she asked us not to think of conflict as 'warfare' – she describes domination as a 'victory' for one of the two sides, and as the 'easiest', but not usually a 'successful', way of dealing with conflict. It is another balanced Latinate, 'not this, but that' con-struction, and it seems as if Follett absents herself from the text, while quickly and authoritatively dismissing that with which she is herself uncomfortable. She returns, again in a shared identity with the reader, 'as we can see', only as she concludes by hinting at recent history, 'what has happened since the war'. She thus forges an implied connection between the Great War and attempts to solve personal or business conflict through domination, and then moves on to begin the next paragraph, and a discussion of the 'second way' of dealing with conflict, compromise.

She is fully back in the text and alongside the reader in 'we understand' and 'we settle', but still emotively portraying conflict as compromise and as war: 'each side must give up a little in order to have peace'; trade unions have 'tactics' and expect to have something 'lopped off'. Although the tone, as she describes this second way of dealing with conflict, is initially familiar, 'we understand well', and placatory, 'it is the way we settle', the notion that it also involves a kind of defeat, 'gives up', in order to achieve a peace that is really no more than a temporary truce, 'that . . . the conflict may go on', is overtaken in the next sentence by the coldness of 'tactics' and finally the brutality of 'lopped off'. The subtext pulls both conflict as domination and conflict as negotiation into the negative environment of the war metaphor, and hints at something quite different to come in the 'fruitfully' that points to a third way.

'Fruitful' is a word that she first used in paragraph one where it described the, as yet undisclosed, third and best way of dealing with conflict – integration – and it introduces a root metaphor that is developed several pages later, where re-evaluation, part of the conflict-solving process of integration, is described as 'the flower of comparison' (p. 38). In the paragraph that follows (p. 39) where integration becomes 'a spontaneous flowing together' it has already merged into a discussion of desire. Desire is imaged in this way as wholesome, natural and to be enjoyed. We should, Follett repeats several times, be able to see 'the whole field of desire': a 'field of vision' full of differences of which we should be able to see the whole vista in order to understand it, but also because it is presented as a pleasant place, one that we would enjoy. By the time we reach page 48, the whole range of human emotion has become the 'emotional field' that methods of reconciliation must take into account. There is an openness, a sense of freedom and liberation in the repetition of 'the field', the 'whole field' of desire that gains much of its effect from preceding images of boundedness and even imprisonment, for as the lecture draws to a close, the vast undertaking Follett is advocating is only made to seem possible because she has also built a metaphor of place, a place with boundaries that demarcate the reconciliation efforts that she later describes, through the preceding text.

When she first introduces the 'integration' of just 'two desires' (p. 32), she says that both must be found a 'place', and this 'place' will later become the seemingly open spaces of a 'field'. Thinking that is based in domination and negotiation is 'confined within walls (p. 32), the 'boundaries' (p. 33) of confrontation. When 'differing' is understood as 'fighting', when 'two desires both claim right of way' then in order to progress conciliation differences must be brought 'into the open' (p. 36). Yet even as we find ourselves so poised between this open space and the confinement of a restricted place that we are unable 'to construct a map' (p. 49) of the future, we are all the while engaging with two other powerful root metaphors which weave around and within that of place: conflict as warfare and conflict as a legal issue.

Wars waged in the battlefield determine the side that will own the contested place, and conflict which is resolved in the court, as in Follett's anecdote of a murder trial, may condemn the accused to imprisonment, to loss of freedom. Both metaphors engage intimately the first time we meet them when Follett writes: I . . . ask you to think of conflict . . . without ethical pre-judgement; to think of it not as warfare . . . (paragraph 1, p. 30). The war metaphor continues in the scene (already noted) that Follett develops on page 31 where 'domination' is a 'victory of one side over the other', where 'each side gives up a little in order to have peace' and 'compromise is the basis of trade union tactics'. It returns with impact on page 36 where differing is not to be thought of as 'fighting', and its resolution is not to be thought of 'conquering'; yet as is the contrary way of language, the more often the words tell us that something is not so, the more inclined we are to remember that it might be so. And Follett stays with the metaphor on page 37, when she describes the union/employer relationship as the 'fight-set' and a 'danger' and then says: 'As long as trade unionism is a defensive movement, as long as employers' associations are defensive movements . . .' there will be 'evasion' disguised by 'diplomacy' to confuse 'the other side' (p. 37).

Introducing an analogy of the trade union movement, the Socialist Party in Italy before Mussolini, Follett says that it is easier for the trade union to fight than to suggest a 'better way of running the factory'. Just as the socialists 'preferred to stay fighting', 'to attack', for 'the "thrills" of conquest', without which 'no side' is 'left swelling its chest, so too no one had conquered, no one had "won out"' (pp. 45–6). Furthermore the person with 'fight habits' anticipates 'further fighting' and 'the possibility of conquest next time'. On the next page there is mention of 'the fight element', labour and capital as 'a fight', 'traditional enemies' and finally of 'the "weapon of the union" etc.' (p. 47). It all culminates in an image of the 'bullied' (p. 49), which is also what we should strive to avoid.

Generally in the argument, where the text discusses legal power, and the subtext speaks in warlike metaphors, and these two abstracts seem to engage in a struggle of their own, fighting power is presented as winning out over legal power, as in the following example. Farmers who, like the trade unions, are presented in a war image, are said to be in a 'struggle with marketing co-operatives' (p. 43), but the farmer cannot be 'held in line', for he has been 'carried off his feet by victory'. In the end though, the use of legal power will 'defeat' the movement, for the farmer will 'rebel' against this sort of 'coercion'. It is 'legal' power that is described here as coercion, and spirited rebellion is, in this context, lauded. A similar link, balance and outcome emerge through several other short passages in the text.

We first met, in the subtext, notions of judgement versus war, of legal and moral forces contending with brute strength, in paragraph one where Follett asks that the reader think of conflict as 'neither good nor bad', and that the reader both withhold ethical judgement of conflict, and also not think of it 'as warfare' (p. 30). On page 32, she returns to the image of judgement in an anecdote of a murder trial, where the conflict that is seen as significant, and is resolved, takes place between potential juror and judge. In the end neither judge nor juror was 'left as victor' (p. 33): prejudgements were not vindicated. In another example of the confrontation of the legal and the war metaphors, Follett discusses the Leob–Leopold case (p. 42), and the symbolic meaning of death versus life imprisonment. She concludes by noting the irony of the outcome in that the sentence of life imprisonment should be understood as a 'victory', not a 'defeat'. The 'case' and the punishment meted out as a result of the 'sentence', a legal metaphor, is presented in the context of a confrontation that is also to be understood as 'war'.

Contrasting sharply with these pervasive images of warfare and the courts is a much more subtle image of recreational games. The employers who have to 'deal' with those who play games of concealment, must 'put [their] cards on the table' (p. 38); 'playing the game differently' as they learn to think of it as being 'like a game of chess' (p. 43). Follett goes into detail as point by point she compares the 'anticipation of response' to a game of chess' (pp. 43–4) and then moves on to a similar analogous explanation of linear response as a game of tennis (p. 44). Chess and tennis are games associated with leisure and privilege, and both follow on from the anecdote of the man who 'liked motoring', but was married to a woman who liked walking, though both played 'tennis in the morning' (p. 43). Integration is thus placed in the context intellectual, monied and civilized leisure pursuits while domination and compromise remain in the savagery of the war zone.

As I unpick this text it seems to be reworking itself into a vignette of Edwardian Fabianism: while the educated pacifists, comfortably at home in the text, discuss the discoveries of psychology, the subtext is buried in the trenches of a bitter struggle for power and territory.

The point here is that although much mention is made of integration, and it is strongly and without reservation the method of conflict resolution that Follett favours, the image in which it is mostly graphically presented is that of the game, something recreational and enjoyable, but not nearly as powerful as the words and 'game' of war in which its alter ego parades. Ironically her text falls into the very trap that, at one point, she describes as an 'obstacle to integration' (p. 45): war is more exciting, and more dramatic, than peace. Many of us, says Follett, 'enjoy domination. Integration seems to be a tamer affair' (p. 45). 'Attack' linked as it is here with 'tamer' suggests savagery and the jungle environment, linking with the earlier image of the savage era we should have left behind in history. It is set against the conciliatory actions of the trade union chairman whose 'true integration' led to the evening ending 'rather dully, flatly'. Although Follett seems to be providing a very honest account of the way things actually happen, does not inspire the excitement of 'brilliant inventiveness' (p. 45), does not in fact throw 'much light' on integration as a captivating drama. As Follett herself also says in the drama metaphor of the subtext, 'the highest lights' in a situation, the 'dramatic moments' may be a 'good curtain', but not a 'controlling moment' (p. 40). So her drama metaphor not only builds into an extended metaphor of leisured recreation, but also supports her belief that it is important to find the significant rather than the dramatic features of industrial controversy. Perhaps the many 'controlling moments' in Follett's argument are not the 'highest lights' in her texts: reason and the authority of the mundane are sometimes drowned in the wash of anecdote and metaphor.

Follett's own argument seems to demonstrate this precept, for rather than making dramatic statements about powerful and expert people, and influential decisions or events, her arguments are muted into the tones of private, personal experience; domestic situations, and the industrial workplace of the humble and the, too often, unheard.

Much of her argument is illuminated and enlivened by anecdote. Chatty and personal, domestic and shop-floor based, the knowledge Follett draws on is sourced from her experience of, and thinking on, the mundane, everyday world of ordinary people, at home and at work. She speaks of a friend who 'annoys' her (p. 36), and of another friend who has learned to distinguish her real from her imagined needs (p. 41). Yet a third friend provides her with the chess analogy (p. 43). When she confronts her own personal needs and conflicts, as in whether or not to open a library window (p. 32), and her attempt to complete an 'adjustment' to her electricity bill (p. 47), she speaks directly to readers.

Into these personal revelations she sprinkles samples of her conversations with, and observations of, those who work at humble tasks. She speaks, affectionately of the unpretentious, coining the terms 'up-hillers and down-hillers' as she describes a conflict over unloading cans at a creamery platform (p. 32). She chats about shop-floor union debate, 'take another case' (p. 33), and discloses detailed talk about the wages of working 'girls' (pp. 36–7), and union negotiation (p. 47). Against these gentle images of modest people she juxtaposes anecdotal images of the long-drawn out and unproductive deliberations of wage board (p. 37) and trade union (p. 46). In the contrast, the glimpse of the knowledge that we can glean from ordinary folk talking, set against, finally, the 'the chief obstacle to integration – namely, the undue influence of leaders – the manipulation of the unscrupulous on the one hand and suggestibility of the crowd on the other' (pp. 47–8), she leads us towards her view of the road to conflict resolution.

Lifted from context as above, these 'criticisms' may seem harsh, yet in context they are always introduced with the unassuming candour of a seeming 'everyman' rather than an 'expert'. And she is as ready to reflect on her own conversation as she is to comment on that of others. She begins, for example, a sequence of paragraphs with firm admonitions to anyone, including herself, who fails to keep a balanced grip on her argument and anecdote: 'but I certainly ought not' (p. 32), 'I have already given this illustration in print' (p. 32), 'take another case' (p. 33), 'a friend gave me this example' (p. 33), 'by far the most interesting example' (p. 33), 'it is often difficult to decide' (p. 34), and 'some people tell me' (p. 34).

Follett does not forgo all appeal to an established authority, but her recourse is to the knowledge that resides within a tradition of academic learning rather than to the expertise or profile of a particular person or organization. There are times, for example, when the anecdotes which weave through the text and the snatches of conversation which weave through the anecdotes, echo Platonic dialogue on conflict and desire. In a passage on 'The Elements in Mental Conflict' (Plato 1987: 206–17), Plato says: 'We thought it would be easier to see justice in the individual if we looked for it first in some larger field which also contained it' (p. 208). Follett says 'a business should be so organized . . . that . . . in any conflict, in any coming together of different desires, the whole field of desire be . . . viewed' (p. 39). Plato says 'when a man's mind desires anything, don't you . . . say that he has an impulse to what he desires . . . ?' (p. 211), and again 'in that case each desire is directed simply towards its own natural object' (p. 212). Follett extrapolates: 'we have to uncover our subarticulate egoisms . . . see them in relation to other facts and desires, [and then] we may estimate them differently' (p. 39). Their voices, Plato's and Follett's, seem to blend as I weave them together here, into one thought process and one tone.[4]

Just as careful claim, counter-claim and qualification move Plato's theorizing along, so too Follett makes a point, chats about it, qualifies it a little and then shifts ground again. To this extent her authority is a conversation that bridges the more than 2,300 years that lie between them. Her authority depends more blatantly on the contemporary and even *avant garde*, at the time of writing, disciplinary knowledge of psychology.

Follett's discussion of our 'subarticulate egoisms' (p. 39) also takes its place in the psychology story, introduced by the subject of the lecture series, 'The Psychological Foundations of Business Administration', that is almost always either in preparation, or being told, or being submerged only to surface on a new angle. Sometimes it is explicit as in 'the key word of psychology today is desire' (p. 34), 'conflict as continued unintegrated difference is pathological' (p. 35), 'psychology has given us the phrase "progressive integratings"' (p. 35) and 'the "uncovering" which every book on psychology has rubbed into us for some years now' (p. 38), 'contemporary psychology shows us' (p. 40). Sometimes it is overtly present as in 'watch the evolution of your desires' (p. 38), 'Freud's sublimation' (p. 39), 'the conception of circular behaviour' (p. 45) and 'we quite consciously choose' (p. 47); sometimes it plays through the subtext as for example a metaphor of health, 'difference may be a sign of health' (p. 34) which plays against the image of a psychological sickness, 'unintegrated difference is pathological' (p. 35). Follett is here the spokesperson for the new sciences; chemistry, for example, so 'difference does not stay too long crystallized' (p. 35), for only 'integration stabilizes', and a few pages further on, 'unity precipitates itself' (p. 39).

Then too, lest any of the philosophy and psychology and chemistry that simultaneously sites this text in timeless as well as contemporary realms should begin to dominate, humour brings the text back to the tone of a relaxed chat. On page 40, Follett tells the brief story of the southern girl and the 'damned Yankee', she jokes about Cerberus' raw meat diet and the naive hope that he will turn out to be a vegetarian (p. 45), and even the self-deprecatory tone in which she tells of the girls who 'looked nonplussed' by Follett's play with language (p. 47) defuses any suspicion of smug game-playing.

This personal tidbit is almost the last of Follett's conversational anecdotes, and it occurs about midway through her cataloguing of the obstacles to integration. Beginning on page 45, she tells of 'another obstacle' and the third, 'another obstacle' (p. 46). By the time we reach the fourth, 'a serious obstacle which every businessman should consider' (p. 47), her tone has become more directive, and as we meet the fifth, 'one of the chief obstacles', she is no longer qualifying her comments on 'the undue influence of leaders' (p. 47). The last, and 'the greatest of all obstacles' and 'our lack of training for it' is at first baldly stated, and then emotively supported in a cumulative listing, 'barriers of unenlightened interest, of prejudice, rigidity, dogmatism, routine . . .' and uncompromising firmness, 'No, it isn't' (p. 48).

We are given no assurance that the future is controllable: it is 'impossible to construct a map of the future' (p. 49), and yet she says 'we should' twice in this sentence and the next. The long, complex sentence which immediately follows introduces the final paragraph, and opens into the key passage of the whole lecture: 'This is . . . and ourselves' (p. 49). In a finely balanced 'not only . . . but for all . . . not to . . . neither to . . . but to' statement that relies on repetition, 'we are all', and antithesis, 'adapt ourselves . . . mould a situation' and 'necessary . . . little importance', for its authority and impact, Follett not only restates the conclusion to which her argument has led, but also builds into a climactic rhetorical question. She follows it with another triple reinforcement of the negative situations that we 'should' avoid, where 'our outlook is narrowed, our activity is restricted, our chances of business success largely diminished' (p. 49). Just as in the opening paragraph she personified conflict, suggesting that we 'set it to work for us', now as she closes she images an 'either–or' as a bully and warns that we should not allow it to constrain us. The text is still talking to us of 'business administration' and 'reciprocal activity': the subtext is still telling a tale of coercion, mastery and liberation.

Reflexive reading

My admiration for, and enjoyment of, the humanity, wisdom and wit that I have found in this text has dominated my response to it. I find understatement reassuring, and have with alacrity welcomed the intelligent conversation with an unassuming author that the text has facilitated, and then deftly transformed into argument that stimulates and challenges and with which I have also happily engaged.

Yet there were many frustrations to contend with as I explored my response to it. I experienced so many layers within, and layers below layers of layers of meaning here, that any one line of inquiry threatened to shatter into a thousand trajectories – all but one of which could not be pursued. When I ignored obvious byways and paths, in the interests of writing a coherent commentary, I was continually aware of doing all the rest of the unexplored text a great disservice.

The aporias that I have paused at, and have then attempted to open up, as in my reading of the first two paragraphs, have largely been vitalized by delight and discovery, not distaste and objection, and have, to a large extent, been stimulated by the visual understandings that the text suggests to me. My dialogue with the text is an individual response to this imagery that takes the form of new images. A nautical metaphor, for example, 'submerged' and 'surface' picks up on 'drowned in the wash' and continues to dominate my response here as in 'steer' and 'drift' and 'tug' and 'float' as below.

More generally, I have of course been aware as I read, that Mary Follett, though much listened to and lauded in her own time, was largely ignored through the remainder of the twentieth century. Until very recently leading management practitioners and theorists were generally unfamiliar with her work, and still only a coterie of admirers are promoting her writings and ideas – a claim that Calás and Smircich (1996) dispute, but one that has been substantially subscribed to (Graham 1995b).

Because she was a woman, and because there is already some debate as to the reasons for her 'disappearance' from the canons of management (Graham 1995b), I was also aware of the temptation as I read to go immediately to the debate, draw on it and perhaps leap to conclusions about partisan response to her theories.[5] On the one hand it was tempting to highlight the domestic, personal ambiance that can be found in some aspects of her text, and on the other it was tempting to profile the gutsy thinking and industrial setting of much that she has to say. So although I tried to steer a nongendered course through the imagery and root metaphors I discovered, to let the text speak to me directly of personified abstract notions, and to allow the play of ideas expressed with wit and irony to determine the direction of my analysis, I was nevertheless constantly nagged, as I read, by the question: 'why was this text ignored by so many for so long?' I was constantly aware of an inevitable drift and tug towards seeming answers as they floated by.

Review

As I look back over this, my second experience of scriptive reading, I see that the most visible outcome of it is that when set alongside my scriptive reading of Taylor's text it is conspicuously different in tone and content. Reflexive comment has already provided me with the opportunity to place my readings in the context of my disparate emotive and intellectual response to either text. Significantly though, the relationship between the first two phases of reading, the dominant and critical readings, is dissimilar in either case. My critical reading of Taylor tells a story that seldom links with the dominant reading: the subtext I reveal speaks most often in the voice of a moral preacher, whereas the dominant story is told by a management scientist. By contrast, my critical reading of Follett expands and deepens the narrative of the dominant reading but seldom counters or questions it. There is a harmony of exploration between the two readings of Follett: they both seem to speak in voices that are not challenged or upset by difference and argument.

This distinction between the way that the dominant and critical readings dialogue with each other suggests that scriptive reading is flexible. The guidelines I have put in place to mark the route that the scriptive reader travels, allow each experience of the same route to be created anew.

Text three: Peter Drucker

Overview

Peter Drucker has often been described as the 'gurus' guru',[6] but to him the label 'guru' is an anathema, for Drucker also holds assured recognition in the canons of management theory, and if any one work firmly holds his place in foundational management theory it is his book, *The Practice of Management* (1955).

This is the third work that I have selected as a text for analysis. Chapter 1 is entitled 'The role of management', and is found in 'Introduction: The nature of management', which includes the first three chapters. But because Chapter 1 is very short (two and a half pages) I have, in a more 'broad-brush' treatment, included in the analysis some of Chapter 2, 'The jobs of management'. Although I considered including the entire Introduction and Chapters 1–3 in the exercise, I decided to exclude Chapter 3 because it has a particular focus on technology, and is therefore something of a period piece.

Drucker's book is 355 pages long, and consists of 29 chapters, with an additional conclusion and a preface. In the preface, Drucker states that although 'we have available today the knowledge and experience needed for the successful practice of management' there is a 'tremendous gap between the knowledge and performance of the leaders and the knowledge and performance of the average' (p. vii). He goes on to state that it is his intention to not only 'advance the frontier of knowledge', but also to narrow that gap.

This is, he says, a 'practical book', based on years of management experience, that aims to: guide leaders to an improvement in their performance; provide novice managers with a vision of what management is, as well as a guide to the management performance that will enable them into a successful management career; and 'enlighten the citizen without direct management experience' as to what management is, what it does, and what to 'rightfully expect from it' (p. vii).

He concludes by sharing his assumption that since all his readers are 'more concerned with what is right than with who is right', they will not be upset by the absence of an 'appeal to authority' – Drucker's phrase for the footnotes, acknowledgements and other references that he warns have been omitted from this work. Without any indication that he is intending an irony, he completes the preface with a long paragraph of acknowledgements. He lists the many 'friends in American management' to whom he owes a 'special debt'.

Dominant reading

Drucker provides his own very succinct summary of each chapter of his book in the several italicized sentence fragments with which he heads each chapter. Though an interesting guide to the intentionality of the argument that he constructs, these fragments do not give any indication of the relative weighting that he attaches, in the chapter, to the points he lists. In the first chapter, 'The role of management', for example, he lists the four main points that he will make, covers the first three in the first three paragraphs, and then devotes seven paragraphs to the fourth and final point.

His first point is that management is the 'dynamic element in every business' (p. 1). He explains that by this he means that managers determine business outcomes. His second point, that management is 'a distinct and leading group', he places, briefly, in a historical context, in order to emphasize that this is a new and developing role for management, and his third point, 'the emergence of management' builds on this historically contextualized claim as he writes of the rapidity with which this 'new institution' has arrived.

Drucker's fourth and final point in this chapter, that the free world has a vital and extensive stake in management, is elaborated on in the following ways. His first claim, paragraph four, is that management 'expresses the basic beliefs of modern western society'; that is, that economic control of resources will lead to the betterment of humankind. This belief, he then says (paragraph 5) is not materialism as it has previously been understood, but quite new in that resources are seen as an opportunity to exercise control over nature.

In the remaining five paragraphs of Chapter 1, he goes on to say of management that it is indispensable and fast-growing, that the survival of the 'free world', militarily and economically, will depend on it, and that maintaining the pre-eminent economic and social position of the United States will depend on 'continuously improved management performance'.

Chapter 2, 'The jobs of management' is again introduced by summary sentence fragments, which belie the, somewhat rambling, logic on which the passage is actually constructed. Drucker does, for example, note the 'first function' and the 'first job' of management, but does not advise readers that he will in fact go on to describe the three functions, which he sometimes also describes as the three jobs, of management. After making a broad claim that most people, including those engaged in business, do not know what management does, he states that he will explain what it does (its job), by first explaining what it is (its function).

It is, he says, 'the specific organ of the business enterprise'. He claims that the purpose of the business enterprise is economic performance, and to this extent at least it must be distinguished from the governing organs of the other institutions, government, army and church, for management must be judged by the economic results of its decisions, actions and behaviours.

If the above is understood, as Drucker intends it should, to be the first function of management, then as he argues it, it follows that the first job of management is to manage a business.

From this point on Drucker's argument and logic tend to loop back and forth as he sidetracks into what management and managers should not be by making comparisons with the other major institutions noted above. Subheadings guide the reader into 'Managing managers' as the second function (p. 9), and to 'Managing worker and work' as the final 'function' of management' (p. 11), but as he introduces the last subsection, 'The integrated nature of management', Drucker describes all these functions as 'jobs': 'The three jobs of management: managing a business, managing managers and managing worker and work' (p. 12). As I read it this confuses the earlier distinction that Drucker intended to make between 'function' and 'job': between what management is and what management does.

Along the way though, the significant points that Drucker raises in relation to these functions/jobs of management are as follows: the skills of management are not transferable to other institutions; although managers can learn to improve their performance, management is an art not a science, and there should not be any attempt to make it into a 'profession'. There should be severe limitations placed on the social authority and responsibility of management (p. 7), for although what is possible is 'one pole in managing a business', the other pole is 'what is desirable in the interests of the business' (p. 9).

Managing managers entails recognition that human resources are capable of enlargement, so their growth and development must be an objective (p. 10), as must attention to the total environment and contribution of all workers (p. 11).

In all of the functions of management described above, Drucker also notes two complications. There is a time dimension, the need to work in both the present and the future, for present action determines future outcomes and it is the decision-making manager who is more directly challenged by this demand than is any other leader (p. 12). It is also necessary, even while distinguishing the three jobs, and time factor, of management, to be always aware that in the work of management they are integrated, and that the management of managers and of workers and work is of vital interest to society. In these two management functions, society's 'basic social beliefs and aims are being realized' (p. 13).

Drucker concludes that business is a 'multi-purpose organ' with three major, but always integrated, jobs.

Critical reading

Drucker's text opens into a sweeping generalization as he pronounces that, 'the manager is the dynamic, life-giving element in every business' (p. 1). His tone is authoritative for he plays the role of the omniscient author (his 'all-knowing' voice comes from somewhere outside the text) as he definitively tells us what a manager 'is' in the emphatically short, opening sentence. In just ten words, he encapsulates all managers in every business in an organic metaphor, 'life-giving', that also accommodates a mechanical worldview in the ambiguity of 'dynamic'.

My first instinct was to read 'dynamic' as pertaining to the mechanical, operative power of matter in motion, but as my eye moved on to the word 'life-giving', 'dynamic' seemed to morph towards its more philosophical usage, suggesting 'the mind as being merely the action of forces' (*OED*), and even the theological notion of inspiration, the dynamical as 'endowing with divine power, not impelling mechanically' (*OED*).

This is a startlingly inclusive opener, accommodating as it seems to do, the two worldviews that are most often set up for debate on the institutionaliza-tion of management and organization theory, views that are characteristically expressed in organic and machine metaphors; and it sets the scene for the development of both as root metaphors that interweave throughout the passage. The organic metaphor is conveyed in words such as 'survival' and 'nature' (p. 1); 'organ', 'begotten', spirit', and 'grew' (p. 2)'; 'getting old' and 'stagnant' (p. 3); 'decide, act and behave', 'alive', 'organ', 'essence', 'vital' and 'nature' (p. 4); 'grow' (p. 5); 'environment' (p. 9); 'spirit' (p. 10); 'fruition' (p. 120) and 'vital' (p. 13).

The machine metaphor weaves through the same pages in words such as 'powerful engine' (p. 1); 'tool' (p. 2); 'purely mechanical' (p. 8); 'human resource' (p. 9); 'managers are also the costliest resource' (p. 10), and culmi-nates in a description of the worker:

> It [the final function of management] implies consideration of the human being as a resource – that is, as something having peculiar physiological properties, abilities and limitations that require the same amount of engineering attention as the properties of any other resource, e.g. copper.
>
> (p. 11)

Drucker immediately goes on to qualify this statement in a listing of all the attributes of 'the human resource as human being' that distinguish this particular 'resource' from all other resources. He notes the human attributes of 'personality, citizenship, control . . . motivation, participation, satisfactions, incentives and rewards, leadership, status and function' (p. 11). In a dominant reading this point in his argument might be read as supporting his claim that to 'consider the rank-and-file worker in the same light as other material resources, and as . . . standing under the laws of mechanics . . . is a serious misunderstanding' (p. 10).

In a critical reading the copper analogy forges an image of people as 'resources' that is supported by the root metaphor of the organization as machine outlined above. It seems that the message intended by the author argues with the message conveyed by the text.

Both the organic and the machine metaphors entangle with a war metaphor that begins to emerge more and more strongly even as the dominant text seems to move magnetically into an overt discussion of a 'cold war'. In the past, 'economic change has been seen as a 'danger' (p. 20), only economic 'advance' can make the 'cold war' bearable, our 'survival' depends upon this 'advance', and we must recognize 'the danger' of simply trying to 'defend what we have' instead of attempting to 'advance further'. The 'tougher job' of management, steering 'formerly colonial and raw-material producing countries' into economic prosperity, is conspicuously placed in the context of a perceived communist threat to 'the entire free world' (pp. 2–30).

Drucker, Austrian by birth, seems to speak for the 'modern west' (p. 20), but his focus is America. When he says, 'management will be decisive both to the United States and to the free world' (p. 2), the placing of 'both' indicates a seeming weighting of the USA as of importance equal to that of the rest of the free world. More than that, the 'free world' trails after the United States, the supposedly non-free world is nowhere to be found in his equation, and a few paragraphs further on Drucker writes of the United States as 'leader' and in the final paragraph of the world 'outside the United States' (p. 3). 'Outside' suggests, especially in the 'cold war' context where this phrase is placed, foreigners, non-belongers. The text assumes American readers.

A number of assumptions are both suggested by the various extensions of the metaphors so far commented on, but are also discernable in the broader, more overtly stated, themes of the text. One of the most interesting of these assumptions, because it is seemingly contradicted by the dominant reading, has already been outlined above: it is the notion that the workers in a business are 'resources', that their 'properties can be justly or even usefully compared with those of copper', and that they require a similar amount of 'engineering attention' as any other resource (p. 11). Spelt out in such graphic detail, the image of workers as a separate class of people, different from that of management, connects with a suggestion that began to emerge on the first page of this text, where Drucker says of management that it is a 'distinct and leading group'. He sets it in direct opposition to 'labor' (p. 1), which, once we discover that it is a 'resource' like any other resource, is what management is 'charged with' (p. 2) making productive.

'Charged' is an extraordinarily powerful word that carries several layers of meaning. Drucker has already, just four lines previously, described resources as traditionally thought of as 'God-given'. In the space of this one paragraph, we have moved into the 'modern west' and its revolutionary view of resources as a 'tool' of control over nature. So the word 'charged' is invested not only with the notion of 'received', or at least inherited, passed down, authority, a divine contract to deliver, but also carries two further meanings: it suggests electrical energy, the power to energize and make something happen; and it also denotes a legal challenge. To be 'charged with' suggests being made to account for one's actions. There is an implied accusation that a person, or group of persons (in this case, managers) is responsible for a particular outcome. When, in this one paragraph, management is said to 'reflect the basic spirit of the modern age', and is presented in biblical language, 'begotten', there is a relentless build towards acceptance of the divine right of managers to manage. This one word, 'charged', read contextually, assumes that managers are to possess power over 'resources' (which include workers), that is divine, legal and physical.

I read 'charged' as an extraordinarily powerful word, and not just because of the layering of meaning within and beyond it that I have begun to describe above. This is Drucker's definitive statement as to what management is – it is 'the organ of society specifically charged with making resources productive'. In this role it is a statement that links back to the opening sentence, which also, in a definition, tells us what a manager is, the 'dynamic life-giving element in every business'; and to the conclusion to Chapter 2 where management is said to be 'a multi-purpose organ that manages a business and manages managers and manages worker and work' and 'that must "discharge" all of its three jobs through the same people at the same time' (p. 13).

The word 'dynamic' suggests science, physical force, drama and divinity. A few lines further back, Drucker's text was presenting economics as a 'performance', as an 'illusion' when achieved by 'mismanagement'. As I make pivotal connections between the words 'dynamic' and 'charged' and 'discharged', finding in them suggestions of extraordinary power, ranging across the physical, the legal, the mechanical, the moral and the spiritual, I think too of the musical connotations of 'dynamic': as the degree and quality of sound in a musical performance it anticipates the need for the 'harmony' (p. 11) of present and future time. I return to my reading of the paragraph in which 'charged' first makes its entrance, and am reminded that the sentence concludes, 'management . . . reflects the basic spirit of the modern age'. 'Reflects' is a gentle mirror image of the forces unleashed by 'charged'. It holds up a mirror of life as does a dramatic performance, and is an emanation of light, physical and symbolic.

This then is the power that the subtext describes as enabling managers as the 'activating organ of the enterprise' to manage workers and work (p. 11). In a dominant reading the image of the worker as a 'human being' who requires 'motivation, participation, satisfactions, incentives and rewards, leadership, status and function' (p. 11) is the image that Drucker seems to portray. Yet even when he argues that mismanaging the worker in the expectation of economic gain is 'illusory' (p. 13) because it is not only ultimately destructive of capital, but also because society has a vital interest in realizing its aims via the functions of management, this same counter-pointing subtext breaks through. In stating that the mismanagement of workers and work will create 'class hatred and class warfare', Drucker assumes the notion of class in the context of management.

As I read it, the group of people who are to be led by management – 'a leading group in industrial society' (p. 1) – has here been classified into a social stratum: 'class' denotes social, not organizational, hierarchy. So while a dominant reading of his text may concur with Drucker's statement that 'management's authority and responsibility are severely limited' (p. 7) or should be, lest they 'help into power a dictatorship that will deprive . . . all . . . groups in a free society of their authority and standing' (p. 8), lurking in the subtext is his representation of a 'lower' order of persons (lower than management persons). He writes of a 'superior management', the 'only' order of persons which 'can prevent our becoming smug, self-satisfied and lazy' (p. 3). The descriptors 'smug, self-satisfied and lazy' ring with echoes of Taylor's voice, so that even the inclusive 'we' reads like a weak subterfuge here.

A few pages later, Drucker reminds his readers of the proper limitations of managerial authority: 'The scope and extent of management's authority and responsibility are severely limited' (p. 7). But this flat observation does little to counter the image that has been steadily building, flattering managers by reflecting them as beings of a superior order, persons 'above' the worker. Their 'spectacular rise' has given them 'high visibility', for they live on the fourteenth floor, and are thought to be 'people at the top' (p. 4). Although Drucker tempers these images of managers by telling us that they are inadequate, his text continues to build the laudatory version, and the overt statement is smothered by the more emotive hierarchical subtext.

Management's exciting status is loudly proclaimed on page one. Educated, emulated even by the highest echelons of government ('And when the Eisenhower Administration was formed in 1952, it was formed consciously as a "Management Administration"', p. 1), management is introduced as 'a leading group', 'an essential, a distinct and a leading institution', a 'new institution', 'indispensable', non-controversial, 'grounded' in business basics. Like the ruling classes through the ages, it should see it itself as the defender of the faith, of the 'basic beliefs of modern western society', and be ready to 'advance the human spirit'. In pursuit of this goal managers will gain 'control over nature', 'win the cold war', and create economic prosperity around the globe (pp. 1–3). All of this richly condensed meal is consumed within two and a half pages. While inflating the ego of the manager it may leave the critical reader with indigestion.

Yet it is only after they have been left for a while to revel in this grand image of self-importance that managers are told to limit their responsibilities in the most acceptable of all possible ways – the social sphere where to act beyond an economic brief would be a usurpation of the rightful responsibilities of the other great institutions: church, government and military. Drucker says that management has 'partial rather than comprehensive social responsibility' and that management should not 'claim to be the leading group' (p. 8). The text says that 'management – almost alone – has to live in both present and future' (p. 12), and 'without it we would not have a business enterprise or an industrial society' (p. 13). As we learned in his opening statement, 'management will remain a basic and dominant institution perhaps as long as western civilization itself survives' for 'management also expresses basic beliefs of modern western society' (p. 1).

A different kind of confusion arises from within the organic metaphor. An 'organ' physically belongs somewhere, is part of the 'body', so when management is repeatedly described as the 'specific organ of the business enterprise' (pp. 4–6), the business enterprise is understood to be the body of which the management organ is an essential and intrinsic part: integral to it, not superior to, or apart from it. This identity, Drucker tells us, 'sets it apart from all other governing organs of all other institutions'. This is a clear and helpful image until Drucker also tells us that 'management is the organ of society'. Just as neither a head nor a hand can be attached to two bodies simultaneously (or at least not without the intrusion of the grotesque), so too with this metaphor of management.

Strangely, the imagination's circus act, as described above, has already been suggested by a particularly startling metaphor that almost leaps off the page. In the opening paragraph of Chapter 2, Drucker describes the popular image of what managers do as bearing a striking resemblance to 'the medieval geographer's picture of Africa as the stamping ground of the one-eyed ogre, the two-headed pygmy, the immortal phoenix and the elusive unicorn' (p. 4). Outrageous as well as unexpected, these images are in no way typical of this text, but are yet all the more memorable for their solo performance on an otherwise sombre stage; and as Drucker piles up the grotesque with the mythological, the cumulative effect is to alienate the reader; to prompt an emotional dissociation from the suggested ignorance and superstition of the picture-book world of long ago.

We are snapped back into the familiar world of sane management when Drucker immediately juxtaposes a short direct question: 'What then is management: what does it do?' – a few lines further back Drucker had suggested that the images he conjured up were those in the minds of the 'well-informed and intelligent' and 'otherwise sane men'. So now, back within the neat confines of his sensible, balanced question, we are perhaps relieved to be in the company of an author who, he implies, will give us a picture of management with which we can identify. His question is our question and he will provide the answer.

Drucker's voice in these pages is occasionally inclusive, but predominantly authoritarian. The opening tone and pace, definitive, expert, seemingly objective and impersonal, is consistently and at length expressed in the unqualified use of the verb 'to be' and is returned to throughout the text. 'The manager is . . .', 'Management is also', 'The emergence of management . . . is . . .' and 'Management will remain . . .', 'This belief . . . is . . .' and 'Management . . . is' are the opening words of each of the first six paragraphs. Such repetition hammers home the author's assurance that there is nothing to argue about here, and the relatively short sentences and uncomplicated syntax support Drucker's uncompromising stance.

Balancing the accessibility that this syntactical style affords, is a Latinate vocabulary that adds a weighty, learned ambiance. Drucker lists, for example, management's competence [f. L. *competere*: to be qualified, suitable], integrity [f. L. *integritas*: wholeness, soundness, perfection], and performance [f. L. *performare*: to shape thoroughly] in a sentence that is constructed in the Latinate form of 'both to . . . and to' (p. 2). The sentence which opens the next paragraph is built around a 'not only . . . but also' construction, and this too, is a pattern that is consistently repeated throughout the text.

There is also repetition throughout these pages in the pairing and triple phrasing (which reinforces the points being made) and in the stark antithesis of phrases (which highlight by contrast) as in the following examples, all of which are found on the first page: 'the *resources* of *production* remain *resources* and never become *production*'; '*determine* the success of a business, indeed they *determine* its survival' (paragraph 1). In paragraph 2 (nine and a half lines) we have pairings such as the image of management as 'a *distinct* and a *leading* group' with a '*comprehensive* and *distinct* system'. There is also a combination of repetition and antithesis in the pairings of '*capital*' and '*labor*'; '*management*' and '*labor*'; the '*responsibilities* of *capital*' and the '*rights* of *capital*' and the '*responsibilities* of *management*', the '*prerogatives* of *management*' and '*education* for *management*', '*management administration*' and '*Eisenhower Administration*'. Even the verbs are repeated: 'We no longer *talk* of . . . we *talk* of . . .' and 'when the Eisenhower Administration was *formed* . . . it was *formed* . . .', as well as opposed as in 'We . . . *talk*. . . . We *hear* . . .' (italics added).

These repetitive pairings reinforce Drucker's message through both emphasis and contrast, and by the time we reach the third paragraph they are building to a climactic triple statement. Paragraph 3 (six and a half lines) builds to a seemingly irrefutable positioning of management as 'a new institution', repeated three times, 'an essential, a distinct and a leading' institution, also described as 'a leading group'. The first sentence of the paragraph is a definitive statement to this effect: 'The emergence of management as an essential, a distinct and a leading institution is a pivotal event in social history.' Poised then at a moment in history when something new is going to be the turning point in our social development, we are assailed by the purported importance of this moment, by the ringing echoes of the triple statements that complete the paragraph:

> *Rarely, if ever*, has a new basic institution, a new leading group, emerged as fast as has management since the turn of this century. *Rarely in human history* has a new institution proven indispensable so quickly; and *even less often* has a new institution arrived with so little opposition, so little disturbance, so little controversy.
>
> (p. 1, italics added)

The repeated concepts here of a new group, of new leadership have already become a familiar drum-roll. Additionally, in the italicized phrases in the quotation above, we see Drucker extolling the unique event to which we are witness and the extreme qualities of this happening, its speed, indispensability and total acceptability. And it is this last attribute that is celebrated in the oratorical cumulation of 'so little . . . so little . . . so little':

> Rarely in human history has a new institution proven indispensable so quickly; and even less often has a new institution arrived with *so little* opposition, *so little* disturbance, *so little* controversy.
>
> (p. 1, italics added)

Throughout Chapter 1, Drucker's voice reverberates with such classical rhythm, with elegant simplicity, balance and resonance. If we return a moment to paragraph 2 for example, we find that it is constructed around sentences syntactically arranged as follows: 1, simple definition of management based on a descriptive pairing ('dynamic, life-giving') and qualifying phrase of place ('in every business'); 2, perfect balance of the paralleled repetition and antithesis in 'we no longer talk of [this]' (capital and labour), 'we talk of [that]', 'management and labor'; 3, a second, longer, parallelism and apposition (adding to the weighty sense of balance being achieved by the paragraph) of 'the responsibilities of capitalism' and the 'rights of capitalism' with the 'responsibilities of management' and the 'prerogatives of management'.

Yet along with all of this emphatic authority, as he makes these points, Drucker's voice becomes inclusive with the use of the first person plural pronoun. 'We talk', 'we hear' and 'we are building' with him, so that readers are made to feel their ownership of the knowledge described. As soon as this comfort zone has been established, readers are again almost entirely excluded from Chapter 1, while Drucker, the distant expert, explains, describes and defines on a broad canvas, and it seems to be assumed that readers are still in step with an argument in which Drucker himself seems to have little personal involvement. But 'we' are brought back in when the need for 'us' to 'improve, 'to progress' is proposed as the antidote to 'our' becoming 'smug, self-satisfied and lazy', and Drucker himself is again present in the appeal to his readers, 'truly', on which the chapter ends.

In Chapter 2 a similar pattern of omniscient overview, expert knowledge and a comfortable yet mentoring relationship to readers continues. Scattered through these few pages we find, for example, personal, chatty asides to the knowing reader ('as we shall see they don't even tell us that' (p. 4), and 'Henry Gantt was the prime example' (p. 7); reference to the author's familiarity with huge corporate enterprises on both sides of the Atlantic (such as United States Steel and the British Coal Board, p. 4); an implied author–reader dialogue conducted at a conversational level, 'True, the work of the manager' (p. 6), evidence of the author's political involvement, the Roosevelt debate (p. 6), the author's summary dismissal of management theory as 'scientific management' (p. 7), use of statistical research, as on investment in managers (p. 10), and notes of a hortatory enthusiasm, 'we must, however, never allow ourselves to forget' (p. 13) that are quite Churchillian.

Drucker supports his arguments not only with the authoritative effects of syntactical constructs already described, a rhetorical reinforcement of key-words and concepts conveyed in a voice that impresses, moves and challenges the reader, but also (despite his disclaimers in the preface) with appeals to authority: political, the Eisenhower Administration (p. 1), social, Jonathan Swift (p. 2) and philosophical, Plato (p. 10).

Several subtexts, of which the dominant reader may be unaware and yet with which she may be persuaded to identify through the effectiveness of a rhetorical performance such as that indicated above, were discussed earlier in this critical reading. Some subtexts however, are as much an aspect of rhetorical persuasion as they are of textual perspective.

An example of such a subtext, one that persists throughout this text, revolves around Drucker's view of management, managers and the managed. From his opening statement and throughout this reading, managers are flattered by a portrait of themselves as extraordinarily powerful, able and versatile. In Chapter 1, I read that they are 'dynamic and life-giving', a 'leading group', 'an essential, a distinct and a leading institution', 'indispensable', accepted by all, 'a basic and dominant institution', entrusted with 'human and material resources', working for 'human betterment', 'new, distinctly modern, distinctly western', reflecting 'the basic spirit of the modern age', and 'truly, the entire free world has an immense stake in the competence, skill and responsibility of management' (pp. 1–3). Chapter 2 continues in the same vein, opening with a sentence that restates the 'crucial importance', 'high visibility' and 'spectacular rise of management', moves on to the unique, creative and applied qualities of managers and management (pp. 4–9); on again to the manager as architect of the 'Good Society', leader of the organization and embodiment of its 'spirit', 'costliest' of all an enterprise's resources, multidimensional, multifaceted, and, by the time I reach page 13, seemingly a totally admirable, essentially necessary, unusually able, person.

Just as the manager and the managed are assumed to be of different class orders, so too we have another 'us and them' dichotomy set up in the first three pages. 'The west', 'western civilization' and 'western society' are all introduced on page 1, while the 'modern west' with its 'new', 'distinctly modern', 'distinctly western' 'materialism' is featured in the first half of page 2. All of this is incorporated into an appeal to nationalism and the contribution that management must make to maintain the pre-eminent position of United States leadership ('the United States is the leader today, economically and socially' (p. 2) of the 'free world' in a 'cold war of indefinite duration'.

This appeal continues with an image of a fallen Great Britain 'doomed to decline for lack of vision and lack of effort' (pp. 2–3), a Europe that needs to 'regain her economic prosperity', 'formerly colonial . . . countries' that have yet to develop into 'free nations' and the ever-present threat of Communism. By the time Drucker reaches his conclusion, that 'the entire free world has an immense stake in . . . management' (p. 3), managers may well be assured that they are the leaders, the potential saviours of the world and its future.

Management's role then is not just that of economic administration, for Drucker envisages a future in which managers in their control of resources, of 'nature', will bring about 'human betterment and social justice' (pp. 1–2). In the management of managers there should be growth and development that will lead to the 'Good Society' (p. 10). All of this is clearly stated in the text. What is not so clear, but seems to me to emerge from the subtexts, is just what role the manager should assume in this context. In a dominant reading I note that Drucker would limit the authority and responsibility of the manager (p. 7), repeatedly profiles management as a leading institution, but occasionally reminds us that it is not, nor ever should be, the leading institution (p. 8), and claims to support the independence and self-determination of all human kind. In the subtext, as noted above in my discussion of Drucker's view of the 'working class', this is a group that, despite his protest to the contrary, he graphically categorizes with 'any other resource, e.g. copper' (p. 11).

This categorization is so explicit, it immediately conjures up, and throws into relief, Drucker's subsequent image of the employee as 'the whole man' (Chapter 2). In this later discussion, Drucker spends some time explaining that how we view a worker, a human resource, depends upon whether we put the emphasis on 'human' ('a moral and a social creature'), or on 'resource' to be 'utilized' like copper or water power (p. 232). Recalling this passage (Drucker entitles it 'Employing the whole man', with the subheading 'The worker as resource') I see all of the precursors to it suggested in Chapters 1 and 2, not as an issue as to which of the two words ('human' and 'resource') should be emphasized, but the fact that humans are classified as resources in any respect. In all that Drucker says of humans as resources, they are treated as fodder for the 'engine' (p. 1) of management that, in pursuit of material advantage (p. 2), utilizes 'resources' as 'tools' to gain 'control over nature'.

As he visions the material, the good, the ideal, society into which the institution of management must lead the world, 'in this book we will bring together both present and future' (p. 13), Drucker advises that we discard the theory and theorists of the past, and their mistaken ideas about management. He indicts 'the early pioneers of "scientific management"', in particular naming Henry Gantt, and the 'German "Rationalization" movement of the twenties', as well as the 'technocracy' of America (p. 7), for the attempted cartelization of the economy, and the resulting limitations on growth. Against this image of the misguided and the misled, he sets up the promise of his own theory. It all leads in to the overwhelming question that he will ask: 'What is management and what does it do?' (p. 13). He promises to answer this question in the pages ahead.

In summary then, a critical reading of Drucker's text reveals that he presents management, the 'dominant institution' of our time, and for the foreseeable future of western civilization (p. 1), as, in addition to its economic role, the rightful proprietor of inherent physical, social, political and spiritual power. Managers, a new leading group, are the possessors of this enormous power; workers and their work are classified into a lower order. The United States is one world and everywhere else is 'the other' world. Material prosperity will lead to spiritual riches, and managers will lead men (*sic*) into the 'Good Society', but only if we abandon the mistaken ideas about management promulgated by past theorists, and learn from Drucker what management is and what managers do.

Reflexive reading

I have found much to enjoy in my reading of Drucker, a master wordsmith. His text is both energetic and sonorous, rolling along with conviction and control, and he pays an attention to word choice and arrangement that is 'truly' (to borrow one of Drucker's favourite words) classical. As I completed my first, dominant, reading I was aware of this enjoyment colouring my response to the text to such an extent that I had been indulging my delight in the musicality of the experience, feeling the emotive impact of it, rather than making mental notes of the theory argued. I therefore had to begin reading again, in order to seek out the substance of the argument, before committing a summary version of the text to paper.

I then found that extracting Drucker's essential argument from the text was not a straightforward task, partly because of the confusions as to word meaning already noted in my analysis, but also because it seemed that notions of, and sometimes images of, for example, 'western civilization', the 'cold war', and medieval Africa, presumably intended to be illustrative, were distracting. They seemed to take on a dominating role that lead away from, rather than further into, the substantive meaning of the passage.

For these reasons my response began to be one of irritation rather than delight. I began to see the word patterns, and the emotions they had initially conjured up, as some kind of betrayal of my own, preferred, rational understanding. In other words, for me this text, more than any of the others read, achieved rhetorical capture, an instinctive reader buy-in, to whatever it was that it was saying, before I had sufficiently determined my own understanding of its meaning, to rationally accept or reject the worldview it conveyed.

From this response I perceived a particular outcome, related to my personal reading of this text, and drew a general conclusion, related to my method-ology and its usefulness. The particular outcome was that my irritation transformed an initially positive response to the text into a negative rela-tionship with it. I found myself seeking out the rhetorical features that had affected my response in a grudging mood, for while on the one hand I wanted to, as it were, 'excuse' my emotional vulnerability, on the other hand I wanted to validate it. I was therefore aware, as I completed my critical reading, that my ambivalence may have resulted in a reading that was not as controlled, as objective, as perhaps were my critical readings of the other selected texts.

My more general conclusion is that this third step in the scriptive reading process, does in its application to this particular text, serve the diversity of purposes that I intended it should when developing my methodology. While there is plenty of scope for other analysts to probe, dissect and generally pick over my interpretation, and indeed I can very well do this for myself too, the awareness of the reflexive reading to come, did, I believe, make me much more self-aware during the critical reading stage. It was this awareness at the time of completing that analysis that allows me to comment now on some of the ways in which my emotional responses may have geared even the more seemingly rational and objective aspects of my analysis.

Review

In this third experience of scriptive reading I particularly noted the interest with which I began the exploration of my reading responses in the reflexive phase. Although I became increasingly aware, as I completed the critical reading, of the ambivalence described above, I did not begin to appreciate its significance until I opened space in which to reflect on it. Further con-sideration, as I completed the comments recorded above, took me back to the two previous scriptive readings.

To this point I have not commented on my decision not to historicize the selected texts. I have nevertheless, in the overview that introduces each text, noted the date of publication. I was therefore prepared, as I began each of the dominant readings so far completed, to allow for some alienation stemming from the different language mores and the cultural environments of times past. Placing the three dominant readings alongside each other suggests two conclusions. First, that Taylor and Follett, both writing early in the twentieth century, promoted markedly different philosophies of management: Taylor put the system first and Follett put people first. Thirty years later Drucker was putting the manager first. Taylor and Drucker have both remained in the vanguard of management thinking and Follett has been largely forgotten. Second, all three texts were written in very different prose styles: Taylor is immediately forthright and accessible, Follett writes a thoroughly considered and detailed argument, and although Drucker's prose rolls out sonorously, his argument is sometimes contorted. Again my dominant reading did not provide me with an explanation for the 'forgetting' of Follett.

With these conclusions in place it became apparent that if I were to find explanations for the historical discrepancy of treatment then it would be the critical readings that would provide the clues. This did in fact turn out to be the case and is discussed fully in the next chapter. For the moment I was content to note another strength of scriptive reading: it potentially allows readers to discover new answers to old, as yet unsolved, mysteries, in this instance the reason for management theory's discard of Follett.

Text four: Henry Mintzberg

Overview

This text is an extract from a book by Henry Mintzberg, *The Nature of Managerial Work*, first written in 1973. I am working with the 1980 edition, published by Prentice-Hall in 'The Theory of Management Policy Series' edited by Henry Mintzberg, and readers are told by the author (p. xvi) that this volume 'is identical to the original book published by Harper and Row in 1973, with one exception' – the three original appendices have been deleted. Mintzberg explains that he regards these (100 pages) as being of interest to the specialist reader, and that he intends this shorter edition to be more accessible to students and managers.

The extract that I have chosen to analyse is taken from the first chapter, Introduction, and consists of most of the first five pages. The Introduction is five and a half pages in length and the final section, which I have left out, is a skeletal summary of the chapters which follow and 'A note to readers' about the design of the book. In choosing to briefly link some of my analysis of the Introduction to a later section of the complete text, the introductory pages of Chapter 7, I have been guided by Mintzberg's own comment on these introductory pages: 'Chapter 7 opens with an integrated summary of all the findings, which ties together the theoretical materials of Chapters 3 through 6' (p. 6).

The book is 198 pages long, consists of seven chapters, and Chapter 1, Introduction, is preceded by a 'Foreword to the series', a 'Preface to the series edition' and a 'Preface to the original edition'.

In the 'Preface to the series edition', Mintzberg describes an incident and makes a comment on it, which is particularly pertinent to my inquiry. He tells of being telephoned by the programme assistants of a TV network and a radio station the morning after the *New York Times* published an article on this book. Both callers 'expressed pleasure that someone had finally "let managers have it"'. Mintzberg comments that, 'of course this book does no such thing' and then goes on to tell of his amusement that it is managers themselves who seem to appreciate the book's message, quoting them as saying, 'you make me feel so good'. He goes on to suggest that the only way to 'explain the book's enthusiastic acceptance by both managers and people who believe there is something wrong with managers is that both have had enough of rationality narrowly defined'. Perhaps, but his words stoked my curiosity about his rhetoric with a very particular fuel, for the rhetorician who can persuade the members of opposing camps that he is partisan to both their causes is indeed masterly.

Dominant reading

Mintzberg's Introduction opens with a quotation from an interview with an executive conducted in 1956. It serves to demonstrate emphatically that a typical manager finds it difficult to explain what he (*sic*) does.

Current understandings of management theorists relating to the work of managers are summarized in the first paragraph, and Mintzberg makes it clear that Henri Fayol's 1916 words, 'managers plan, organize, coordinate and control' still provide the basic and most generally agreed job profile, but that later theorists have added motivating and integrating roles.

Academic theorizing about what managers do, as described in the first paragraph, contrasts sharply with the broadly shared perceptions of the manager in popular American culture as described in paragraph 2. There managers are seen as folk heroes, and are thought to be leading the nation into material and organizational success, even while there are concerns about their leadership abilities. Given the scope and importance of their tasks, this concern is not seen as surprising.

In the author's view though, it is deeply ironic that the work of managers is still not really understood because a plethora of education and training programmes have been designed to enable them to do their job. These include scholarly and management practice journals, public, private and in-house management development programmes, and the services of specialist teams of management scientists as described in the third paragraph.

In the fourth paragraph, the problem illustrated in the first three paragraphs and the prefacing quotation, that we do not know what managers do, is illustrated in the anecdotal evidence provided by the telling of a story about a management science conference that was attended by some of the 'best-known names in management science'. The gathering was challenged by one presenter to explain 'what constitutes the job of top managers', but failed to do so.

Mintzberg concludes that since neither the literature of management nor management scientists nor management practitioners can tell us what managers do, all of the questions that depend upon this knowledge also remain unanswered. He lists first a series of generalized problems expressed as questions, and then formalizes a list of specific questions. The generalized questions, in paragraph 5, all relate to the need to acquire knowledge that will enable the teaching and designing of management systems to support and improve the work of managers.

In paragraphs 6 and 7, Mintzberg moves on to the list of specific questions to which he intends seeking answers in the book. The questions relate to: the activities managers perform; the distinguishing characteristics of managerial work; the basic roles of managers; the variations that exist among management jobs, and, finally, the extent to which management is a science. A set of the specific questions that will direct his inquiry is provided for each topic area and he limits the scope of the research to exclude many middle managers: his focus will be on those who are 'formally in charge of organizations or their subunits' (p. 3).

In the next two paragraphs Mintzberg reiterates what the book is, and is not, about: it is not about 'effective' management; it simply aims to discover the manager's job description. It is also, uniquely, based on empirical evidence and should therefore replace all previous research.

Having established then, that at the time when he began his research no one could explain what a manager does, he spells out in some detail the questions relating to the job of the manager to which he will seek answers. Before summing up the main conclusions that have emerged from his new view of the manager's job, he reminds readers that he did not set out with a 'preconception' of this. The empirical research, which included diary studies, observation, analyses of working records, activity sampling and structured observation across a range of organizational activities and managerial roles, leads to and supports the conclusions. He lists ten of these, and each conclusion is introduced by a summary statement before being more or less qualified.

The ten conclusions are: managers' jobs are remarkably alike; the differences that do exist in managers' work are largely those of common roles and characteristics; managers' work is challenging and non-programmed; the manager is both generalist and specialist; much of the manager's power derives from information; the job threatens to become superficial; there is no science in managerial work; the manager is in a kind of loop – time pressure makes if difficult to receive help from management scientists, exacerbating the problems that the latter could solve; it is for the management scientist to break this loop, and finally, managerial work is so complex that only precise understanding of it will allow for its improvement.

In the remaining four paragraphs, Mintzberg outlines the design of the book's chapters, particularly as this relates to the ordering of the material found in it, and reminds readers that he is writing for non-expert audiences with chapter summaries of his propositions provided for the 'casual reader'. This section of the Introduction is not analysed in the critical reading that follows.

Critical reading

Mintzberg introduces his introduction with a passage from an interview that plays on the verb 'to do'. 'Obviously' a piece of data from field research (the participants in the dialogue quoted are named as 'observer' and 'executive') the assumption that the reader will recognize it as such, initiates a writer/reader relationship based in shared knowledge of research and its methodologies. Balancing the formality of this 'classroom' contextuality, is the informality of the conversational dialogue:

> EXECUTIVE: That's not easy
> OBSERVER: Go ahead anyway (p. 1)

The dramatic form of the whole exchange (it is set out as if both characters were taking part in a play) binds reader to author in the shared intimacy of their dual identification with the expert knowledge of the 'observer' and his careful probing of the subject 'executive'. The dramatic form also suggests action, and building tension, as the characters in this play engage and the reader awaits an outcome. Already the reader is involved in this inquiry; in pursuit of answers that the executive seems unable to provide.

The reader who is a manager has here been both provoked and soothed: provoked because the hectic schedule and seemingly endless responsibilities of the manager have been passed by in the vague summation of the job as 'I must see that things go alright' (p. 2); and soothed because the subtext seems to read 'My job is so complex, so varied, so responsible, it cannot be described in a casual bit of chat'. Yet 'presidents' are not usually lost for words, as is this executive here, so reader/author identification builds through the recorded exchange, culminating in the over-riding impression that the executive is the butt of a gentle authorial joke. The reader is being spoken to in the encouraging, but fractionally condescending, voice of teacher to student, or counsellor to client: all of the power base resides with the observer, who directs the dialogue, insists on answers, and in so far as the author is also represented in his voice, has established control of the situation which we are about to explore as the text opens into the rhetorical question: 'What do managers do?'

All aspects of this tonal play: the 'doing' – but not reflective or verbal – executive; the leading role of expert observers, and the relaxed ambiance of the scene being played out as it morphs into dramatic tension, and resolves in humour, are immediately echoed in the relationship with his readers that Mintzberg establishes in the first paragraph of his text. It opens with a generalized but direct question, 'What do managers do?' and assumes reader familiarity with the question in a variety of relatively intimate situations: family (children), work (staff specialists), and schooling (university students). We are in familiar, even cosy territory here, but an explicit threat to the manager is also expressed in the description of students as those 'who one day hope to replace him' (p. 2). So manager–readers are both made to feel the comfort of the familiar, but also worried enough by the threat of usurpation to want to continue reading with the expectation that they will become equipped to meet challenges to their position.

On first reading, the opening question also seems to be a rhetorical question (a question that does not expect an answer, serving to emphasize what is in fact an assertion with which audience affirmation is assumed) and is indeed here a statement about something of which speaker and audience have shared knowledge and understanding. Here, Mintzberg is really saying something like: 'Well, of course we all know what managers do; we just don't waste valuable time trying to explain it in words.'

Three lines on, and Mintzberg has moved from the generalized, universalized situation – all managers and those who people their immediate environment – to the specific, and a direct address to his readers. 'Ask it' sounds imperative, Mintzberg directing his readers and assuming their compliance. He is the authority now, mentoring his acolyte reader, and simultaneously reinforcing the more personal tone of the relationship, and the reader's assumed participation in conversation with him. All of these developing aspects of his relationship with his readers are contained in the simple statement 'you are likely to be told': 'you' is a direct address to the reader; 'are likely' is casual conversation, and 'told' brings us back to the mentor/student relationship. The author's use of the second person pronoun, 'you', following the imperative, 'ask', clearly brings his immediate interpersonal relationship with his reader into play, the informality of the chatty tone allowing the expert/amateur distance to be bridged.

But then what 'you' are 'told' is the cited words of an old (1916!) authority, Henry Fayol; words with which 'you', the reader may indicate dismissive familiarity, 'Fine . . . but what do managers really do?' Mintzberg has now begun to flatten the hierarchical distance that was developing by extending the conversational mode, and simultaneously allowing that his reader has some expertise too, and a familiarity with classical management theory.

Status and respect restored, the reader is now probably ready to beaver along beside Mintzberg with the implicit understanding that when Mintzberg suggests burying 'yourself in one of America's better management libraries for a good part of one year' and reading 'perhaps two hundred books and articles' both reader and writer understand that it is actually Mintzberg's own experience that he is describing. The specifics of 'one year' and 'two hundred books and articles' give us the clue here, and yet it is also in the sentence opener, 'if you are intent', conjuring up the image of that author on just such a mission. Readers are flattered by the implication that, like the expert author, they might be inclined to undertake such an activity. 'Burying' yourself, suggests death – a total removal from the world of action (where managers 'do' things) – and 'emerging' able to recite literature, serve effectively to emphasize the gulf between book-learning and the kind of field work in which Mintzberg has based the research outcomes described in this book. 'So remains the state of our understanding', concludes the author without qualification: we have book learning but no knowledge of what real managers do.

'State' suggests a grand territory and aptly introduces the unqualified claim in the next sentence, that 'the manager is the folk hero of contemporary American society'. We are now in popular territory, in the 'down home' backyard of every citizen, with a rhetorical appeal to nationalistic identity being prepared. It is made explicit in the next two sentences: though 'we know so little of what he does' (the mystique of the hero who is beyond the ken of local know-how) yet we believe that he is the embodiment of our national pride, the 'American genius'. Our hero is a stranger, wrapped in the mythology of the lone ranger who rides into town, performs his hero deeds and disappears again into the sunset. We do not 'know' him but, awed by his anonymity, we admire his deeds: his 'success' is our success and we are grateful ('America owes').

In the space of three short sentences our local hero, the manager, has arrived on the national stage. From hometown to Washington, it is 'America' that owes 'her material and organizational success' to managers, for their leadership ('we look to the manager') is yoked to that of the president himself. In the question put by a 'popular periodical', 'Is the Presidency actually too much for one man?' every man, or at least every American citizen, is evoked. Mintzberg insists that this question is being 'echoed' throughout the nation, for 'in the corridors of a thousand government and industrial bureaucracies' Americans are turning to managers. In just one paragraph, as we try to grasp the current 'state of our understanding', the scale and scope of management, and its national importance has grown exponentially. From the familiarity of 'the folk' back home, to the remote corridors of industrial and political power, and to the superhuman role of the White House itself, the work of managers is lauded. All success and the essence of vital leadership is now encapsulated in this 'corp' [*sic*] of ten or more million individuals.

The manager, this entity bestriding America, enlarges his territory as he (*sic*) steps into the next paragraph where he immediately becomes a world citizen for he is 'trained in programs throughout the world'. But he is embattled. In the paragraph described above, his territory is the nation, and he is in charge: in the one that follows, the manager becomes the victim, the laboratory specimen beloved of the controlling denizens in academia's empire. Here the management 'corps' is trained, 'exposed' and 'surrounded' by the investigating and teaching teams of management scientists. In the world of action and affairs the manager is 'hero' and 'leader': in the world of scholarship he is caught in a military metaphor of siege and ineptitude. Yet the list of besieging scientists is not to be taken too seriously, for Mintzberg can't even be bothered completing the list of bodies making up its rank and file: 'planners, information systems designers, operations researchers, an [*sic*] so on'. Detailed description, the naming of names, trails off into the colloquial 'an so on'.

Yet even as this 'wanted' person is pursued and seemingly ('ostensibly') moulded by professionals, we are reminded that he is the seer, as well as the specimen: his experience is the fountain of management knowledge (for the practitioners who write to him through *Fortune* and *Business Week*); even while he is the subject of endless investigation in the academic journals (such as *Administrative Science Quarterly* and the *Journal of Management Studies*). Seer and specimen he may be, but the very next sentence reminds us that he is also human and vulnerable for he is 'tempted'. He is tempted by that which is 'supposedly' designed to help him. Here the suggestion of deceit ('supposedly designed'), of that which is not what it seems to be, echoes the 'ostensibly' qualifier four lines back. The very human manager, on whom the whole world seems to depend for leadership and 'success', is beset by confusions and deceits that have taken on a moral (the notions of deceit and temptation), as well as a physical dimension.

As I read it, two of the major themes that emerge here are held in delicate juxtaposition: on the one hand the manager is admired and depended upon; while on the other hand it seems that managers themselves, as well as all those who are intent upon studying them, do not really know what it is that they are about. To be 'president' is a great achievement, but if it is actually 'too much for one man' then we all have cause to worry – if not panic! Readers have become audience to a potential tragedy of epic dimensions. In classical drama the tragic hero is a great man, one we 'look up to' and on whom we depend, but he is also human and so we identify with him. His heroism is seen in his deeds, and his human frailty in a character flaw that may lead to his downfall. We are awed by the roles he fulfils, and afraid because his failure will cause us to fall too.

Mintzberg's manager is a 'folk hero', someone to love and admire, but neither he nor his army of advisors seem to know what they are doing. Readers are both captivated and afraid.

Why then might readers, whatever their preconceptions of management, choose to comfortably identify with the sentiment of either or both themes, rather than panic? I suggest that reader identification may be a response to two particular rhetorical strategies at work throughout the text: the careful balance and control that is always maintained, combined with reader involvement sparked by dramatic impact. Balance, largely achieved through careful syntactical arrangements, suggests author authority based on the recognition of both sides of an argument or different aspects of a subject, and drama, often based on the building and breaking of tensions in the narrative of the text, invites emotional involvement. Where the text exhibits both drama and balanced comment then the reader may engage with it, both emotionally and rationally, giving the reader a holistic experience resulting in a sense of completion and satisfaction.

The first paragraph moves from the attention-grabbing opener, a rhetorical question, to cumulation, the piling of one example upon another in order to give weight to the point being made – in this case the number and range of the people who are all asking the same simple question, 'What do managers do?' Having emphasized the importance of 'the question' in this way, the author follows on directly with a logical 'if this, then that' statement, in the form of an imperative (command) 'ask it', followed by its outcome, 'you are likely to be told'. Invocation of an authority (Fayol) adds further substance to the authoritative tone being established, and the whole pattern is repeated in another rendition of the 'if this, then that' logic, followed by a citation from 'authority'.

In the next paragraph short, almost staccato sentences dramatically change the pace of what has been, up to this point, a more leisurely and descriptive introduction. Simple statements, less or little more than a line in length, convey certitude. Sentences begin with the vocabulary of logical argument: 'so', 'yet', 'hence' and 'yet' again; while unqualified simple statements such as 'the manager is' do not brook disagreement.

In the first paragraph the reader was addressed as 'you' and it was assumed had a level of knowledge inferior to that of the author: she is told what to expect if she pursues the 'simple' question. Now, in the second paragraph, as the 'logic' of the author's claims about the state of our understanding of management are relentlessly pressed home, the dichotomy of the second person 'you' as reader, and the assumed 'I' of the author, is replaced by the inclusive first person plural, 'we'. It is 'our' understanding that is here described. 'We' join forces in not understanding the work of the manager who is now the other, 'he'. It is 'we' who look to 'him' for leadership, and 'we' who are concerned about his ability to lead 'us'. As subject and lead actor in this paragraph, 'we', author and reader, enjoy a shared identity that is partly defined by the 'other' of the object of our inquiry, the manager.

Emphasis throughout the first paragraph is on the verb 'to do'. The insistent repetition of it in the chorusing question of the first paragraph echoes the six-fold repetition of it in the prefacing quotation, and establishes a significant boundary for the whole text: we are to understand managers and management not by what a person 'is' (though we are briefly told that too: 'the manager is the folk hero of contemporary American society') but as what a person 'does'. All of America's 'better management libraries' will not tell us the answer to the question in the chorus line, 'What do managers do?' but the repetition of the question and the echoing reverberations of 'do' throughout the passage insist on the importance of the question and the need for universal recognition of it.

By the time we reach the end of paragraph 3, we have travelled from home to workplace to university; from the best management libraries to the folklore of the community and out to the whole of the American nation and its president; from management-trained graduates and management journals, scholarly and practitioner, to corporate trainers and management scientists. Yet with the author we are led to conclude, 'All this and still we do not know what managers do'.

We need to break here, to take a moment out from the frenetic scope and pace of this narrative, while we digest this rich meal, and a narrative pause is just what paragraph 4 provides. That we don't know what managers do has become a 'problem', but one that an anecdote will illuminate, so Mintzberg tells us about a conference incident. The 'sharp focus' that he claims the anecdote will provide is introduced in a sentence that builds an appropriate emotional bedding: 'After h<u>ou</u>rs of r<u>ou</u>ndab<u>ou</u>t discussion by s<u>o</u>me of the best-kn<u>o</u>wn names in management science' is dominated by the sonorous assonance of 'o' sounds, and sleepy murmuring 'm's and 'n's: 'know<u>n</u> <u>n</u>ames i<u>n</u> ma<u>n</u>age<u>m</u>e<u>n</u>t'. The text soothes, slows and quietens response, only to snap back into focus with sharply pointed 'p's of '<u>p</u>artic-i<u>p</u>ant <u>p</u>osed a question that <u>p</u>ointed <u>p</u>recisely'. We are invited into the inner circles of management science (peopled by some of the best-known names in management science) where we discover that they, like us, do not know what managers do. This is reassuring – in so far as our shared ignorance puts us in elevated company – but also, tension begins to build again with the insistent repetition of the (still unanswered) question, 'What does a manager do?' becoming a drum-roll of impending demand. The roll spills out in a crescendo of questions (paragraph 6) that seem to almost fall over one another in their haste to hit the page: 'if/ how', 'if/how' bounces along through the whole of the paragraph in a litany of repeated negatives. 'We do not understand', 'we do not know', and 'we cannot influence' are paired with impossible actions: 'how can' we 'measure', 'design', 'explain', 'claim', 'expect', 'influence' and finally and significantly, 'hope'? The impossible sequence ends on a despairing note as it recognizes the inability to hope in the face of problems that 'appear insurmountable'.

If this were the tragic drama suggested above, then we have already arrived at the first climax as the scene explodes into these frenzied action statements. With Shakespearean control Mintzberg rescues his readers from emotional overload in the quiet voice of reason which introduces the next paragraph: 'We must be able to answer . . .'. From the chaotic surge and break of all that we do not know and therefore cannot do in the 'if this/then that' of the paragraph, Mintzberg precipitates a crystalline series of simple sentences, that he sets out in stepped indentations each featuring a main question, and a subset which follows on from it.

The main questions relate to, in order: the activities of the manager; the characteristics of managerial work; the basic roles of the manager; the variations in managerial responsibilities, and the extent to which management is a science. Since the declared purpose of the book is to 'answer these questions and to stimulate others to seek more precise answers to them' (p. 3), it might be expected that the title of the work, *The Nature of Managerial Work*, would be a key to this focus. In that it suggests an exploration of our understanding of managerial work, 'what managers do', the title seems to me work well: but Mintzberg tells us that his book is about the nature of managerial work. To me, this suggests a philosophical inquiry in the tradition of Alexander Pope or John Locke. It echoes perennial questions about the nature of being, and treatises on the nature of God, of man and of natural law all seem to assert themselves in an intertextual web of meaning that suggests this work belongs in the very company that it eschews, that of the academic library and philosophical thinker.

Clearly Mintzberg intends to reveal what a manager does (managerial work): not what a manager is. But I find the distinction arbitrary. Perhaps what a manager is should be integral to this discussion and research. If it is possible that what a manager does is to essentially be a certain kind of person, that the essence of the person who fulfils the role of manager 'is' what a manager 'does', then discussion that blurs this hides an assumption. Mintzberg's text assumes that what a manager is, is what a manager does, and his powerful rhetoric sweeps the readers into accepting this assumption.

If what a manager 'is' is as important, perhaps more so, as what a manager 'does', then there is an extraordinary contrast in Mintzberg's treatment of these two vital aspects of 'him': what he 'is' is tossed aside in a casual aside; what he 'does' becomes the subject of huge scientific inquiry. The assumption is that 'doing' takes precedence over 'being'. We are told in one simple, seemingly casual statement, what the manager is: 'The manager is the folk hero of contemporary society'; while the author commits a book and many years of research to tell us what he does. Why he should be a folk hero, a powerful and intriguing image (if indeed he is), is neither regarded as of interest in itself, nor as the fodder for further investigation.

A second assumption that runs through the subtext of the whole book does concern the nature of management work, and this despite the author's claim that 'this book is written without preconceptions of the manager's job'; that 'the results of empirical research do the talking' (p. 4). The assumption is that the manager's work is a negative experience, and it is an assumption that features prominently in the ten conclusions listed on pages 4 and 5 and numbered in parentheses below.

It is identifiably predictable (1 and 2). That it is 'challenging' as commonly thought is conveyed in one and a half lines, while six times as much text is given to an immediate qualification of that statement as the author insists that the manager's duties are 'regular', 'ordinary', 'maintaining' (3). As a specialist, the manager requires skills which 'unfortunately, we know little about', and the implication is that since we have 'done little to teach' what we know 'little about', managers cannot be managing well (4). The manager is seen to derive his power from his access to information, but even this is seen to be problematic – 'unfortunate' because his information reception is verbal and he lacks effective means of dissemination. That the manager must take full charge of the organization's strategy-making system is presented as 'the problem' (5).

In the next conclusion (6), the beleaguered manager faces the 'hazard' of superficiality, a 'heavy' workload, 'unrelenting' pace of work, and the brevity, variety and fragmentation of his work. The concluding sentence here, a Latinate 'not this . . . but that' statement (bestowing a reasonable authoritative tone to the claims made here) first states what the job does not do, 'the job of managing does not develop reflective planners', implying that it should do so, but rather 'breeds' (a word more commonly associated with animal husbandry than with managers) 'adaptive information manipulators'. Manipulation suggests deceit and yoked with 'breed' creates an image of a world in which something unpleasant is being intentionally produced. When the author tacks on the qualifier 'prefer a stimulus–response milieu' the image becomes that of the laboratory, rather than the farmed, animal.

The manager also lacks science. That he has 'no' science (an absolute statement) is repeated for emphasis in the next conclusion (7). It could be that intuition and imagination as guides to management work are more valuable than explicit routinized systems, but it is not made to seem so here. The paragraph begins and ends with indictments: 'there is no science . . .' and 'the management scientist has no influence . . .'.

The image of the loop (8) is yet another negative image. Caused by work 'pressures' and 'difficulties', and leading to 'superficialities' that serve only to increase the size of the work burden he carries, the problems represented by the loop simply increase, and only the management scientist, as yet unheard by the manager, can 'break the loop', as is claimed in the following conclusion (9).

In the final conclusion (10), a way forward is indicated. From paragraph 1 to paragraph 9 the author has distanced himself from all the negative implications of his summary conclusions on the work of the manager, by referring to 'the manager' in the third person as 'he' and 'his'. Now, with a change of direction suggested, Mintzberg reverts to the inclusive 'we': 'we shall improve it significantly only when we understand it precisely'. In a perfectly balanced sentence (the subject actors 'we', and the object 'it' hold the shapely structure in place as 'improve', qualified by 'significantly' confronts 'understand' qualified by 'precisely') that shouts the authority of knowledge and control of the media, and the conditional 'we shall' challenges us to face the 'only when'.

As I skim back over what I have read and written here about these ten conclusions, pulling together the themes that seem to me to have emerged from the subtext, my first conclusion is that we have been presented with a particularly negative view of the job of management.

Management is boringly predictable. The excitement and charm of difference are submerged in the image of sameness that lumps all managers, foremen to presidents, into one 'peas in a pod' profile, for – as is illustrated in the italicized words in the next three paragraphs – such differences as do exist, are differences within the perceived essential sameness of their practice: 'as *commonly thought*', they have '*regular ordinary* duties', and they '*maintain* a status system', through the '*common* practices' that are '*almost all* the activities that managers engage in' and which all 'relate back to their roles as manager . . . [who] is *both* generalist and specialist', and for whom the 'prime occupational hazard . . . is *superficiality*'. Managers 'work essentially as they always have' (pp. 4–5).

Managers are unskilled: '*Unfortunately*, we know *little*' and have 'done *little* to teach them'. '*Unfortunately*, the manager' '*lacks* effective means' and 'has *difficulty* delegating'. They are overworked automatons who face the '*hazard*' of '*superficiality*', have an '*unrelenting* work pace' and have a job that '*breeds*' '*manipulators*' who act on a '*stimulus–response*', non-reflective basis (pp. 4–5).

They are also scientifically ignorant, and caught in a destructive *loop* that is caused by job *pressures*, that *force* them, make things *difficult* for them, and *lead* them to *superficiality*; that, in turn *leads* to '*increased work pressure*' and '*more complex problems*' and '*even greater work pressures*' (pp. 4–5).

All of these numbered points (there are a reassuringly definitive ten of them) are hammered home with frequent repetition – for example 'common' (point 3), 'general' (point 4), 'information' (point 5), 'superficiality' (point 6) – that results in a breathless cumulative image of the problematic jobs of management. Rising tension and resulting panic, as the list almost topples over, is resolved in the perfect syntactical balance of the quietly assured conclusion: 'We shall improve it significantly when we understand it precisely' (p. 5).

There is obvious need to 'break' the 'loop' (point 9) and to avoid the temptation to 'prescribe' 'simple remedies' for management's 'difficulties' (point 10). Here, in the concluding paragraph of Mintzberg's 'major conclusions' is the metaphor which sums up his view of managerial practice: it is sick, its 'difficulties' described as if they were a disease in need of a cure, in need of the interventions of the medicine (*prescriptions*) of the management scientist. Ironically, woven through this metaphor, and picked up in the word 'temptation' is the image of the management scientist as the tempter, the devil himself. 'We' in paragraph 10 are abjured to 'avoid the temptation' (a phrase that echoes the Lord's prayer) of seeking simple cures, in a word that also echoes the third paragraph where management scientists were 'tempting' managers with courses 'supposedly' designed to help them.

From all of this it is to be understood that we need a 'new' science of management, one that will not masquerade as that which it is not; one that will honestly help managers to pull themselves out of the morass of problems that beset them. So management is in a mess: but it is the fault of management scientists, not managers themselves. They are the victim patients of the false medicine-men, and a saviour, the author, is waiting in the wings.

Here, in a tangle of metaphorical associations, the tentacles of which curl out into all parts of the analysed text, is the scenario that gives the lie to Mintzberg's bemusement at finding himself lionized by both managers themselves and their critics. The managers see themselves in the metaphors of siege and confusion as in paragraph 3, 'he is surrounded', and the critics see that management and managers are neither knowledgeable nor skilled. Both groups of readers – because of the emotive strategies employed to bring about identification with the text – tend to find in it the image of management that is acceptably familiar to them: readers write their own texts.

Although I could repeat this exercise, picking up the more positive aspects of management commented on, every time a positive point is made it is immediately undermined by an 'unfortunately' or a 'but' followed by an outbalancing negative statement. The point here is that building something up only to then shoot it down leaves the reader with a negative impression. If the same paragraphs were reconstructed along the inverted lines of 'although this . . . yet that', the reader would be left admiring the manager's achievement. Paragraph 4, for example, could be inverted and rewritten as: 'Although we know little about the manager's skills, and management schools have done little to teach them . . . yet the manager is both generalist and specialist' and would then leave the reader with an impression of the manager's achievement.

In the first section, Mintzberg reports that the manager's home is not a 'sanctuary' (p. 29) implying that the manager needs a place to escape to, where he will be protected from confrontation and danger, and that managers feel 'compelled' to work at an 'unrelenting pace' (p. 29). On the next page 'unrelenting' is repeated and 'subordinates . . . usurp' the manager's time as if the latter has no control over his environment. This notion of powerlessness and the image of unattainable 'sanctuary' are both caught up in the further idea of imprisonment in the reminder that for the manager there is 'no escape'. As if the marked route to a place of peace and respite has been lost, we are told in the next paragraph that the manager has no 'mile posts' to indicate a stopping place (p. 30). It seems that he must 'always keep going'.

In the second section of text, pages 170–3, through which I have tested my reading of the subtext in Chapter 1 as conveying a negative view of managerial work, I have noted the following in the first paragraph: the manager lacks support (he is 'alone'); a large part of his job is boring (he has 'house-keeping duties'); he has too much to do ('added to all this'); does not know what his job is ('there are no clear mile posts'); there is no end to the job ('never an indication . . . always a nagging thought') and his 'burden' is great.

The mundane character of his job suggested by 'house-keeping' and 'nagging' extends into a root metaphor of physicality and lower-order occupation in the repetition of the word 'burden' (paragraph 3), combined with the image of the manager as a 'major obstruction' in the 'flow' of decisions and information. As a 'real danger' in an 'unfortunate' situation, recalling the 'hazards' of the introduction, the humdrum toiler seems to become a non-sensate block in a swirl of natural action.

If I skim back over all of the analysis now completed, two themes clearly begin to emerge from my exploration of the subtext. The first is that Mintzberg's positive introductory images merge in a root metaphor of the manager as a 'folk hero', hard-working and widely respected, a national leader of huge importance in the US, but this is rapidly countered by thoroughly negative images of managers who are incredibly burdened and besieged. The second image of management and managers as recognized through doing rather than through being, reflects an assumption that a systems or mechanistic approach to the study and implementation of managers and their work will improve both job skills and outcomes.

Reflexive reading

An anecdote, and his thoughts on it, that Mintzberg, in the preface to the series edition had shared with his readers, may have influenced my reading of this text. Mintzberg tells us that the book was enthusiastically accepted both by 'people who believe that there is something wrong with managers', those who expressed pleasure that someone had finally 'let managers have it', and also by the managers themselves who said:

> You make me feel so good. All the time I thought I was doing something wrong. While *I* was constantly being interrupted, *they* were all planning, organizing, coordinating and controlling.
>
> (p. xvi)

By way of explanation for this seemingly perverse assessment of the book in the two different camps, Mintzberg says that the only suggestion he can make about its appeal to both groups is that 'both have had enough of rationality narrowly defined' (p. xvi).

Perhaps, but the challenge to provide a more substantial explanation is one I found irresistible and it therefore probably guided a proclivity to look for those rhetorical elements that would explain this broad appeal. As I read and commented, I persistently found myself imagining my reception of the text as that of a manager and then rereading as if I were a management skeptic.

Two other external factors may have had a particular impact on the agenda that (unwittingly) I may have brought to my reading here. Before embarking on this reading I had completed an exploratory reading of *Musings on Management*, another text authored by Mintzberg (1996). Despite the fact that it is a witty piece which initially I enjoyed reading, and which had some pithy points, my reading was in some measure both mocking and destructive, and I had shared it with both a public audience and the author himself.[7] An instinctive sense of justice and 'fair play' made me want to redress the balance by allowing an author whose ideas I respect to be presented with a more flattering analysis of his rhetoric than was the case with *Musings*. This feeling was heightened by the consciousness as I analysed, that Mintzberg had already generously agreed to read through my reconstruction of his text.

Moreover, as a management theorist myself, and one who, not unexpectedly, believes in the value of the kind of meticulous research that supports Mintzberg's view of the nature of managerial work, I hoped that the persuasive elements of the text would not prove to be particularly dominant or significant, and would perhaps significantly distinguish Mintzberg's writing from the other subject texts.

Review

Looking back over my fourth experience of scriptive reading I was particularly aware of the relationship between the dominant and critical readings. My respect for Mintzberg's scholarship as portrayed in the dominant reading is shadowed by the hovering ambivalence towards his rhetorical skills. In the critical reading, where I explore this, the balance and control that he maintains over his narrative, counterpointed by the impact of developing dramatic tension, explains my reader response.

Recognition of this enables me to appreciate the antithetical responses of dominant readers: those who have identified with the text as appreciating the challenges imposed by their managerial roles, as well as with the management critics who found support in the text for their indictments of managers. In the third, reflexive, phase of my reading, I was able to provide some detail of the background to interest in this ambiguity, as experienced by other dominant readers, that had sparked my interest in exploring it critically.

As I completed my analysis of this text, I noted that scriptive reading had enabled me to both identify with the diverse responses of dominant readers, and also explore my own responses.

My interest in what was beginning to emerge as a historically developing theme in management theory was also furthered by my critical reading of Mintzberg's text. Drucker had promised that management would be the new leading institution and managers the new world leaders. Two decades later Mintzberg assumes that this is the role and status of management and the manager, and adds another dimension to it. In his text the manager appears as a romantic folk hero, as well as a world leader. My critical reading intimates the genesis of the hero manager.

Text five: Rosabeth Moss Kanter

Overview

This text is an extract from a book by Rosabeth Moss Kanter, *The Change Masters: Corporate Entrepreneurs at Work*, first published in 1984. The book is 432 pages long, consists of twelve chapters, arranged in five parts, and Chapter 1, 'Introduction', is preceded by 'Acknowledgements' and a definition of 'Change Masters': 'Those people and organizations adept at the art of anticipating the need for, and of leading, productive change' (p. 13).

The passage I have chosen for analysis, is lifted from the first pages (17–23) of the first chapter and is simply entitled 'Introduction'. It introduces not only the work as a whole, but also Part I, 'The need for an American corporate renaissance'. Each of the five parts of the book consists of two or three chapters.

The general thesis of the book is that corporations that value people and encourage their participation in the pursuit of company objectives, will be more successful than those that do not. Kanter identifies innovation as the key to growth, and advocates recognition and support of it at all levels of corporate activity. She claims that the American entrepreneurial spirit of the past has been suffocated, but should be resurrected, and that a new set of management skills will be required to manage in the 'integrative, innovation-stimulating environment' (p. 35).

Kanter's own summary of her argument is laid out in the 'Introduction' (pp. 35–6).

Dominant reading

A quotation from William Anderson, Chairman of the NCR Corporation, introduces Kanter's 'Introduction'. In it, Anderson cites Arnold Toynbee on the rise and fall of nations: nations that do not continue to adapt their response to new challenges fail.

Kanter's personal experience of corporate America is then reported as evidence that the question to which all of corporate America wants an answer is: how might corporations stimulate their people to more innovative action? Furthermore, she has found that corporate recognition of the importance of their need for innovative people seems to be a response to recognition of corporate crisis. When corporations operate in a stable environment they can depend on systems, rather than individual people, for their economic success, but as the pace and nature of change accelerates, it is to people that they must look for creative idea power.

Kanter concludes that empowered individuals initiating micro-changes help their companies to be leaders, and that companies should therefore aim to build a culture that enables these effective individuals to become problem-solvers. Her research has demonstrated that 'companies with reputations for progressive human-resource practices are significantly higher in long-term profitability and financial growth than their counterparts'; and although it is impossible to determine causality in this equation, she argues that innovative, company-initiated actions provide the context for further innovative acts.

Progressing her argument, Kanter moves to a consideration of the state of research and development. While unprecedented social and economic change is taking place throughout America, short-term profit-making is pursued and research and development is neglected. Both government and large corporations should invest in innovative research and training that places as much emphasis on social and organizational innovation as it does on technological and product innovation, for innovation should be understood as 'the process of bringing any new, problem-solving idea into use' (p. 20).

Describing company innovators as 'corporate entrepreneurs' (p. 21), Kanter notes that technological, product and service innovation tends to occur early in an industry's life cycle, whereas because the more mature industry tends to focus on performance and cost-saving, creative ideas are found in the manufacturing process, work methods and quality control. But she points out that opportunities exist for internal entrepreneurs in both resource-rich and resource-lean environments, and that the need to empower people to act on their ideas occurs across all sectors of business because of the pervasiveness of environmental change.

Reminding readers of Drucker's notion of effectiveness as 'doing the right things' she emphasizes that there is a greater need for long-term development than there is for short-term productivity; that the former demands the more exciting innovation, and that despite the pressures in the contemporary environment to be risk-averse (and she equates innovation with risk) it should be recognized that 'maintaining status quo is itself risky' (p. 23).

With a reminder of both the entrepreneurial spirit responsible for America's past successes and the need to now develop that within large organizations, Kanter concludes with an emphatic restatement of the importance of the people, at all levels of an organization, who can contribute to an innovative approach to the future.

Critical reading

The title, of this text, *The Change Masters*, grabs attention. It is masterful, masterly and asserts power. 'Masters' command, dominate and control. Their command connotes superiority and even subjugation, because one cannot achieve mastery without something to be master of. The change that is subject to their control may be skill, theory or individual people, but wherever it is found the word 'master' assumes domination. And yet 'change' itself is an abstract force. To be 'master' of it lies well beyond any human capacity, so the breathtaking impact of this title suggests extraordinary power.

In the subtitle, immediately juxtaposed with this notion of extraordinary power, a notion of power that lies well beyond the experience of ordinary mortals, we find the 'corporate entrepreneur at work'. In its succinctness, this image of superhuman power is fast attached to the entrepreneur, so it is the entrepreneur who takes on extraordinary status here. The title assumes that readers aspire to the power that entrepreneurs possess.

The title of Part I, 'The need for an American corporate renaissance', immediately supports these suggestions. Change is not only needed, but will herald a new age. It will be initiated by, born from, the work of the masters of change, corporate entrepreneurs. 'Renaissance' literally 'means rebirth' and because the Renaissance was a time of excitement, adventure and new knowledge, all of this is what corporate America too is in need of; is what entrepreneurs provide, and importantly, is what entrepreneurs control, is that over which they have mastery.

In the yoking of the nation of America to the corporate world, a second dominant theme of the passage is introduced, for the persistent appeal to nationalism, a feature of the prefacing quotation, 'the United States faces such a challenge', weaves throughout the whole of the text and culminates in the invocation to the entrepreneurial spirit as the saviour of the American nation that 'alone ensures our survival' (p. 23). In the first paragraph the author claims personal knowledge of the whole of 'corporate America'; in the second, knowledge of 'every sector' of corporate America, and in the third, recalls recent domination of the world by American companies: 'American companies seemed to control the world'. We are presented with images of the world events and powers, 'OPEC and foreign competition and inflation and regulation' (p. 18), that threaten this American domination, and with a litany of the 'most progressive' giants, 'led by IBM, General Electric and Xerox', who could lead America out of the 'doldrums'. Innovation should be a 'national priority' (p. 19) because 'where America leads, it leads because of innovation'; 'the United States is ahead even of Japan', and thus America must 'play to national strengths' (p. 20).

Supporting the scope and range of this appeal to nationalism, is a geographical metaphor that is also introduced in the first paragraph in an extended image of the author as travelling expert. Kanter claims familiarity with 'settings as different geographically and culturally as' – and she lists businesses representative of east coast and west coast, high-rise city and fishing-boat village, snow-capped mountains and sea-shore, imaging them from 'dingy' to sophisticated. This is all the world of American business, and its global environment is picked up in the repetition of the word 'world' in paragraphs 3 and 4. It is within this global 'environment' (paragraphs 6 and 7) that nationalist pride is called upon to rescue America's economy from the 'doldrums', a state of depression or inactivity, but literally meaning a region near the equator in which sailing ships are often becalmed to the point of desperation for lack of winds.

A further use of this geographical metaphor is found in Kanter's image of America as 'disturbed', even threatened, by other nations: 'world events . . . threaten to overwhelm us'. Only when 'American companies seemed to control the world' can individuals be ignored without 'peril' to the American economy. In a changing world 'environment', like adventurous explorers it is American entrepreneurs who could move the nation into 'uncertain realms' (p. 18). They 'take the lead' (p. 19) in establishing enterprise 'zones' (p. 20).

If America is to 'secure' its future, 'American organizations' must empower people to innovate on all 'fronts', for it is these 'corporate entrepreneurs' who will 'help their organizations to experiment on uncharted territories and move beyond what is known into the realm of innovation' (p. 23).

American nationalism grips through the text in a rhetorical appeal that moves assuredly about the root metaphors of the text. It combines with a geographical metaphor suggesting exploration, adventure and the discovery of new realms, to conjure up conquest and colonization in an appeal to past greatness, 'the entrepreneurial spirit responsible for American success in the past' (p. 23). America was won by conquest and readers are reminded of all the 'fronts' on which people are required to operate. Exploration, discovery and domination glance one into the other in what becomes a rhetorical appeal to a romantic view of the American dream of greatness: the 'American entrepreneurial spirit' (subtitle of the second section of the Introduction) is called on to dominate that part of the globe popularly denoted the 'new' world.

The old world is denigrated: 'individuals constituted . . . sources of error', they were 'taken for granted or ignored', companies did not trust their people, and some companies were inclined to 'stifle or ignore' the ideas of their people (p. 18); 'America's economy is slipping', 'past practices cannot accommodate' 'social and economic changes of unprecedented magnitude and variety' (p. 19); and 'our economic future is . . . neglected as ventures are milked for short-term profits' (p. 20). The new world, presented as there for the taking, will be fuelled by 'new' energies and successes: the word 'new' is repeated eight times on page 20, and the word 'innovation' (derived from the Latin *novus* meaning 'new') is repeated sixteen times on the same page. It is a new world imaged as one of trust, creativity and people power (p. 18); success, people-affirming programmes and profit (p. 19); challenge, stimulation and vitality (p. 20), and is the antithesis of the innovation that was confined to a 'marginal and unexciting role' (p. 22) in the old mechanical organization.

A generalized antithesis, much of it based on hyperbole (exaggeration) begins to emerge, for in her advocacy of the notion she is promoting, the corporate need for innovation, Kanter pits the old against the new, images of stability against change, boredom against excitement, 'dysfunctional', 'negligible' innovation against 'acceptance and implementation' (p. 20). Some of the hyperbole that sweepingly generalizes the whole 'world' of these contrasts is apparent in the claims that thud heavily through the final paragraph of page 19: 'innovation . . . a national priority', 'clear and pressing need for more innovation', social and economic changes of unprecedented magnitude and variety', 'past practices cannot accommodate'. When unqualified claims of this magnitude sweep through a text: 'America leads because of innovation', 'our emerging world requires more social and organizational innovation' (p. 20), and support vast contrasts (in this case we are presented with all of America and the nation's place in the whole of the world) the reader is emotionally engaging with one of rhetoric's most powerful strategies. One of the easiest ways to highlight the attributes of one entity is to set it against its opposite. Black looks blacker placed alongside white than it does in apposition to grey. When black is said to be blacker than black, and white whiter than white, then the intensity of each is magnified. Kanter tells us, for example, that we face 'unprecedented change', and is comfortable with loose comparatives and superlatives such as 'most' progressive (p. 19), 'most' people (p. 20), 'fewer' people (p. 20), 'more' difficult (p. 22) 'most' fully (p. 22), and 'more' innovation (p. 23).

Syntactically this same emphasis is achieved through contrast in the Latinate 'not this . . . but that' sentence structure, also widely employed by Kanter: for example 'to assume that the "system", not the people', 'not assets but sources of error', 'designed not by machines but by people' (p. 18), 'whereas short-term productivity . . . innovation requires . . .' (p. 20), 'productivity is not . . . the mechanical output of a production facility; it is rather . . .' (p. 22), and 'not because it produces more profits, but because . . .' (p. 23).

In the new world that the text assumes we all aspire to, to be a leader, to demonstrate a 'willingness to take the lead' (p. 19) individually and nationally, is assumed to be a shared goal (p. 20, paragraph 2). Taking the lead, and competitive values (similarly lauded) entail defeating others to first place: 'the United States is ahead even of Japan' (p. 19). This ethos, this need, to be seen as first, pre-eminent in the world of affairs and money-making, premised on the assumption that competition is 'good' and will result in more profit, and that profit is in itself an inherent 'good', is supported by two other root metaphors in this text: metaphors of sustenance and health and, even more familiar, the organization as machine versus the organization as organism.

The America that Kanter has portrayed as being endangered by foreign competition, is also being 'milked' by its own corporates as they pursue short-term profits (p. 20), and this despite the fact that in resource-rich times, customers are 'hungry' (p. 21). In this metaphor both profits (the milk that is 'milked') and resources (that customers would consume) take on the attributes of food, so when Kanter immediately follows up her accusation (this is an awkward mixed metaphor for 'milked' also suggests the 'cash cow' cliché of Boston Matrix fame) with suggestions as to how the problems of the resource-lean, as well as those of the resource-rich corporate environment might be addressed, the connotations of 'lean' replay the image of 'hungry'. In a further extension of the same idea, the repetition of the word 'health' (p. 22) and even 'survival' (p. 23) suggests that the organic interdependency of American society and the corporates is at stake here. The metaphor of need and ingestion as hunger and food in both the corporate and the societal environment, is seen to build into the deeper metaphor of an organic versus a mechanical worldview.

Although an old familiar in organization theory, Kanter's metaphors in this text also build into the rhetorical use of antithesis as outlined above. Just as in the rich versus lean contrast, so too the apposition of machine and organic life in a third root metaphor identified in this text, highlights similar contrasting images.

On page 18, the machine metaphor is explicit: the ideal organization of the recent past is described as one that was 'running automatically to turn out predictable products' until 'the smooth workings of corporate machines' were disturbed by world events. On the same page the organic metaphor sprouts in words which describe the company in words such as 'stimulus', 'environment', 'responsive' and 'adaptive', and grows in words like 'milked' (as explained above), 'vital', 'playing', 'at root', 'change or adapt', 'abundant', 'matures', 'older and more stable', 'health', 'stemming' and 'grass roots' in the pages that follow. The metaphor of the 'clockwork' (p. 17) operations of the mechanistic organization that introduces the passage is recalled in the 'routines and rules' that 'subordinate individuals' in the final paragraphs of this text (p. 23), where experiment and creativity are to be the 'infusing' 'spirit' of organizations that rely on 'intelligence' to 'move' them into 'uncharted territories', away from the old 'mechanical systems'.

The worldview that Kanter is subscribing to, the assumptions that are conveyed in the images and metaphors discussed above, include: nationalistic pride is threatened by the success of other nations; American corporations should be 'first' in the world; success is based on competition; the business goal is profit; management theory of the past, a belief in systems, routines and the 'mechanized' organization must be replaced; change is overwhelming and is exciting.

As she leads the reader through her argument, the author's voice in this text suggests that she intends to relate to the reader on a number of different levels. Her first pose is that of the omniscient national commentator, as she takes us on a tour of corporate America. With her we visit all corners of the nation, for she is immediately present in her text ('my travels' and 'I have been struck by') and demonstrates her intimate knowledge of the nation she is seemingly addressing. It is a huge and, she implies, exotic land of such vast contrasts and distances ('in settings as distant geographically and culturally') that few could know it as well as her 'travels' have enabled her to do.

Kanter suggests that she has been travelling as a consultant, or mentor, for everywhere she has 'been struck' by the same question (the implication is that it has been addressed to her), and she reveals that she is as conversant with a dingy engine plant in Detroit as she is with a Minneapolis electronics factory. The colloquial 'I have been struck by' conveys the image of an expert who is in touch with the factory floor, even while writing for managers. We will shortly discover that she is indeed a researcher engaged in discussion with the highest echelons of management – 'In 1981 I asked an expert panel of sixty-five vice-presidents of human resources in major companies . . .' (p. 19) – but in this introductory paragraph she portrays herself as having more in common with the epiphany of St Paul, than with careful academic research, for her 'was struck by' recalls St Paul's fall to the ground as he 'sees' his life-changing revelation.

That Kanter, like St Paul, may have visionary powers, is immediately picked up in the next paragraph where the 'ever-louder echo' of 'the question' of the previous sentence is played upon in the voice of a visionary who now reminds us of the visionary romantic poet Wordsworth. Kanter's 'in every sector, old and new, I hear . . .' 'echoes' Wordsworth's lines in 'Intimations of immortality': 'I hear, I hear, with joy I hear!' (Wordsworth 1936: 460).

It is perhaps significant that the age of Romanticism witnessed the rise of individualism, for Kanter continues: 'I hear a renewed recognition of the importance of people, and of the talents and contributions of individuals, to a company's success. People seem to matter . . .'. Wordsworth was the declared poet of the people: he saw himself as the voice of the common person.

The authority that Kanter assumes in her role of the expert who speaks for Everyman is supported by rhetoric that resonates with pairings (bringing together both ends of every spectrum commented on and all within it) sometimes for reinforcement, 'geographically and culturally', 'talents and contributions' and 'taken for granted or ignored'; at other times to highlight opposites as in 'old and new', 'the system not the people', and 'human error or human intervention'. Combined with frequent alliteration such as 'high-rise headquarters', 'dingy Detroit', 'sportswear showroom', 'renewed recognition' and 'corporate crisis' (all examples lifted from the first three paragraphs), all of this serves to emphasize and pull together the assured tone in which these opening statements are delivered.

By the time we reach the third paragraph though, the personal tone of the first person 'I' has been replaced by the voice of a remote omniscient author as the scene she describes moves from the nation of America to a global setting and the history of management theory. In place of the listing of American companies and the conversational tone, 'people seem to matter', of the visionary who speaks for the people, 'I hear', readers are now distanced by the assurance of 'indeed' and the hieratic, weighty cadences of Latinate syntax 'only when . . . can', 'not assets but sources of error', and Latinate vocabulary – responsible, legacy, individuals, constituted, intervention, automatically, predictable, unexpected, occur – which weigh in heavily through the third paragraph and establish that we are now in the company of an august teacher.

Another two paragraphs and the teacher who stresses the importance of 'trust' (paragraph 5) metamorphoses into the evangelist who will tell us how: 'This book shows how . . .', 'it describes how people can help . . .', 'even small-scale innovations add up . . .', 'this book is also about the circumstances that make it possible . . .'. The emphasis here is on the role of the teacher/visionary who makes new possibilities seem reachable, and reassures the reader that even small achievements are worthwhile. The story she tells to illustrate the truths she is promoting links again with revelation in the use of the word 'strike', 'let me cite one striking finding . . .', for now the author is not only personally present again in the text, but is humbly asking the reader's permission to quote from her own experience.

But the story she tells is no parable: its main purpose is to establish the author's research credentials as she details the substance, scope and significance of her research leadership: 'my research team'. Seeming to acknowledge a weakness, 'it is impossible to be entirely sure', she does so only to wave off doubters dismissively (the evangelist is momentarily back with us) in an airy short sentence: 'I doubt that this is the case'. 'Case' suggests a legal opinion, and the syntax of the simple sentence expresses certitude. The 'I think . . .' which immediately follows sets the tone for the next few pages, as the argument is progressed by a voice that assures readers her thoughts are incontrovertible: 'economists argue' (p. 19), but 'neglect' the one important issue; 'most people think' (erroneously) (p. 20) and this is 'unfortunate' but the author is always certain, and emphasizes her certainty with intensifiers such as 'indeed' (twice) and 'certainly' (all on p. 20) as sentences openers.

Kanter reinforces the authoritarian tone that she is developing here by her use of periodic sentences (sentences in which the main point is delayed until the end, thus building a fast dramatic pace) and cumulation, the piling of one example upon another to add weight to the argument. Both of these features are found, for example, in: '– and the extent to which they encourage their people to solve problems, to seek new ideas, to challenge established wisdom, to experiment, to innovate is crucial' (p. 20); and in the inexorability of: 'in the present environment, with scarce resources, low profits, reduced growth, and pressure to increase current profitability, the capacity to invest resources in the future and promote broad innovation is even more sharply reduced than would normally be the case' (p. 22).

She also continues to assert her difference, her unique expert knowledge, in phrases such as 'most people' (repeated), and 'typically' as generalized groupings of the erroneous, 'unfortunate' ideas of others, and contrasts this with the 'fewer people' and 'fewer still, if any' who share her own insights. The dismissive tone of these other opinions is conveyed in the stark structure of relatively short compound sentences, which contrast with the more intricate patterns of the complex sentences in which she expresses her own ideas, in the long third paragraph of page 20.

Then, in the next paragraph the tone of her statements changes again; it becomes assertive, dogmatic as she defines innovation and enlarges on her definition, and on page 21, she begins to instruct readers on the opportunities for innovation: 'Corporate entrepreneurs can find', 'there will typically be', and 'look at', the commanding use of an imperative verb.

The use of italics that Kanter has tended to rely on when she intends to stress a point is somewhat condescending, for it assumes that the reader needs guiding to these key statements. When, as now, a single word is italicized ('The *form* that innovation takes . . .' and in the next paragraph, 'business *must* be innovative') her voice takes on a scolding note. Readers are to do as instructed, as *told* by the author, one who is still showing us ('I show', p. 22) the errors of the past: 'much [of the] attention [that] has been focused on this problem . . .'; and the 'confusion' that has been both cause and result. Her

confidence is conveyed in balanced Latinate 'not this . . . but that' constructions which demonstrated that she has weighed the evidence and is giving us
the benefit of her measured opinions.

In the final paragraphs, as the visionary returns to the text but now
with a strident, evangelical voice, the same balancing act is maintained in
'if this . . . then that' statements: 'if America is to build . . . [innovation] is a
necessity' and for 'more innovation' we need 'entrepreneurial spirit'. Yet this
element of reason is now no more than an underpinning to what becomes
an increasingly emotive harangue as the passage draws to a conclusion.

As she lines up the conditions needed and the actions that must be taken
if this new world is to be realized, Kanter draws her readers into complicity
with her use of the first person plural pronoun, 'we need', but then immediately returns to her mentoring role in the admonishing 'keep in mind' which
opens the next paragraph. Then, posing her 'open question' (whether organizations can accommodate entrepreneurial individuals) she both exaggerates
('let alone') and emphasizes ('especially') the challenge entailed.

'Nevertheless', she insists, 'we' (the reader is included again) 'need' (there
is no option here) to take up this challenge, 'to innovate'. A carefully balanced
antithesis ('mechanical systems' versus 'intellectual effort') follows, bridging
a dramatic move to the staccato repetition of sentence fragments, all designed
to emotively hammer home her dogma: it is about people (italicized), 'all
people', 'people at all levels' and 'ordinary people'. 'People' is repeated three
times in three lines, as is 'all': 'and that in turn means people. All people. On
all fronts. . . . People at all levels'. The repetition and the sentence fragments
suggest impatience, no time for further discussion and the pressing need for
action now.

The repetition of 'all' and 'people' also conjures up again a vision of
American individualism and America's proud record of democracy: '. . .
of the people, by the people and for the people'. Lincoln's voice rings through
the phrasing and word choice, and it is the 'ordinary people at the grass roots'
who are to contribute, invent and even strategize.

That readers are not alienated by this onslaught is perhaps because we are
made to feel part of the new order being advocated. The direct address of
the last paragraph on page 22 ('but think') in which author and reader are
differentiated and which continues on into these final paragraphs ('keep in
mind') is blended into a cosy use of the first person plural 'we' as she draws
her readers into her vision of the future: 'we need to reinfuse' and 'we need
to create conditions'. Finally it seems this vision is about 'All people. All
fronts.' We will fight side by side, on into 'uncharted territories' (p. 23).

I have already noted that Kanter's argument often seems to be buried
in the emotive blast that carries the reader through these pages. It is perhaps
the impact of this forcefulness that prompted me to begin my analysis by
engaging with it. But there is argument weaving through this onslaught.

Kanter sets the scene with an 'appeal to authority', the wisdom of Arnold
Toynbee, cited by the chairman of a large American corporation, William S.

Anderson, captured in the prefacing quotation. She goes on to support her arguments with references to personal experience, her travels throughout corporate America (p. 17); her knowledge of the history of management theory (p. 18); and an image of the contemporary global scene (p. 18).

She then makes her promise, 'this book shows how' (p. 18), and provides a taste of the recipe for success that she will provide. By the time we reach page 19 we are being bombarded with names, numbers and the results of number crunching to demonstrate the establishment profile of Kanter's completed research. She concludes the section with a return to her own thoughts, and a definitive conclusion, one which plays with the word 'innovation' in a display of cleverness: 'Improved organization designs and human-resource practices can be a company's *innovation-producing innovations*' (p. 19). Whenever Kanter intends the reader to take particular note of a particular idea, or the conclusions at which her thinking has arrived, she italicizes a word or a point: see, for example, pp. 18 (×3), 19 (×2), 21, 22 (×2).

As she progresses her argument in the next section of the Introduction, Kanter's stance suggests that of the debater. Opening with a sweeping generalization, 'we face social changes of unprecedented magnitude and variety, which past practices cannot accommodate', she quickly dismisses other contemporary – 'the early 1980s' (p. 20) – commentators on the economy and calls up the troops who support some aspects of her recipe for future action: first Senator Paul Tsongas (p. 20), then Proctor and Gamble (p. 21) and finally Peter Drucker (p. 22).

Along the way she cites a few examples of American innovation, and then, in a series of carefully constructed paragraphs, explains how, where and when innovation can be achieved. Although dressed in specifics, the argument here could be summed up as quite simply that innovation is the application of any new idea, in any sector, by any person at any stage of industrial or organizational development.

By the time we reach page 22, we are expected to know what innovation is, so Kanter can now safely remind us of what it is not, secure in the surety that we can weigh old, limiting notions of innovations in the balance and find them wanting. This she does with an emphatic denigration of the 'mechanical' organization, and its emphasis on production, a move which, in recalling the history of management theory in the opening paragraphs, provides the link that brings her argument full circle, and leaves the reader with a sense of completion, an argument clinched into completion.

But there is still a page of short paragraphs to go. These Kanter uses for an exhortation which has little to do with logic (though seeming to have been spawned by the preceding argument) and everything to do with seeking emotive consent to, and identification with, the argument she has laid out up to this point. In a paradoxical twist of logic in the final paragraph of page 22, Kanter images the 'standard equation of innovation with risk' and the 'usual propensity for large firms to be risk-averse' in times of economic

recession, as in danger of becoming exaggerated 'under present circumstances'. Her solution to this 'standard equation' is simply to recommend
that it be inverted: she states that 'maintaining the status quo is itself risky'
(p. 23).

Her support for this recommendation is a series of paragraphs built
around: an invocation to past entrepreneurial spirit; a lauding of individualism that claims the status of all people 'at all levels' as being of equal value;
and a final challenge to organizations to empower and enable individuals 'if'
they have the stomach for it.

Reflexive reading

My general impression as I first read through my critical interpretation of
this text is that I am angry with it, and that the more I read of it the more
angry I became. The pace of my comments is at first relatively measured, but
the tempo increases as I become more emotively embroiled in a confrontation
with it.

It is significant that I began here with an exploration of root metaphors
rather than with the argument of the text. This was an instinctive response,
which obviously I followed through on, and one that was sparked by the
prominent role that metaphors played in the composition of the text –
so prominent that I found myself having to make a disciplined attempt not
to engage with them during the write-up of the dominant reading.

There was therefore perhaps some stored frustration waiting to be
unleashed. That said, it was not entirely a latent negativity with which I began
the third reading here, for my love of metaphor ensures that whatever the
use made of it, I relish my anticipation of analysing it.

Nevertheless, as the analysis proceeded and I found myself embroiled in
American nationalism, the prioritization of competition and profit-making
as unquestioned 'good' values, a dismissive discard of historic understandings
and a romantic vision of the 'new world' waiting to be conquered, I became
aware that I was in alien company and felt in myself the stirrings of a confrontational approach.

As my analysis moved on to an examination of the voice of the author,
these stirrings became a storm of discontent. As a reader I do not enjoy being
preached to, condescended to and instructed, especially when it seems that
I am simultaneously supposed to be impressed by a parade of expertise and
status.

I discern three aspects of my own identity, noted in the generic section
of the reflexive reading, that may have influenced my interpretation of this
text: my own national identity, my gender and my love of European
literature. It is a proudly American text, and an enjoyment of American
domination of the world is assumed. All other nations are foreign competition, so as a reader I am excluded, marginalized by the text, because I am
not American.

In terms of gender there is, I think, disappointment in my response. As noted in Chapter 4, I determined to include two women authors in my selection of five texts, as I was interested to discover whether or not my analysis might reveal some gender differences in terms at least of worldview. This did not prove to be the case here; in fact quite the reverse, for my interpretation discovered jingoism, images of conquest and competition, exploration and action that are all inherently seen as the preserve of the male need to dominate his environment. Yes, people are said to count, but in images that recall Abraham Lincoln, rather than conjuring up a future Anita Roddick – surely one of the more innovative innovators of an ilk that Kanter might have been envisioning for us. There is nothing here, that I can find, that suggests that this woman theorist offers a challenge to male-dominated thinking.

My response, in this gender context, may also have been geared to an unfulfilled expectation created by an intertextual dialogue that continued, unbidden, as I read. I was aware that, before selecting this text, I had noted Gary Hamel's evaluation of and admiration for, it. In his comments on the '50 books that made management' (Crainer 1997) Hamel says of this work, 'Rosabeth Moss Kanter's *The Change Masters* has been dubbed the "thinking man's *In Search of Excellence*"' but, claiming that this is a largely futile comparison, he goes on to cite the conclusion of the *Sloan Management Review*, that it is 'of immeasurably higher quality than such competitors as Peters and Waterman's best-selling *In Search of Excellence*' (p. 135). He sums up: 'Kanter's analysis of "corporate entrepreneurs at work" is thoroughly academic. Its prose is slow and occasionally cumbersome, its references lengthy and intricate. It oozes authority.'

In selecting this text for analysis I had then, expectations that were, as I read, soundly trounced.

Third, and finally, texts like this remind me again, as I noted in Chapter 2, of Plato's reasons for banning poets from his ideal republic (Plato 1987: 435): he banned them because he saw that they are dangerous. Their words can seduce, can move 'men' to act against their better judgement (and that of the state!). Though I love the seductive power of words, when I do not like the values, the worldview, of the seducer, the wordsmith, when I feel that 'sweet reason' (my own worldview!) has been betrayed by word power, then my response is to: 'take arms . . . And by opposing end them' (*Hamlet*, III, i, 59–60).

Review

A particular facility of scriptive reading is immediately apparent in the reflexive phase completed above: it provides space for me to comment on the gap between my expectation and my experience of this text as a dominant reader, a gap that led to emotively charged responses in the critical reading, occasioned by the disillusionment that flowed into the gap. In the dominant reading, Kanter says that she is for people, not systems, so it seemed that her theorizing would perhaps link back to that of Follett. That it did not, as exposed in the critical reading, sparked a sense of betrayal. Explanation of subjectivity does not equate with exoneration of lack of objectivity, but a certain sense of fair play is served in the honesty of talk between the three phases of reading.

That said, the hero-manager who dominates much of my critical reading seems to have developed an extravagantly posturing status in the decade since Mintzberg wrote of him (*sic*). Kanter's text picks up on the jingoism of Drucker's worldview, and builds glamour and adventure into managerial status. Utopian adventures here are premised on the colonizing of new territories, and presumes the subjugation of all those who are not as competitively able as the leader who is well served by people participation.

While each of the three phases of scriptive reading continued, as in previous readings, to dialogue across their tripartite placing, so too my reading of Kanter's's text continued to echo and reflect themes that had been developing historically across all five texts. The hero-manager, introduced as Taylor's the best of good men, is now a world leader (echoing Drucker); a romanticized action-man (echoing Mintzberg), and a glamorized, powerful, territory-grabbing adventurer, poised to lead the way into a utopian future of American-controlled prosperity and global domination.

A review of scriptive reading

As I completed my final scriptive reading I returned to the review I recorded after I had completed my first scriptive reading – of Taylor's text – and reconsidered my initial assessment of the efficacy of this approach to reading. Reviewing my scriptive reading of all five texts, I found that I have consistently been comfortable with the balance of justice, perception and honesty that it has allowed me to maintained throughout all of the analyses.

I found that in each case my dominant reading has ensured that I am participating in an on-going conversation about these texts with the management community. If the critical readings were stand-alone interpretations, then barriers to further dialogue about the texts with other readers would potentially rest on the accusation that I have *mis*-read the texts.

As each critical interpretation of the texts progressed, I found that even the short extracts I had selected from the five original texts were so rich, offered such an infinity of possibilities for analysis, that I was experimenting with both very intensive analysis (several paragraphs on one word) and analysis that, seeking thematic connectives, ranged across several pages. I discovered that where the dominant reading had discovered a relatively 'prosaic' text, then the critical reading demanded an intensive reading approach: when the dominant reading encountered a richly figurative 'purple patch' (a heightening of style that makes a passage stand out from its context) my analysis became more free-ranging. I found that scriptive reading allowed the flexibility I demanded of it in accommodating this approach.

I also found that my critical interpretations of the texts have explored meaning not previously commented upon and have therefore opened up avenues in which new conversations about familiar texts can proceed.

The third, reflexive, phase of each reading has ensured a transparent context for the critical readings. It suggests that in on-going dialogue, reader-response to my texts will be initiated in an unprotected environment.

6 Performance, perspective and persuasion

If the doors of perception were cleansed
  everything would appear to man as it is, infinite
For man has closed himself up, till he sees
  all things thro' narrow chinks in his cavern.
William Blake, 'A Memorable Fancy',
The Marriage of Heaven and Hell, 1793

On completion of the scriptive readings as described in the previous chapter, I turned to a consideration of what had emerged as being of interest across all five selected texts. My focus at this stage of the reading process became the five critical readings. Although the dominant and reflexive readings continue to play an active role in my considerations they are assigned supporting, rather than protagonist, parts. Scriptive reading draws on an eclectic mix of literary theories and practices that inform a particular reader-response to any one reading; together with the critical reading, the dominant and the reflexive readings are an integral component of this. But in my inquiry, from this point on, the dominant and reflexive readings will contribute to my interpretations chiefly to the extent that, as part of the total reader-response to the text, they shed light on the critical reading.

The dominant reading is both one component of an individual reader's interpretation of the text in question, and is also intended to be representative of other familiar interpretations, serving as a reminder that the standard, everyday reading of the management theory perused is typically bounded by conventional understandings. Set alongside the critical reading, one of its functions is to demonstrate how much more of the text's meaning is exposed by critical reading. It highlights the limitations of familiar interpretations.

Yet, significantly, both the dominant and critical readings, as stand-alone interpretations, are valid, as are an infinity of, as yet unwritten, interpretations. Interpretation is a creative act on the part of the reader. The author cannot control reader-response, but can aim to influence it, intentionally and without intention, through both judicious and unconscious use of rhetoric.

Placing the reflexive reading immediately after the critical reading makes transparent any circumstances that may have impacted on the interpretation described in the critical reading. Discussion of these circumstances enables other readers to be circumspect in their inclination to identify with, or reject, meaning found in the critical reading.

Process of comparison

As my reading of each of the five selected texts progressed, a number of shared assumptions, rhetorical attributes and author/reader roles and relationships began to emerge, and I recorded these in note form. Less distinct to begin with, but increasingly evident as I read my way through the texts, and then began to reread my own interpretations, were those attributes which seemed to be atypical of, and significantly different from, most of the other texts. I noted these also as and when I sensed their appearance. When my scriptive reading of all five texts was complete, I returned to my notes and considered their relevance to the three Ps, performance, perspective and persuasion, which denote the main aspects of textual meaning discovered in the critical reading.

Although many passages in the texts are thick text, so layered and diffuse that any meaning fractionated out from them in a partial reconstruction of meaning runs the risk of betraying the original, as much as does a paraphrase or dominant interpretation, I have nevertheless, to facilitate further discussion, separated out for comment points of similarity and difference across the texts as they have emerged from my reading of them. As I mapped these attributes on to three matrices, I also returned to the original texts, rereading them to affirm and extend the findings in my notes. In the discussion that follows I describe these findings under headings that reflect the three Ps of the critical readings. In 'performance' I discover the 'who' of the text, the persona of the author, and the author's relationship to the reader, as played out in the text; 'perspective', the 'what' of the text, denotes the constructed worldview I have discovered in the text, particularly exploring root metaphors; 'persuasion', the 'how' of the text, denotes the means, the literary conventions of the *lisible*, readable, text that carry this constructed worldview from the text to the dominant reader. A summary of my discussion, the final version of the three matrices, completed under these headings, is presented in Figures 6.1, 6.2 and 6.3.

Performance

Notions of the presence, or absence, of the author in the text, of the authorial persona or voice, is a contemporary recognition of Arisotle's description of the ethos, the personal character of the 'speaker' in the text. As such, because the voice of the author determines the relationship established with readers, it may also be seen to function as a means of persuasion. If, for example, the voice seems to be knowledgeable, is sympathetic and engaging, then the reader will be inclined to give credence to the arguments presented.

The voice, the persona – *persona*, in classical theatre was the Latin word for the mask worn by actors – of the author, builds a writer/reader relationship that is the outcome of tone, the author's attitude to the reader, a sense of how the author stands in relation to those addressed. In discerning this relationship I found it useful to keep Barthes' notion of the 'author' function in mind. Barthes distinguished authorship from the more clerical activity of 'the writer' by ascribing a priestly function to the author: when readers are

Voice	Taylor	Follett	Drucker	Mintzberg	Kanter
1. Academic Management Theorist	■	■	■	■	■
2. Practising Management Consultant					■
3. Scientific Paradigm	■			■	■
4. Phenomenological Paradigm		■	■		
5. First Person Presence	■	■	■	■	■
6. Third Person Disguise	■		■		
7. Manager's Point of View	■	■	■	■	■
8. Employee Point of View		■			
9. Nationalistic Identity	■		■	■	■
10. Author as Mentor	■		■	■	■

Figure 6.1 Matrix 1: Performance

assumed to be the consumers of the text as product, rather than the producer of their own texts, then it is more likely that the author will write as a seer, or mentor to the learner–reader.

All five authors create for themselves a learned, pedagogic presence, for they support their arguments with research and workplace experience recognized by scholarly and/or professional bodies, speaking to readers in voices that establish their places in an academic community and bringing the credibility of those bodies into their texts. For a visual impression of this conclusion, and as a summary of the evaluations on which it is based, as described in Figure 6.1.

Academic management theorist

As described in the dominant readings, all of these authors write as management theorists, laying out concepts for consideration and precepts for action. They compose logical arguments supported by research and workplace experience.

Management did not emerge as a distinct discipline until midway through the twentieth century. It is therefore interesting to note that Drucker comments on this (p. 1) and then writes of management theory in the voices of both historian and philosopher; Follett, whose voice is also that of the philosopher, specifically that of the political philosopher, invokes the learning of psychology, and frequently speaks in that language; Taylor speaks only of his own theory. He is the theorist, and speaks in his own voice of his own theories.

Mintzberg promises to review 'current literature' on managerial work in a later chapter, but is dismissive of it, and definitively does not speak as a denizen of it (pp. 1–4); and Kanter alludes to it briefly and dismissively: 'after years of telling citizens to "trust the system" many companies must relearn' (p. 18). Like Taylor, they both speak as individual theorists with distinct voices.

It is then, a general characteristic of these texts that the author speaks as a management theorist, but does not speak for established management theory.

Management practitioner/consultant

Only Kanter, as she speaks directly from her text of her personal experience, wears the mantle of the management consultant. Taylor, Drucker and Follett all speak as informal observers of the workplace and its mores – they are conversant with its people; while Mintzberg displays familiarity with management education, literature, conferences and (his own) research.

None of these authors speaks as a practising manager, but all display familiarity with, and involvement in, management practice.

Scientific and phenomenological paradigms

Two of the five authors overtly write as management scientists who collect, collate and analyse factual information. Taylor writes: 'As engineers and managers we are more intimately acquainted with these facts than any other class in the community, and are therefore best fitted . . . [to educate] the whole country as to the true facts' (p. 18), and Mintzberg writes, 'unlike virtually all of its predecessors this book is based exclusively on the evidence from empirical studies of managerial work' (p. 4). Both authors discuss what they determine to be facts, provide definitive answers to the specific questions that they have posed, and set out their conclusions in lists of numbered points.

Kanter attempts to slip into their company when she details the number of companies and kinds of information that her research has utilized, and blames 'the kind of data I had access to' for not being able to 'untangle causality, or be entirely sure that reputation reflects reality' (p. 19); her voice is positivist as she makes definitive statements and recommendations.

Drucker also tends to make definitive statements as he sets out his argument. As he expands it, roving about social and political history, and then moving on into a critique of the 'cartelization' of the economy and management theory, his voice becomes more critical and philosophical.

Follett does not write as a management scientist. She is an entertaining story-teller and home-spun philosopher. She speaks of human experience, common and individual, and eschews the facts, figures and definitions that the positivists arrive at. She introduces a world of paradoxical confusions, ambiguities, qualifications and approximations, as she invites readers to share their discernments and understandings.

First person presence and third person disguise

One of the ways in which authors become realized in their texts is through directly sharing personal experience with readers. Of these five authors only Follett allows readers the intimacy of shared personal history and relationships

Follett often and in detail refers to stories told to her, discussions she has taken part in, and conversations held. Many of these invite the reader to share the personal and even the domestic people, places and situations of her life. She tells stories that introduce her friends (for example, the friend who mistakenly thought she wanted to travel to Europe), and shares casual encounters with strangers (for example, the person with whom she shared a room in the library) that contribute to her theories, and also allows actors – for example, the man who liked driving and his wife who liked tennis – to speak representatively of domestic experience as she understands it. She shares her feelings, 'a friend who annoys me' (p. 36), 'I do not like' (p. 47); tells us what interests her 'by far the most interesting examples (p. 33), 'another interesting case' (p. 37); and shares her hopes 'I wish indeed'.

Her argument is a patchwork of personal anecdote, psychological theory and philosophical discussion.

All of this is conveyed as she seemingly enjoys a conversation with her readers. She leads this conversation, and yet author–reader hierarchy is diminished as she respectfully requests the reader to 'consider' her ideas.

In contrast, Kanter remains impersonal and professional as she refers to her 'travels around corporate America' (p. 17) and her own 'expert' research (p. 19); Mintzberg writes about circumstances and objectives that relate to his book, but always objectifies himself and his work as for example in the remote 'this book' (pp. 4–5); Drucker shares his reading and his thinking but not his life experience; and Taylor – though he tells the stories, for example, of the 'golf caddy boy' (p. 21) – attempts to hide in anonymous distance when he says of himself, 'the writer was much interested' (p. 21).

But all of these authors acknowledge their presence in the text when, assuming identity with their readers, they write in the first person plural pronoun 'we'. Follett, Mintzberg and Kanter also further personalize this presence when they speak of themselves as 'I'; whereas Taylor and Drucker writing as the omniscient author, one who is outside the text, hide behind the objectifying third person pronouns 'he', 'she' and 'they'; and Taylor, perhaps just writing within the conventions of his times, removes himself even further from the text when he repeatedly writes of himself as 'the writer' (pp. 18–21).

Yet each author is a distinctively recognizable presence in the text. Taylor's tone is that of the pedagogue: imperative, committed and emotive, so his text is a treatise. Follett is always courteous to her readers and to her subject. She questions with gentle respect and engages her reader in an on-going dialogue. Drucker sets out his serious, even weighty matters, as an argument adopting resonant tones relieved by a little chat, while Mintzberg is curt, definitive and energetic as if preparing a business report. Kanter's mentoring tone merges with the hortatory echoes of the sermon.

All five authors move into, away again, and sometimes return to the use of the inclusive 'we', as they assume a ready-made author/reader identification. Taylor is the only author who refers to himself as 'the writer', but Kanter establishes similar distance when as an omniscient author she declaims: 'This book shows how . . .' (p. 18) and also when she absents herself from the text at length while imaging a world picture and generalizing about 'most people' (pp. 18–19). Mintzberg is comfortably inclusive until he begins to set out his summary of his research. Having assumed that 'we' will 'develop a new view of the work of the manager' when confronted by his research, his objective listing of his ten points contributes to his pre-emptory, authoritative tone.

Follett and Drucker tend to move discreetly back and forth from being personally present as 'I', to comfortable identification with their readers as 'we'.

All of these authors assume a nongendered identity in their use of the inclusive pronoun 'we', although Taylor rarely brings the reader back into the text after his insistence on the first page that 'we' all recognize and share the problem of waste, and Kanter speaks of 'most people', clearly differentiating herself, until she reaches the hortatory final paragraphs in which she declaims the need for collective action.

All five authors, following historic convention, write consistently of both managers and workers as 'he': it would be remarkable if this were not so of those writing before the 1960s, but Kanter publishing in 1984, clearly might have chosen to do otherwise.

Follett's text is unique in that a number of the anecdotal illustrations she includes allow her both to tell women's stories for them – as of the 'lowest paid girls in the industry' (pp. 31–2), and the woman who like tennis (p. 43) – and for them to tell their own stories – as of the friend she disagrees with (p. 36), the friend who was 'going to Europe' (p. 41), and the young woman to whom she did 'wish to make a complaint' (p. 47).

Each of these authors is fully present in the text, and speaks in a very distinctive voice, so in each case the tone of the relationship established with readers is markedly different. At the same time, what these texts have in common is this same distinctiveness of voice, and the way in which the authorial presence established controls the author–reader relationship.

Workplace identity: Manager and employee viewpoints

Whatever persona authors adopt, in an organizational context their texts about management may reflect particular, or diverse, points of view. They may, for example, choose to study and comment on any one management or workplace practice or theory from the viewpoint of employee, customer, shareholder or any number of other stakeholders, and may change from one stance to another.

In these five texts, four of the authors speak consistently, and almost exclusively, from a managerial point of view, while the fifth, Follett, moves comfortably back and forth between managerial and employee viewpoints. Taylor, Drucker, Mintzberg and Kanter all tell anecdotes that revolve around employees. They consider their usefulness and sometimes their welfare and well-being, and generally they write of the greater good for the greater number. But in all of this the employee is spoken for by the voice of managers. We do not hear the voices of employees: there is no listening role for managers.

Follett is unique in that she not only shares the intimacy of personal domestic experience from her own life, as described above, but also, in the short narratives she uses to illustrate her theories of conflict, difference and integration, she contrives to bring the voices of employees into her text. The employees whose voices we hear are captured directly in snippets of dialogue, but also echo through the stories told of workplace behaviours as experienced and interpreted by workers, and these are interspersed with stories of behaviours, both management and union, to demonstrate that sometimes the experiential understandings of the former are more profound than those of the latter. Her text is also unique in that she enables the telling of women's stories. Women speak directly and indirectly, in diverse roles.

All five authors write from a management perspective. Follett alone also writes from employee and other stakeholder perspectives.

National identity

All of these texts are written by North Americans, one of whom, Mintzberg, is Canadian. Follett, lived many years of her academic and professional life in England and Drucker is Austrian by birth. As might be expected, national culture plays a part in informing a writer's worldview.

Taylor opens with an address from President Roosevelt given to 'the governors at the White House' (p. 5), and reminds us of American success, prosperity and pride in political, industrial and sporting (he links America with England here, p. 13) contexts. Drucker expresses his nationalism in sweeping generalizations such as 'the United States is leader today' (p. 2), by assuming a position in the context of the 'cold war', and by differentiating the United States from others 'outside the United States' (p. 3). Kanter personally and firmly locates herself in and of an all-American environment 'in my travels around corporate America' (p. 17), while assuming an American-centred world of success, and leadership that excludes those who do not share her American identity. These three writers, Taylor, Drucker and Kanter, all tend to define themselves, and their assumed readers, by national identity. Their voices are American voices, and those who do not share their emotional commitment to their nation are not included in the 'we' of the text.

Henry Mintzberg locates himself firmly, but not obtrusively or emotively, in North America. His 'executive' is a president and his library is 'one of America's better management libraries' (p. 1); managers are the folk heroes of 'contemporary American society', the subject of American magazines and journals, and work in American organizations (p. 2), but although he locates these managers, Mintzberg himself does not identify with them or with 'their' America: his role is that of observer and commentator.

Mary Follett, also an American, refers to American places, 'Massachusetts' (p. 31) and the Harvard Library (p. 32); politics, 'the Democratic party' (p. 35); and companies 'the Edison Electric Light Company (p. 47); but she is just as comfortable outside as inside the United States. She mentions reading the London *Times* (p. 33), a European happening and its outcome at a London conference (p. 39), quotes the quintessentially English author, Kipling (p. 40), and is casually familiar with European politics as in her references to the 'socialist party in Italy' and the 'English Labour Party' (p. 45).

Follett and Mintzberg do not establish their own national identity by excluding 'other' nationalisms outside the 'we' of the text, but all of the authors in these texts assume the primacy of the Western world for it.

In summary, the nationalism of three of the American writers Drucker and Kanter, is exclusive of non-American readers. Mintzberg, a Canadian, is identifiably American, but writes from a critical perspective and Follett, an American who lived many years in Britain, speaks as a cosmopolitan.

Author/reader relationship

The power relationship between author and reader as evoked by the text is built up by the tone of the author's voice. Tone conveys the writer's attitude to the reader, a sense of where the author stands in the speaker/listener or writer/reader relationship, and the author's perception of the reader's intelligence, sensitivity and status. Subtle clues reveal our conception of, and attitude to, the matters being discussed. So the author's tone suggests an assumed reader-role, one that may include varying degrees of power-distance from the author. As they emerge from my critical readings, the assumed author/reader relationships in these texts suggested by authorial tone are as follows.

All of these authors are pedagogic, but Frederick Taylor is an imperative pedagogue. His impatient, evangelical style assumes that readers can be drawn from their ignorance into his enlightenment by his argument, a trait that he shares most immediately with Kanter.

Mary Follett is gentle, questioning and always respectful. Her learning and civility are never on parade, but are nevertheless the controlling forces in the text. Even the inclusivity of her text, drawing the reader into a climate of careful participative consideration of all people and all arguments, is dictated by her control of text and tone.

Peter Drucker's tone is serious, resonant and eloquent, and it is this classical poise that establishes his control of text and reader as he scopes his argument to stretch somewhere just beyond what he seems to assume is the reach of his learner-reader.

Henry Mintzberg adopts the tone of a pragmatic, energetic manager. His definitive, even curt, comments seem to model the style of effective management that his text pursues. So it seems that there is some 'line authority' at work here as the reader falls into step as trainee manager, foil to the manager expert played by the author.

Rosabeth Kanter, like Taylor, is evangelical in her call to arms, but where Taylor blusters, she is the grand dame sweeping across the pages in hortatory gestures. But as the reader I find myself cast in the role made familiar by Taylor. Sitting in the congregation, looking up at the pulpit, the one voice is redemptrist (Taylor), and the other is pentecostalist (Kanter).

Summary findings (see Figure 6.1)

All five authors speak as academic management theorists, and only one, Kanter, speaks as a management practitioner. Three authors write from within the scientific paradigm, and two write from within the phenomenological paradigm. All five authors write in the first person and only one, Taylor, hides behind the third person. All five write from the manager's point of view, and only one, Follett, also sometimes writes from the employee's point of view. Four authors maintain a nationalistic stance and one, Follett, does not.

Perspective

I am primarily interested here in 'looking through' the text, in searching out root metaphors, the worldview(s) embedded in, and conveyed by, management theory. If an 'eternal truth' that 'we all serve' is assumed in management theory, then the exposure of root metaphors might discover the image of our world that they purvey. My critical reading searches out the tap roots fixed deep down in the foundations of management theory, roots that pass through the rich seams of knowledge found in the archives mined by the archaeological critic, and feed the stems, the leaves and the decorative blooms of the surface metaphors that sprout above the ground where they can be 'looked at'.

I suggest that in my scriptive readings Utopia is the elemental root metaphor in these texts, and that this utopian vision is made to appear desirable and achievable by the intricate weave of meaning in the linings, the embroideries, the total tapestry formed by the root metaphors that I discuss below. The argument, the *logos* of the text, makes the imaginary seem realizable, and the emotive ambience, the *pathos*, that the texts generate may seduce readers into an assumption of shared intimacy with an author intent upon stimulating the vision, reassuring of success and energizing to action.

Explained in the context of metaphor theory and utilizing Richards' terminology, 'our world' is the subject (the tenor) of this root metaphor, and it is 'represented' to us (in the vehicle) as management theory. Where attributes from the two domains are linked and new meaning emerges we find Utopia. The assumptions buried in the subtexts of the theory as I have reread them are the shared attributes that link the tenor to the vehicle domain. In this linking the assumptions underpinning management theory become the assumptions that also underpin the worldview the texts present. Other readers, finding different meanings, would make different connections across the domains and thus discover other root metaphors.

As discovered in the subtexts of my readings, the attributes of the worldview constructed by management theory are set out in Figure 6.2, and as described below.

Worldview	Taylor	Follett	Drucker	Mintzberg	Kanter
1. Discard History	■		■	■	■
2. Pre-eminent Theory	■		■	■	■
3. Problematic Practice	■			■	■
4. Ultimate Question	■		■	■	■
5. Utopian Vision	■		■		■
6. Material Motive	■		■		■
7. Managers as Rulers	■		■	■	■
8. Workers as Resources	■		■	■	■
9. Competitve Character	■		■		■
10. Business Righteousness	■		■		■

Figure 6.2 Matrix 2: Perspective

History

All of these texts make references to the past, to responsibility for and experiences of, mistakes and hardships, but two of them are particularly denigrating of it in their imagery. They suggest that we should discard the past and that we have little to learn from it.

Taylor reminds us that our natural environment has been despoiled by men who are the ignorant and lazy citizens of an uncivilized nation; and Kanter shows the past to be a stagnating, untrustworthy and dysfunctional place, founded on practices that have no place in the future. Drucker's image of the past initially seems to suggest no more (nor less!) than incompetence and laziness, but in the context of the ever-present cold war threat that runs through his text, there is another subterraneous implication: 'doom' (p. 2) awaits if trends in the more recent past cannot be turned around. Mintzberg does not provide an image of the world, past or present, beyond that of management, so although, as noted below, he denigrates the management theory of the past, his text is neutral. Follett is different again, for although she suggests the brute force of industry, and sets it in apposition to the harmony of the arts and civilization, all of the past is here a metaphor of the present, and from the past itself, she reminds us, we do have much to learn. She draws on the history of political struggle, military battles and legal judgement as she provides her readers with insights into the nature and resolution of conflict.

Taylor and Kanter then provide particularly harsh images of a primitive, barbaric and even savage past; Drucker and Mintzberg do not find anything of importance to learn from history; and Follett, although she refers to the primitive physicality of earlier times, is alone in suggesting that there is knowledge and experience in our collective heritage that we should access and draw on.

Management theory

Collectively four of these texts (Follett is the exception) tell us to abandon past theory for we cannot learn from it. They advise readers to discount all previous management theory for past theorists have taught in error: the management theory they have taught is now irrelevant or wrong. The four authors suggest that management theorists do not see their discipline as either having evolved from other disciplines or as building on its own theory, and so they dismiss the erroneous theory of the past and, like the guru writers, they suggest that they have something new and different to offer. Taylor warns that 'no great man can (with the old system of personnel management) hope to compete with a number of ordinary men who have been properly organized' (p. 7). Drucker refers to 'scientific management' only to denigrate the widespread 'cartelization' that he sees as its legacy. Mintzberg lists the management libraries, the executive degree programmes, the business magazines and journals, and the academic conferences that cannot tell us what a manager does, dismisses them as having nothing useful to tell us, and then informs his readers that he will find answers to his question without their help. Kanter blames 'turn-of-the-century organization theory' and its 'scientific management' legacy for leading American companies to believe that 'individuals constituted not assets but sources of error' (p. 18).

Follett's work is in this respect distinct. Throughout her text she refers to psychology and the understandings that we can gain from it, for example, 'psychology has given us the phrase "progressive integratings"' (p. 35). Follett refers to events in history (pp. 36, 39, 45) from which we can learn, and she cites legal cases assuming that her readers accept that knowledge is bedded in collective experience as well as learning.

Management practice

That business management practices are problematic is primarily signalled by the metaphor of health that pervades three of the selected texts. If 'business is sick' then it must be looking for a 'cure'; so problematizing practice leads into the notion (as below) that diagnosis of the illness will lead to the discovery of the antidote – in the form of the new theory about to be promoted, and the Utopia that it will enable.

Taylor, Mintzberg and Kanter all present the practices of management as a cause of business failure. They write of afflictions and incapacities, and prescribe medicines that they promise will 'cure' business ills. Mintzberg is the most meticulous in delineating a negative portrayal of the work of the manager, but Taylor too sweeps his brush broadly across the canvas of workplace practices that are in need of healthy management reform.

Kanter's view of the problems facing management are also found in geographical images such as that of the becalmed ship (the 'doldrums'), but she too relies on the health metaphor as her images of food, portraying the hunger and survival of business, merge with more explicit references to the health needs of the economy necessitating more competition and innovation.

Looking through these three texts, it seems that management's challenge is premised on the notion that our world is in trouble. The way we are doing things is 'wrong' and we are the authors of our own misfortunes.

Neither Drucker nor Follett problematize management. Drucker, as noted below, issues a clarion call for recognition of managers as the new leading class. He presents management in a very positive light as a powerful profession and group already leading society into the future. Follett's use of a health metaphor, in the context of psychology, inverts some of the analogous connections noted above. She says, for example, that 'difference may be a sign of health' (p. 34), and that 'unintegrated difference is pathological' (p. 35). And although this problematizes relationships in the workplace and in society, it also removes the problem from the in-tray of management and firmly objectifies it by allocating its origin to the evolution of desire in the human race.

Pre-eminent management question

Four of the five texts either claim to have discovered the one essential question that must be answered, and/or to promote the one essential precept that must be recognized. Each particular theorist effectively argues that the issue presented is the one that must be prioritized in management thinking and action.

Taylor's 'one best way' is represented in a chiasmus (a perfectly balanced parallel and antithetical phrasing): 'in the past the man has been first: in the future the system *must* be first' (p. 7). Drucker, whose question is, 'what is management and what does it do?' (p. 13), demands that we recognize that 'management *is* . . . an essential, a distinct and a leading institution' (p. 1); Mintzberg says that we '*must* be able to answer' (p. 3) the overarching question 'what do managers do?' (p. 1); and Kanter says that 'business *must* be innovative' (p. 22, original italics). All of these positions are categorically stated and maintained throughout the text.

Taylor appears to qualify these claims in what are effectively weasel-word afterthoughts. He concludes that 'it is not here claimed that any single panacea exists for all the troubles of the working-people or of employers' (p. 29), but the remainder of his text belies his words.

Follett also has a thesis to promote and it is that we should think of conflict as difference and that differences are effectively resolved through integration. Her stance differs from those of all the other authors in that she repeatedly invites readers to 'consider' her ideas. She does not demand that we accept them. She 'suggests' that we think on her arguments rather than insisting that we 'must' accept them. Whereas the uncompromising positions taken up by the other authors indicate that they would be prepared to defend their views in any kind of debating forum, Follett again differs dramatically. In the concluding pages of her text she tells us that the 'greatest obstacle to integration is our lack of training for it', that we need 'to teach the "art" of co-operative thinking'; that because 'in our college debates we try always to beat the other side', participants in business conferences have been trained to come prepared only 'to force through' what they have planned on the basis of '*preconceived* ideas' (p. 48, original italics). Among the barriers she lists as obstacles to the civilized development of self and society through integration are 'prejudice', 'rigidity' and 'dogmatism'.

Vision

In keeping with the confidence described above, and in stark contrast to the image presented as outlined above of our primitive past and presently troubled world, four of the five texts promise us, to a greater or lesser extent, a better, more ideal world, if we accept the doctrine prescribed. Taylor says that if the principles that he believes in 'are correctly applied, results must follow which are truly astounding' (p. 7). He promises that 'under scientific management [we] will be far more prosperous, far happier, and more free from discord and dissension' and that the sooner these principles 'come into general use . . . the better for all the people' (p. 29).

Though Drucker does not, like Taylor, make an explicit promise for the future, he does conclude that 'it is management's specific job to make what is desirable first possible and then actual' (p. 9). Kanter promises an exciting new world of trust, creativity, people-power and wealth; and Mintzberg, though he makes no generalized claims for a better world, does promise – 'we shall improve it' (p. 5) – significant management improvements if we follow his clear directives.

It is Mary Follett who again sits furthest away from the other theorists. She is quite explicit in two comments that are at variance with the above. She is fully aware of the gulf between 'what ought to be', 'what is' and 'what perhaps may be', and just as explicit in placing herself: 'I am talking neither of what is, to any great extent, nor of what ought to be merely, but of what perhaps may be. This we can discover only by experiment' (p. 34).

She also says that although she has suggested that integration is perhaps the most fruitful way to deal with conflict, she does not think it is possible in all cases, and concludes: 'I do not say that there is no tragedy in life' (p. 36).

Motive

One of the most overt assumptions, an assumption that is only partially buried, in these texts is that material advantage is the one overriding goal of business and of life. Kenneth Burke writing about 'The nature of monetary "reality"' has claimed 'money is not a mere agency in our civilization, but is a rationalizing ground of action' (1989: 172). He further argues that 'our monetary economy [is] accompanied by a distinctive "capitalist" psychosis' (p. 173). To the extent that Burke's thesis is reflected in assumptions about the most basic functions and goals of business management, it sums up what emerges from these texts when accounting for motive.

Taylor at first simply condemns material waste: 'we can see and feel the waste of material things' (p. 5), but he then goes on to exemplify the 'psychosis' described by Burke when he proclaims not only that 'the principal object of management should be to secure maximum prosperity', but also that 'good' men, the 'best' men will assume, as does this text, that making money is the 'highest' of goals, the surest road to a virtuous life.

Drucker writes approvingly of 'materialism' (p. 2) as the modern western view of 'organized economic advance'. He juxtaposes material advance and the human spirit as if the latter were in some way dependent on the former.

Kanter's prioritizing of profit and economic wealth is built into her assumption that economic competition is what business is all about, and that there is an all-consuming need for the USA to be materially supreme in the world. Thus the force of the material motive is here seen in a national rather than individual or corporate context.

Mintzberg does not seem to assume that effective management is dependent on motive. It seems that management activity is a negative experience, and perhaps the only 'motive' for improving it is to transform it into a less unpleasant occupation.

Follett again adopts quite a different stance. Approval and advocacy of material wealth, economic advance and expanding ownership are absent from her text. Instead there is an emphasis on recognizing and understanding 'desire'; the need to harness the civilizing forces of respect for difference; and the benefits for all harmonious outcomes.

Managers

Four of these texts, Taylor, Drucker, Mintzberg and Kanter assume the rightful place of pre-eminent management power.

Taylor reiterates several times that management is founded on principles that 'are applicable to all kinds of human activities, from our simplest individual acts to the work of the great corporations' (p. 7), and that 'its [management's] principles can be applied with equal force to all social activities' (p. 8). In this sweeping generalization of management 'activities', he includes homes, farms, businesses, churches, philanthropic institutions, universities and government departments. He not only assumes the placing of managers, as the repository of these 'principles', in charge of all these social activities, but also later states that 'engineers and managers . . . are . . . best fitted to lead . . . the whole country as to the true facts' (p. 18). Managers, says the text, are 'over' other men (p. 26), who are 'incapable of fully under-standing', perhaps because they have 'insufficient mental understanding' without the 'guidance' of managers.

Drucker, the author, states that 'management can only be one leading group among several; in its own self-interest it can never and must never be the leading group' (p. 8); but his text belies this advice. When Drucker explains that management's second function is 'to make a productive enterprise out of human and material resources' (p. 9), that making a 'whole that is greater than the sum of its parts has since Plato's days been the definition of the "Good Society"' (p. 10), then we see that managers are to be thought of as leading this development, as did Plato's philosopher kings in *The Republic*. We first meet managers and management as an 'essential, a distinct, and a leading group', in an ambiance of awe and astonishment: 'Rarely, if ever . . . has a new leading group . . . Rarely in human history has a new institution proven indispensable so quickly . . . Management well remain a basic and dominant institution perhaps as long as western civiliza-tion itself survives' (p. 1). The text's message drowns out the disclaimer.

Although as author Mintzberg suggests that the manager is besieged, overworked and unsure of his ability and/or competence, his text suggests the contrary. In his text the manager is both folk hero, symbolizing both the romance of America's frontier past, and the anonymous grand leader with the fate of the nation in his hands. In action and in the diverse roles that Mintzberg portrays him in, the manager symbolizes all that we admire and are grateful for, all that we are aspire to be, and all that we depend upon to secure our future.

Kanter, as author, says that 'people at all levels, including ordinary people at the grass roots and middle managers at the heads of departments, can contribute . . . can help their organizations' (p. 23) and so seems to promote a democratic worldview. Her text says otherwise. All of these people are valued only to the extent that they further the economic prosperity and the power of corporations, American corporations. When circumstances are stable, corporations can safely ignore individuals (p. 1), for only if the 'corporate machine' is threatened, do 'individuals actually need to count for more' (p. 18). The tone is concessionary: individuals are valued only to the extent that they fuel the corporate machine. The text values corporations that are powerful, 'American companies that seemed to control the world' (p. 17), for all of its theory is geared to securing this pre-eminent corporate position and, by implication, that of the 'masters' who control the corporations. The manager is a romantic figure from American frontier mythology, and in this text a 'change master' is the manager who enables 'more kinds of people, at all levels, to contribute' (p. 19). The master presumably sits on the top 'level'.

Unlike all of the managers above, who lead from outside, beyond, or above the group, Follett's text is built around an image of a servant manager. There is responsibility in this role, but little glamour, as the manager facilitates from within the group, assisting the endeavours of those who seek to understand and progress that understanding into positive action.

Worker

As noted in the previous section, on 'performance' in these texts, in four of the five texts the voices of employees are not heard. Relegated to the empty margins of the page they are most immediately known through being spoken for by the voices of management, and the role they are assigned is that of just one of the resources that fuel business growth.

Peter Drucker spells this out in literal detail. But as in the texts of three of the other authors, it is in the context of the machine metaphor that the mechanistic role of the employee most clearly emerges and culminates in his claim that human persons require the 'same amount of engineering as . . . any other resource' (p. 11).

Taylor equates man and machine, 'each man or machine in the trade' (p. 15), and accuses lazy workers, the 'natural laziness of men', of restricting the potential of the machine to produce (p. 24).

Kanter, in the dominant reading, seems to adopt a particularly democratic stance, as she writes of 'All people. On all fronts . . . People at all levels' (p. 22) but even here she assumes 'levels', and assumes a battle in which 'people' are equated to the soldiers who give their lives for the cause at stake. It is always the corporation and its economic advance that is prioritized and the employees, the most innovative and therefore valuable of employees, are valuable to the extent that they fuel this economic growth. We are back with people as resources.

Mintzberg ignores the employees and maintains that it is the manager's work to manage. By implication employees have no role to play in their own management.

In stark contrast to all of the above, Follett invites employees into her text and assumes that, because they have an accumulated store of wisdom to contribute to understandings of their own management, they have as much to say to managers as do managers to employees, and that both managers and the managed are committed to the civilizing of humankind.

Competitive character

Three of these texts, those by Taylor, Drucker and Kanter, rely on metaphors of competitive sport and of warfare as they actively promote corporate success premised on the defeat of others.

Taylor describes the individually competitive sportsmen who 'give their all' in pursuit of the success that industry is advised to emulate; and describes competition from outside the company that should also motivate workers to greater effort. But he also sees internal 'wars' in a metaphor that assumes a competitive relationship between employer and employee.

Drucker, writing in the context of the 'cold war', premises the survival of the free world on the battle of the American corporates to retain and extend their economic domination of the west. He assumes that winning the cold war, taking control of former colonial territories, and gaining economic control over nature are all designed to create economic prosperity and thus advance the human spirit.

Kanter's text assumes conquest and American domination of the world. Workers 'on all fronts' are expected to share the national goal of beating others to first place. Competitors – she instances Japan – must be defeated so that American corporates can dominate the world, which her geographic metaphors suggest is there for the taker.

In Mintzberg's text a metaphor of war is reserved for a representation of the world of scholarship, where the management 'corps' is besieged by hordes of marauding investigative management scientists.

Interestingly, Follett's metaphors of sport and war suggest patterns of behaviour that we can learn from, but what we can learn has to do with co-operation, not competition: 'conflict' should be understood as 'difference' not 'warfare', we should aim to understand the 'rules of the games', and learn to anticipate responses. She later elaborates on this notion, for 'domination' a victory for one of two sides, is not, she says, the most 'successful' way of dealing with conflict. Similarly she reminds us that to continue 'fighting' is an easier option than is finding resolutions to conflicts. Then with consummately ironical twists she engages the war metaphor itself in a struggle with metaphors of legal power and inverted notions of victory and defeat as outcomes of struggle and judgement.

Yet while Follett's concern in her text is the resolution of conflict within organizations as she seeks out and recommends the best way to integrate competing desires, she does also assume a competitive base to business. In an interesting aside, as she discusses the anticipation of response, she notes that 'to beat them to it – is exactly what each firm does try to do to competing firms' (p. 43). Neither approving nor disapproving, she takes for granted that this is what firms do.

Business righteousness

Authors who tell readers the best way of being or tell them how they should behave, may be assuming a moral order, and to the extent that they promote this order, may assume the voice of moral leadership. It is a voice that may ring with the rhetoric of the priest and pulpit, as was noted in my discussion of the author-as-mentor, in the previous section, but is also sometimes a voice that is so bedded in the text as to be, though barely audible, yet clearly speaking.

Taylor, for example, assumes morality based on a Christian dichotomy of good and evil. He castigates 'men' for their laziness, an evil state, and accusing them of having lapsed through ignorance, reminds us that we bring about our own sufferings. Salvation and reward, achieved through action-based striving to be 'better' come to the virtuous in the form of material reward. Prosperity will make us happy.

Drucker's text rings with received wisdom. The manager, as keeper of God-given resources, has a moral duty to husband capital and reap profits. Champions of the progressive march of capitalism, they will 'advance' the 'human spirit' if they successfully orchestrate economic prosperity.

Kanter's text is secular, but permeated by an assumed 'oughtness'. The route to her vision of a better world is peppered with rousing, authoritarian instructions, for 'we [Americans] must' be first, must control and dominate the world. To be 'master' is mandatory. Everything else must be subjugated to economic priority if we are to look forward to a new world based on trust and creativity.

Competition and domination do not light the way to Follett's new world. She images battlefields in order to persuade us not to go there. She is 'for peace' and integration will 'flower' in a 'field of desire'. Her vision of this new place images an openness where we take time to enjoy our differences. It is an aesthetically pleasing world, intellectually rigorous, and emotively satisfying.

Summary findings

Beginning with Taylor's 'one best way', four of the five texts have set out to show that they offer 'the way and the light': take heed, they seem to say, and go forth equipped. They simplify 'the message' to a recipe for success. Follett is different. She draws on her knowledge of psychology and instead of presenting something 'new' and dramatically successful, explicitly says that although her ideas may help us to learn and progress, some conflicts cannot be resolved: 'I do not say that there is no tragedy in life' (p. 36).

These same four texts also proclaim the need to forget the 'old' wisdoms, on which our presently problematic world has foundered, and to join with the mentoring author in determining the 'best' way to direct employees.

Three texts of the texts, those written by Taylor, Drucker and Kanter, tell readers that managers are a 'race apart', that managers are extraordinarily powerful, and that they have superior roles and understandings.

One text, Mary Follett's, is out of step with the other four at every stopover on this leg of my discursive journey.

In the next chapter I discuss these commonalties and differences in more detail.

Persuasion

The suasive devices, semantic and syntactical, that an author can choose to work with are so numerous that text analysis inevitably involves selecting just some devices, and results in comment on just some of the rhetorical effects of these devices. Critical readers are also aware that the semantic and the syntactical can never legitimately be fully separated out, as I may appear to have done in the matrices (Figures 6.1, 6.2 and 6.3). What language says, and how it says it, are inextricably mingled. Metaphors, for example, the most powerful of all the persuaders, have already been discussed under the banner of 'perspective', while the voices and personas of the authors have been discussed in the section on 'performance'.

So although the threads of rhetorical persuasion may be teased out a little further, as in my comments below, many aspects of the devices I discuss and the uses to which they are put, impact on many other aspects of the other two Ps, 'performance' and 'perspective'. Likewise, some of my comments in the previous two sections continue to be relevant here. Barthes' metaphor of text and text analysis, for example, is a salutary reminder that all analysis involves the arbitrary division of that which is not essentially divisible. Barthes suggests that we should think of 'text as tissue' (in French *tissu* connotes both 'fabric' and 'web') or as a skein of different voices and multiple codes, and this to me suggests density and holism which cannot be maintained in a laying out of fragmented parts.

For this reason, the matrices are only useful if they are read within the total context of the reading process I have described. Thus the explanatory comment that follows each of the subheadings below is intended to be succinct: to provide just enough description of the categories of suasion covered to indicate what I see as the main impact of the strategy described. I comment on aspects of persuasion that I have identified as being predominant across all five selected texts. These are not the only devices present in the texts, and nor are they always the devices that are consistently and predominantly found in any one text. I have singled them out for comment because a majority of these management writers have utilized them.

As I constructed the third matrix (see Figure 6.3), my intention was to identify the devices that I consistently noted in individual texts. And this is what the matrix does display, but what it does not sufficiently do is to indicate the use of a device or devices that is in some way startling, memorable or atypical, so where this is significant I have commented below.

Suasive devices	Taylor	Follett	Drucker	Mintzberg	Kanter
1. Inclusive Language	■	■	■	■	■
2. Appeal to Authority	■	■	■	■	■
3. Logical Argument	■	■	■	■	■
4. Emphatic Devices	■	■	■	■	■
5. Dramatic Tension	■	■	■	■	■
6. Narrative Illustration	■	■	■	■	■
7. Emotive Imagery	■	■	■	■	■
8. Irony & Humour		■		■	

Figure 6.3 Matrix 3: Persuasion

Other than as this particular need dictates, I have not, in this section, made detailed comment on individual use of each of the devices and texts listed in this matrix. What is of interest here is the broader patterns of use, as well as the differences, that distinguish some aspects of some texts. Thus my comments on the devices displayed on this matrix are more generalized.

As the dominant readings demonstrate, all of these texts have traditionally been read as logical arguments. It has been assumed that they appeal to the rational faculties of the mind: that the ideas they set out and connect are the meat of the content devoured by readers. But much of the argument, or reasoning (*logos*), is reinforced by carefully constructed syntax, and emphasizing or highlighting devices such as repetition and antithesis. I comment on these aspects of persuasion below.

Texts appeal also to the senses, and the extent to which they engage the emotions, eliciting a feeling response, may also influence reader uptake of textual messages. *Pathos* is the emotive dimension of the text, for language that moves the reader stirs the emotions towards or away from identification with an idea or an action, and is seen to play a powerful rhetorical role in determining the acceptance or rejection of the text's message(s). *Pathos* is almost invariably at work in all rhetoric but I comment on particular aspects of it below.

Ethos, in classical rhetoric the persona of the author as present in the text, as has already been discussed, is a central component of performance. It is the third arm of the classical troika of *logos*, *pathos* and *ethos*, and may be a powerfully persuasive component of the text, but as I have already discussed it fully in the first section of this chapter, I have not retraced that ground here.

Inclusivity

The use of the first person singular pronoun 'I' brings the author into the text. It gives the reader an opportunity to relate to the author as an individual, a person whose thoughts, emotions and experiences are displayed to the reader, but it does not assume that the author's views and values are shared by the reader. When the corresponding plural pronoun 'we' is utilized then the tone changes to an all-inclusive assumption of shared identity. All five authors write in the first person plural 'we' and make use of the companion possessive pronoun, 'our'.

Another form of direct address, the rhetorical question, performs very differently. Rhetorical questions are an oratorical device because they assume a predetermined answer: when, for example, Taylor asks 'what other reforms . . . could do so much . . . ?' he is not looking for an answer, but for affirmation of the thesis he has already put, and is assuming that his readers will shout their agreement in the form of an affirmative answer. Follett asks, 'why not?' Drucker builds to a climax in the form of a question (p. 130), and Mintzberg too opens with a question.

What these two forms of direct address, inclusive pronouns and rhetorical questions, have in common is that both allow the author to play an assumed lead role, to assume that the reader will fall into step as a follower, and that this assumed agreement of writer and reader will go unchallenged by the reader.

At a more general level, texts are sometimes described as being written in an hieratic ('high') or demotic ('low') style. The latter, because they speak to readers in their own language, also suggest inclusivity: demotic style is determined by word choice and syntactical structures that are modelled on the language, associations and rhythms of ordinary speech. Texts written in this way are seemingly familiar, speak to us in comfortingly accessible ways, and carry the authority of folk wisdom and insight. Often they suggest the tone of a casual conversation or a chatty story. Their power of conviction lies in the everyday common-sense reality they seem to convey.

Taylor writes of 'quitters' in sport, and 'soldiering' in the workplace, assuming that we are familiar with these colloquialisms. Follett relates casual conversation and Mintzberg quotes informal dialogue. Drucker tends to maintain the sonorous role of his dignified prose, and Kanter abandons her mentoring role only to assume a hortatory pose as she exhorts her readers to accept her message.

Authority

Use of the second person pronoun 'you' establishes a further change of tone as the authors distances themselves from the reader, and may become authoritative if they speak in the imperative, seeming to issue instructions. Where authors speak directly to readers it usually has the distancing effect of placing author and reader in clearly differentiated roles. Addressed as 'you', or put into the role of recipient to imperatives (verbs such as 'take' or 'leave' which issue commands), a clear author/reader hierarchy is established: knowledge and authority reside with the author. In a context where this assumed leadership is reinforced with other rhetorical strategies, such as those outlined on these pages, it may well be that this form of address, and the role assumption that it expresses, seems to emerge from, and simply reinforces, just such an already justified distinction.

All five authors either imply this kind of writer/reader relationship at various points throughout the text, or directly address the reader.

Where authors wish to establish even greater distances between themselves, their texts and their readers, they may employ the anonymous pronouns 'he', 'she', 'one' or 'them', as do all five writers on occasion. When authors seem to completely remove themselves and the reader from the text (Taylor speaks of himself remotely, as 'the writer') this has a particular rhetorical effect for it is a rhetorical device designed to suggest objectivity and inarguable factual evidence. It is most often the rhetorical style of scientific argument. Although they seem to come and go, none of these authors have stayed completely outside their texts, and when their authoritative presence is tempered by the easy familiarity with which they establish a relationship to the reader as described above, then the reader may be both comfortable and flattered. The authoritative author is treating the reader as a familiar.

An argument may also be made to seem authoritative if 'authorities' outside the texts are named, quoted and referred to. Such an authority may be a historical figure of some stature, for example a political or civic leader of renown, an eminent thinker, a famous visionary or a representative of the arts, or a theorist on whose research the text is somewhat dependent. In these texts we meet authority that ranges from the presidential (Taylor), to philosophers (Follett), historical knowledge (Drucker), corporate consulting (Kanter) and management scholarship (Mintzberg).

But I did not find that all of these theorists draw on, or build on established theory. On the contrary, as already noted, four of them advise readers to abandon disciplinary knowledge of the past for it has taught in error and must shoulder some of the blame for current problematic practice in management. The rhetorical effect of this stance is of course to suggest that here is something quite new: that the insights conveyed carry the imprimatur of great thinkers, but are new to management.

Two authors appeal to more abstract authoritative entities: Follett invokes the learning of psychology and Taylor appeals to an anonymous moral righteousness that seems able to determine what is good, better and best for all.

Much of this authority may be conveyed in a voice that exudes hieratic style. Determined by word choice, sentence structure and syntax, and other formal features, such as rhythmic patterns and component sounds, hieratic style is also sometimes described as 'high' or 'grand style' and is employed by speakers or writers who communicate from a level 'above' that of their readers. It is recognized as being more 'literary' than everyday speech, and typically incorporates Latinate words, and hypotactic sentence structures. In hypotactic style the logical and syntactic relations between members of sentences are expressed by words (such as 'which', 'because', 'when', 'then' and 'while') or by phrases (such as 'as a result', and 'in order to') or by subordinate clauses. In my analyses of the selected texts, I have most often noted their Latinate features in this context, because the cadence and balance of such features lull the reader into a secure acceptance of the arguments portrayed, while the polysyllabic vocabulary lends seeming weight to the argument(s) promoted. In all five texts I noted examples of hypotactic style.

Logic

A well-wrought argument, one that is constructed along clearly logical lines in neatly linking paragraphs, makes a powerful appeal to the rational faculties of the reader. Where there is no distraction from the power of a logical progression and linking of ideas, because the passage is also seemingly dispassionate and objective, the 'evidence' on which conclusions are reached may seem 'scientifically' irrefutable. But although 'scientific prose' is generally free from emotional appeal, this does not create neutrality: it deliberately asserts the value of a non-rational appeal to the authority of reason. It is a carefully crafted rhetorical invention. In science, the denial of emotion is a passionate tribute to our belief in it: a powerful advocacy of its methods and goals. In other words, the exclusion of emotive appeal has its own very particular rhetorical appeal, and in essence is no less contrived than is any other rhetorical strategy.

My dominant readings expose the skeletal frame of the argument put forward in each text. Each reading clearly progresses through a logical argument. Moreover, the two texts that lean furthest to a positivist mode of inquiry, Taylor's and Mintzberg's, also specifically remind readers of their logic as they progress through the main points of their arguments, and although they seem to rely on 'facts', my critical readings demonstrate that even their most 'scientific' paragraphs are highly rhetorical.

Emphasis

There are a number of ways in which, in these texts, ideas and assumptions are reinforced. The first is repetition: sometimes a keyword is repeated several times within a short space as with 'evil' (Taylor), 'conflict' and 'difference' (Follett) and 'all' and 'people' (Kanter). Sometimes an idea or concept is described in a number of different ways as is the institution of management (Drucker); or is illustrated in a number of different ways as are the problems of management (Mintzberg).

'Listing', where one idea or example is piled upon another and another, tends to have a cumulative effect. There is, as with hieratic style generally, a general weightiness about this kind of device that may leave the reader feeling a little breathless, perhaps overwhelmed by the sheer weight of evidence. Mintzberg piles up negative image upon negative image as he presents the overwhelming challenges managers face.

The rhetorical effect of antithesis is to heighten the qualities of the subject by throwing it into relief against its opposite, by providing contrast. Numerous examples of antithesis are scattered across all five texts and they include the setting of one word against another as in Taylor's great men versus ordinary men; one attribute against another as with Mintzberg's positive versus negative traits of the manager's role; one entity against another as with Drucker's workers versus managers; one concept against another as with Follett's justice versus war, and Kanter's mechanical systems versus intellectual effort.

Drama

Dramatic tension can be created in any number of different ways, from the simple use of contrast as above, and cumulation also above, through to the emotional tension sparked by conflict and its awaited outcomes in storied illustrations and the creation of situational scenarios that allow textual actors to determine the tenor and pace of everything from argument to description. Even at the basic level of sentence structure, tension can be created when the main point of a statement is delayed until the end of the sentence (periodic), and this contrasts markedly with the easy, descriptive, style adopted by the writer of loose sentences. In the latter the main point of the statement is made at the outset, and everything that follows is descriptive; the reader already knows what is at issue and has time to ponder on it as the statement is enlarged upon in the remainder of the sentence. Where there is no tension, no eagerly awaited outcome, readers are less likely to engage with text. All of these texts are dramatic in different ways.

Taylor sets up an image of a deeply troubled, even corrupt world and his text moves, in super-confident steps towards a material Utopia. Images of suffering, laziness and evil wait for the antidotes of his recipe for happiness, provided as he guides the concerned reader back to the reassurance of order and plenty.

Follett not only inserts a series of illustrative conflict situations into her text, each one of which waits to be resolved, and tells a series of anecdotal stories, each one of which pulls the reader into action that builds to a climax, but also heightens our perception of dramatic undertones by building into the subtext the dramatic metaphor that my critical reading surfaces.

Drucker's drama is the drama of pomp and ceremony. The cumulation of phrase on phrase as the new institution, the new leading group, the power and importance of management and managers grow as the prose swells, and the era of management is ushered in.

Mintzberg adds a dramatic dimension to his argument by introducing it with a dialogue script, and then setting up the stage for the entry of the hero-manager. Theatre makes way for a close-up of the manager at work as his hard-hitting catalogue of problems builds to a climax awaiting resolution.

Kanter also draws back the curtains on the image of an expansionist America, active on all 'fronts' as a new order is instated. Her text suggests the drama of the pulpit as her story builds to an insistence on the realization of her visionary Utopia.

Narrative illustration

Rhetorical use of short stories (anecdotes) serves a number of persuasive purposes: stories may entertain, illustrate concepts, provide historical or other authoritative support for the argument, or allow authors to portray their personal life or work experiences as they build a profile and relationship with the reader. All of these texts engage in story-telling. Sometimes the story is a little vignette, inserted into the main narrative and sometimes it is intimately woven through the argument. Lively anecdotes – such as Taylor's moralistic parable of the golf caddy – entertain readers while simultaneously emphasizing values with which the reader is being persuaded to identify: the golf caddy is materially rewarded for his work effort. Stories such as those of Mintzberg's would-be managers, beleaguered by dusty tomes of argument, are presented as prototypical of those whose unthinking acceptance of the status quo makes them responsible for their own sad fate, whereas Follett's militant farmers and tennis-playing wives, symbolize the confrontational and the cooperative, respectively. Kanter's story of her own research introduces readers to her expertise and her status as consultant and researcher, while Drucker's potted history of the rise and fall of nations enables him to profile the expanding role of the 'new' and 'leading' institution of management.

Mintzberg's middle managers, Follett's unionists and women in service, and Taylor's sportsmen and 'soldiering' workers are all 'characters' to whom we can easily relate. Their work and lives and language are representative of shared human experience, and their roles and activities are familiar, so they are able to play out the concerns of their authors: the problems of managers (Mintzberg), the handling of conflict (Follett) and the need to motivate workers through reward (Taylor). Conversely, the stories told by Drucker and Kanter image worlds beyond the experience of the average reader. They serve to stimulate the imagination and introduce the reader to new ideas via old and impressive narratives.

Emotive imagery

The images found in a text include all the material that relates to the senses, not just the visual, although it is the most commonly discovered. Particular words may carry emotive connotations, and metaphors are of course the most powerful conveyors of emotive images and have been discussed as such in the five analyses. Metaphors are particularly notable because in them can be found many of the assumptions that inform the text. Managers and management practices are, for example perceived as destroying competitors in metaphors of war (Taylor, Follett, Drucker, Mintzberg, Kanter); playing by the rules in the game of business (Follett); as adventuring, conquering and colonizing in metaphors of state and empire and in geographic metaphors (Follett, Kanter); as the cure for human ills in metaphors of sickness and medication (Taylor, Follett, Mintzberg); as providing efficient business systems and workplace practices in mechanistic metaphors (Taylor, Drucker, Kanter); and as developing business in a naturalistic, people-focused environment in organic metaphors (Follett, Drucker, Kanter).

In one surprising image of a grotesquely mythical Africa, Drucker's text suddenly throws up an image that shocks the reader into awareness. It is not the image itself that forges a link with an associated idea (in this case what managers do) but the shock of its sudden appearance that indelibly writes the associated question, 'What is management?' into the reader's awareness.

Irony and humour

Irony assumes reader complicity in unstated assumptions. Its powerful appeal depends on shared writer/reader understanding of what is meant versus what is said, and should the reader miss the cues that point to it, then not only will its rhetorical effect, the binding of writer/reader sympathies in this common understanding, be lost, but the overt message too may be misinterpreted. It is a subtle, witty overture to the intelligent reader and there are few examples of it in my reading of these texts.

Follett touches lightly on the paradoxical notion of the engineer's relationship to friction and when she juxtaposes notions of war and justice she expects her readers to follow subtle inversions and seeming contradictions.

Humour relaxes readers and predisposes them to be receptive to other textual meaning. Again it is a shared experience, one that, because it is enjoyable, creates empathetic writer/reader bonds, and some of this bonding may be achieved in a common identification against the subject that is the butt of the joke. I found only brief and isolated examples of humour to which I responded positively: Follett's jokes and the 'damned Yankee', and

Mintzberg's sympathetic exposé of the executive who cannot explain what he does.

Summary findings

The understated humour and lightly satirical tones of Follett and Mintzberg, respectively, are the only rhetorical strategies I have noted, and commented on, in the texts that are not common to all five texts. In all other respects the persuasive rhetoric of the five texts is remarkably consistent and effective.

Disclaimer

In the matrices that followed my discussion of each of the three Ps, performance, perspective and persuasion, I have visually mapped the similarities and differences that emerged across all five texts. Although aspects of meaning were separated out in this manner for discussion, in fact of course all three Ps of scriptive reading are always intertwined and interdependent. Nevertheless, in order to facilitate on-going discussion and dialogue about meaning in these texts, in the next chapter I continue to discuss their commonalities and differences.

7   A metanarrative of management theory and a differing voice

Oh God! I could be bounded in a nutshell,
and count myself a king of infinite space.[1]
Hamlet, II, ii, 263–4

As I noted, elements emerging from my reading of perspective in four of the subject texts, I was aware that my analysis had mined several seams of a common management theory narrative. I sensed a narrative of my own forming around a few nuggets as I unearthed them from their root metaphors; and a utopian narrative began to shape itself into a fairy tale. And I also listened to another voice, Mary Follett's, speaking in measured tones from the wings, but her story is unique and follows later.

Perspective: A utopian metanarrative of management theory

The management theorist who sets out on a quest for management knowledge and know-how should unpack and discard all past learning. He[2] should not take anything he thought he knew with him because managers and management theorists cannot learn useful lessons from history. Commerce, industrial and electronic, has changed and is changing all that we thought we knew about the world so dramatically, and so rapidly, that if he is to follow a road to future success, he must reinvent the future of the world he will manage. Discarding his past should be easy because it has been ignorant, brutal, savage and uncivilized, whereas the remade future can be ordered, controlled and materially prosperous.

Old management theory is the deceiver, for the manager's past inadequacies, ineptitudes and ignorances were fostered by the teachings it promoted. In the light of the new understandings the management theorist will glean as he reads this particular text, the management 'other', the irrelevant, the erroneous, theory of the past can be junked with the rest of history.

The manager's understanding of management theory, and the way he manages, are of course inextricably woven together, so it follows that his contemporary management practice is problematic. Since management practice in the past has been responsible for business ailments, weaknesses and suffering, the medicine of new theory must be taken if a cure is to be realized.

Our hero-reader is not unprotected in this problematic territory. Help is immediately available: a prescription is prepared and waiting, for in the text he will find THE pre-eminent question. The holy grail, the answer to the one crucial question that must be answered, or the one crucial element of our human situation that must be understood, is waiting to be discovered in the text.

With the magic charm (the pre-eminent question) safely pocketed, the reader may proceed, sure of the promised access to the apple of knowledge and entry to the ideal world beyond. The reader is to be given a map to this utopia, a place where there will be more (more work, more profit, more competence, more competition, more material advantage) constructed by the enactment of the assumed values upon which this dream future will be built.

In this new world order the newly instructed manager will rule. The power of his managerial status, subscribed to and endorsed by the text, may ascribe multifarious roles to him. He may become a seer or a witch-doctor; an adventurer, explorer and conqueror; and a mentor and life-style educator. He will assume magical powers of imagination, of physical strength, of moral fervour and of rational intellect.

He will rule over his employees. His story, management theory's story, will always be told in his voice, written from his perspective, for the voice of the employee is not heard. He is advised to listen to his employees, and to work alongside them, so that he, the manager, will be able to manage them more effectively. Ultimately the worker is always the resource fuelling the business machine or growing the business plan which he controls. Even as repositories of knowledge, his employees exist to serve the ends of business. Democratic power sharing is not on his management agenda, nor is there any notion that the goal of business might be to empower and enhance the lives of all who engage with it and in it. There is no suggestion that the business he manages should serve the needs and desires of other stakeholders unless the service is profit-orientated or otherwise self-seeking.

Instead manager and employee, author and reader, are expected to share a common identity, to find a common purpose, as they stand, shoulder to shoulder, against their common 'other', the outsiders, the foreigners. Competition is good, because through it all differences can be overcome or annihilated. As in sport and in battle, the defeat of the other in business serves to affirm superiority, and vindicate the one true path to success.

Management theory can teach us how to live successfully and happily. If we follow the prescriptions of the theorist we will achieve Utopia, and this Utopia is built on the profit motive ensuring that the outcome will be material gain. More is better: money is a 'God substitute' (Burke 1989: 168).

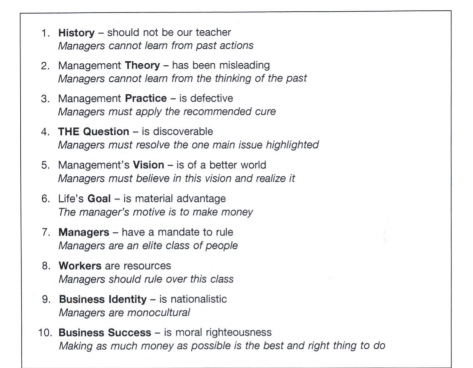

1. **History** – should not be our teacher
   Managers cannot learn from past actions

2. Management **Theory** – has been misleading
   Managers cannot learn from the thinking of the past

3. Management **Practice** – is defective
   Managers must apply the recommended cure

4. **THE Question** – is discoverable
   Managers must resolve the one main issue highlighted

5. Management's **Vision** – is of a better world
   Managers must believe in this vision and realize it

6. Life's **Goal** – is material advantage
   The manager's motive is to make money

7. **Managers** – have a mandate to rule
   Managers are an elite class of people

8. **Workers** are resources
   Managers should rule over this class

9. **Business Identity** – is nationalistic
   Managers are monocultural

10. **Business Success** – is moral righteousness
    Making as much money as possible is the best and right thing to do

Figure 7.1 The ten precepts of management theory

A commentary on the metanarrative

The story of the road to Utopia, a 'good place' that is found 'no-where',[3] that emerges from the subtexts of my critical readings of management theory is a story that has evolved through the decades that my selected texts span. In my reading, management theorists write as the seers who vision the state we aspire to, and the theory they evangelize: the nuggets I unearthed from their root metaphors, writ large on the tablets of the ten precepts (see Figure 7.1), map the route for us. These ten signposts on the route to Utopia emerge from my analysis of the root metaphors that convey perspective, as I interpreted it, in four of the texts (see Figure 6.1). A summary chronology of the tale told follows.

In the beginning there was Taylor. We were admonished to believe in the system, to work our hardest for it and in it. Hard work, competent work and efficient work was equated with good work. Shot through with the capitalistic protestant ethic of hard work as good work (a good worker is a hard worker), Taylor's text promised material happiness for all, in all walks of life, if only we would heed the message and obey the call.

The utopian management narrative continues in the subtexts of Drucker's theory. It is decades since Taylor first preached that 'the system must be first', and although Drucker is dismissive of scientific management, his text assumes that systems of management have been put in place. Now the emphasis falls on the person responsible for ensuring that the system works, the manager. If the system is creed then the system-maker is king. Management, as Drucker then visioned it, was to be the new leading institution and the manager a world leader.

But in the 1950s aggressively competing nations were struggling for world dominance, and Utopia, a free, American-dominated world, could only be achieved if the divine, legal, social and economic powers of the manager were fully recognized and brought into play in all spheres of human activity. Encapsulating the basic beliefs of modern western society and ready to advance the human spirit, Drucker's manager would lead us into the prosperity, the new world also promised by Taylor's text. In Drucker's vision of the future, managerial control of workers and resources, of 'nature', promised 'human betterment and social justice' (pp. 1–2): when managers manage the world, material prosperity will lead to spiritual riches and the realization of the 'Good Society' (p. 10). His text is promissory. He visioned a new leading institution, management, and a new class of leaders, managers, and assured us that their pre-eminent role, inevitable in both present and future eras, would ensure utopian outcomes.

Mintzberg's text does not vision Utopia for us, but it does contribute to the historical development of the narrative in that it builds the image of the hero-manager who will lead the way to this ideal state. His text personalizes Drucker's anonymous leader-manager in images that range from the reassuringly familiar to the glamorous but distant figure of a world leader. We are perhaps seduced by romantic appeal, even while being awed by political power, as Mintzberg's theory paves the way to Kanter's Utopia.

Utopia as visioned in Kanter's text, is American. As the dominant world power, the United States, prosperous, powerful and pompous, is the place we should all aspire to be happy in and in which to manage. Utopia for the individual assumes an adventurous managerial role. Out on the high seas of economic battle, fame and fortune, the exciting manager competes aggressively for aggregating territories and expanding powers and participating people. The latter will find that if they obey the call to contribute all their energies and talents to the overriding managerial goal of competitive economic success, they will be rewarded by the knowledge that they have contributed to the building of a Utopia for managers.

Follett's text does not contribute to the utopian story as told above by the other four texts: Follett has a story of her own to tell. I will return to it shortly but first, a return to the nuggets of management theory from which I fashioned my utopian narrative, my fairy story.[4]

The ten precepts

I found the ten precepts (Figure 7.1) my scriptive reading uncovers woven through the underfabric of our texts. As I picked at tiny knots below the smooth surface of the material text, pulling on individual threads as they became visible, I found, at first, a growing pile of scraps. As I played with them, they began to gleam like polished nuggets and so I wove them into the fabric of a new narrative, a metanarrative or fairy story of management theory. Scraps or nuggets, they encapsulate attributes of the utopian root metaphors which emerged from my readings of the subject texts: for, as I read them, they detail the ten precepts that the student of management theory must understand and enact in order to achieve utopian outcomes.

The route to Utopia, as visioned in management theory, is encapsulated in these ten precepts of management theory. It gains legitimacy through its institutionalization, and is supposedly accessible to the acolyte who subscribes to the creed promoted.

Of particular interest to me is that the precepts I have delineated pertain primarily to the perspective or worldview the texts portray, rather than to attributes of persuasion and performance. This seems to suggest that a text is 'accepted' when the reader identifies with the worldview it promotes: that 'what' is said (including what is said in the subtext) may be more influential in bringing about reader identification than is 'how' it is said or by 'whom'.

Looking at the differences between the four texts discussed above and the one text (Mary Follett's) that seems always to be out of step with the other five, supports this conclusion.

Against the genre: The voice of Mary Follett

Follett's text, like the other four, stitches images of a primitive and restricting past and suggests ways of improving the way we live and work, but there the similarity ends. Her voice shapes a more desirable future built on recognition of our need to learn from the past, and not just from its mistakes: she finds wisdom in all that has gone before. In her text it seems that we live in a world of evolving continuities so that our past is part of our present, and our future will evolve from our collective experience of past and present. There is no drama in the pace of, or nature of change, just an on-going need for recognition of the way things are.

Follett does not trash 'other' management theory, but instead suggests that there is a much broader field of scholarship from which we can learn, and which we can apply to management problems. Psychology in particular could be our teacher and we do need to discover and import new knowledge, for her text moves towards my metanarrative of management theory when she employs metaphors of ill-health to depict the woes of business.

Nor does Follett indict contemporary management practice as the focus of much-needed workplace reform. Her text allows for the way things are, for the potential conflict inherent in all human situations, and suggests that we all 'consider' long enough to come to a fuller understanding of our world.

There is no one question, no one pre-eminent insight, revealed in this text, for Follett indicates that of many important topics she will consider just 'this', and although she has some remarkably strong recommendations to make, following her advice does not guarantee a successful outcome. There is a world of new freedoms and new understandings waiting to be discovered, but Follett warns that she does not say 'that there is no tragedy in life' (p. 36). We can choose to work towards a more satisfying future, but it is still a flawed world, not a utopian dream that lies ahead.

Her text veers most sharply away from my metanarrative in its assumptions about knowledge and power. Employees speak in their own voices, personal friends stroll through her pages, and ordinary, domestic situations and relationships have much to say about management. There is no managerial hierarchy here: she counsels managers towards humble learning from all those with whom they have any interaction. Employees are not resources: they are people. People are esteemed and listened to whatever the task being performed, just as readers are respected and asked to 'consider' with the author.

Similar respect is accorded the 'other' in any dispute, personal, organizational or national, for we should work together to understand difference and resolve conflict. From the integration of desires all parties will benefit.

Money and material gain are never proffered as the motive for adopting the prescribed theory and applying it. It is not business prosperity that is primarily sought here. Follett's text speaks of 'every one of us', of the plus values in our activities that mean progress for the individual, and the role of business in facilitating that progress.

Remarkably, Follett's metaphors of a past and future society are built around metaphors of an abstract concept, conflict, represented in a metaphor of another abstract concept, justice. Conflict called to account, reinterpreted as 'difference' and set to work for us, is the 'defendant' in a long-running case of mistaken identity. If we harness its potential to move us towards more complete understandings we will not control the future or find Utopia, but we will garner more responsibility for our own actions.

A fairer world will evolve from our better understanding of ourselves and others.

Persuasion: Voices in chorus

The metanarrative and the 'other' story that I have related above demonstrate that Follett's perspective, her worldview, is radically different from the generalized picture of perspective that emerges from a synthesis of the other four texts.

Just as dramatically displayed on the three matrices is the simi
Follett's text to the other four when persuasion is the focus of intere
think of persuasion only as a generalized 'toolkit' of devices availabl ₋ ₋₋ ₋ne
author, then Follett's text utilizes suasive devices that are common to all five
texts. Viewed in this way, scriptive reading demonstrates that persuasion,
narrowly defined as stylistic devices, is the one aspect of Follett's text that
shows it to share commonalities with the other four. It is the only one of the
three Ps with which she is consistently in step.

But the picture imaged by the matrix is based on a very narrow view of
persuasion. The voice of the author, the author's performance and the reader
relationship that the author builds in the text may be very persuasive, just as
the message itself, the perspective, the views and values found in the text may
attract or alienate the reader.

Re-reading the narratives I have already related, and with this blurring of
the boundaries between the three Ps in mind, another kind of story – one
that appears in a dramatistic mode reflecting the notion that all of these texts
are 'performances' – moves from the margins and spaces of the texts, in my
reading of them, to a position centre-stage.

Performance: Management theory as an ode

If we read these narratives as we would an ode of the Classical Pindaric
prototype, we see that they are massive and public in their proclamations. In
the odes of Pindar, modelled on the songs sung by the chorus in a Greek
drama, the chorus chants the strophe, the lines sung while moving in a dance
rhythm to the left, and chants the antistrophe while moving back to the right.
In a performance of my *Ode to Management Theory* the metanarrative, sung
by the majority voice in these texts, is the strophe: the antistrophe is here
sung solo by Mary Follett's narrative.

The voices that perform the ode are carefully choreographed into these
scripted roles, so I have borrowed this form to illustrate something of the
dramatic qualities of my reading of the texts. The voices that speak within
the texts, the relationships that I feel these authors constructing with readers,
are here given as the 'stage directions' which produce the kind of tellings I
have described.

Preparing my directors script, I have not slavishly followed the categories
on any of my matrices: as I have previously and repeatedly argued, scriptive
reading should not ever finally be contained by boundaries and stored in
boxes. These are just markers along the way to the discussion of more
meaning. Performance is often an aspect of perspective and persuasion, and
I have therefore, looking back at the metanarrative and the different story
told by Follett, structured this script to reflect this blurring of boundaries.
The stage directions given the performers of the management ode tell of the
distinctive ways in which Follett's voice sings a different audience relationship: the metanarrative tells the strophe: Follett's voice, the antistrophe.

1   Author/reader relationship
     Strophe: pedagogic distance
     Antistrophe: conversation conducted between equals
2   Argument
     Strophe: empirical or anecdotal evidence
     Antistrophe: philosophical logic illustrated by familiar anecdote
3   Concepts
     Strophe: accessible and insistent
     Antistrophe: cryptic and dense
4   Tone
     Strophe: earnest importance
     Antistrophe: irony and understatement
4   Advice
     Strophe: prescriptive and simplistically laid out
     Antistrophe: descriptive and qualified
5   Anecdotes
     Strophe: corporate, nationalistic and international
     Antistrophe: appeal to the authority of everyday, personal and domestic
     experience
6   Protagonist
     Strophe: multiskilled hero, leader and/or seer
     Antistrophe: humble, democratic enabler
7   Action
     Strophe: corporate decision-making conquest and control
     Antistrophe: personal conversation and recreation, and mundane
     work

My comment on a distinctive voice

Given the distinctions listed above, the questions that tease are: since it has
been argued that Follett's work, pioneering management philosophy, was
neglected through much of the half century that followed her death, but has
been resurrected and much admired in more recent times (Graham 1995b),
does my analysis suggest an explanation for this situation?

In the Graham-edited book of Follett's texts (Graham 1995b), Drucker,
Mintzberg and Kanter are all given space for comment. Mintzberg notes that
if we were to 'strip away the name and date . . . she could make the bestseller lists' (p. xiv). My analysis suggests that he is wrong: her worldview
(perspective) and authorial voice (performance) do not romanticize the role
of managers, endorse the power of the business enterprise, or provide clear
directives to achieving utopian outcomes.

This conclusion is starkly thrown into relief by the light that the matrix
of 'Persuasion' (Figure 6.3) sheds on it. The suasive devices that Follett's text
displays are remarkably similar to those demonstrated by all of the other four
texts. Although originally written to be a spoken performance, this text is

always in tune with the other four when we look at the variety of semantic, syntactical and symbolic suasive devices employed in it.

Peter Drucker (1995: 1–10) historicizes her lack of popularity, suggesting that the world of the 'cold war', nationalistic economic expansion and machine-like efficiency was not ready for her enlightened, humanistic thinking. Rosabeth Kanter (1995: xiii–xix), who claims that contemporary feminists such as Carole Gilligan would argue that her voice was ignored because it is female, insists that in fact she was not heard because she did not build a group of 'disciples' around her and lacked the aura she would have acquired as a CEO or high-profile academic, image-making support that Kanter has astutely built her own profile upon.

These explanations are conjectural.[5] My scriptive reading suggests that Follett's worldview, and the root metaphors that convey it, are a more likely reason for the general discard of her voice and theory through several generations. To the extent that she has lately been rediscovered and her theory reinstated, I surmise that as we move into a new millennium, the institution of management and its theorists may be leading the discipline into an era of theory based on an evolving view of what is important, how we might best understand, and how we might best live our lives.

In very general terms then, my summative reading of these narratives depicts perspective, the worldview that I have surfaced from the subtexts, as the primary determinant of reader identification with these management theory texts.

8   Post-scriptive reading

Children, if you dare to think
Of the greatness, rareness, muchness
Fewness of this precious only
Endless world in which you say you live
. . . untie the string.
> Robert Graves, 'Warning to
> Children', 1959

My methodology has built on initiatives and interpretative approaches to text analysis already familiar in the scholarship of management. Other scholars have begun to import critical literary theory into the discipline of management and they have explained and demonstrated methods of criticism based on this interdisciplinary move,[1] but as yet we do not have critical readings that sufficiently account for the role of the reader in the reconstruction of textual meaning. Scriptive reading emphasizes the reader's role in text-making, and is inclusive of diverse reading strategies: it allows for endless reader autonomy and individuality; and is also flexible enough to accommodate our ever-developing understanding of the author–text–reader relationship.

Scriptive reading, while incorporating all that management scholarship has already learned from diverse literary approaches to text analysis, also recognizes that readers are the 'writers' of their own texts: that the reader's reconstruction of the text does not necessarily recognize either the intention of the author, or the autonomy of the text, as the overarching constituent of text-making. In prioritizing the role of the reader, scriptive reading allows that meaning is not only always ultimately elusive, always in the process of being constructed, deconstructed and reconstructed, but also that reading outcomes are as multifarious as are the many readers of any one text.

The methodology on which I have drawn to support my scriptive reading informs my conclusion: that there is no finite meaning to be found in texts. All texts are plurivocal: they suggest multiple meanings. Just as the meaning of a particular word or phrase carries the scriptive reader into realms far beyond that of dominant interpretations, into the elusivity of ambiguity and paradox, and even perhaps to the brink of a metaphysical no-meaning, so too *différance*, acknowledged as the premise of response to the whole text, allows the discovery of more meaning in our texts than has previously been recognized.

Nevertheless, my methodology also supports my claim that although meaning is always in the process of being made, rather than conclusively 'made', we all, individually and collectively, make and share textual meaning on which we communicate very adequately and often with passion. Textual interpretation is individualistic and incomplete, but sharing our meaning-making, explaining the routes we have followed and the premises on which we reconstruct our texts, leads to enlarged understandings in interpretive communities, rather than to chaos and confusion.

Scriptive reading allows for an infinity of textual discovery. No one reading is exclusive of other readings but rather aims to acknowledge and converse with all other textual interpretations. Ironically the more meaning readers discover in a text, the less they may feel that they 'know' what it means. This deepening and widening of the vistas of endless opportunity for textual exploration of management theory may both humble the reader into a growing awareness of how limited our present knowledge of our texts is, as well as challenge management inquiry to support more critical approaches to disciplinary assumptions.

A bigger picture? Constructing more management theory

One of my earliest findings, as I embarked on my review of the literature, was that management scholarship pays scant attention to its foundational theory. Potted versions of the 'classics' are churned out in classroom texts, and there are collections of 'management classics', but there is a dearth of comment and debate on the theory texts that provide us with our management knowledge. I have commented on the few notable exceptions to this generalization, and I have also pointed to a burgeoning literature that maps approaches to the critical reading of guru theory texts. Yet I suspect that a comment from an anonymous *Academy of Management Review* reviewer who rejected a paper based on my scriptive reading of Taylor's text,[2] expresses an opinion and experience representative of the discipline of management:

> I do not believe that the misinterpretation of fundamental texts of management theory is a serious problem in the field today. Much more of a problem is that doctoral students read very little of these texts today . . .
>
> (Anonymous *AMR* reviewer, personal communication, 11 October 2000)

My inquiry indicates first that management theory texts offer us a rich and profoundly important research site, and second that multiple readings of these texts will discover more of their previously unrecognized meanings.

Interpretation of, and debate about, all theory building is essentially important in any discipline. Deidre McCloskey (1998) has said that some of the various reasons for completing rhetorical analyses of economic texts are to understand, to admire, and to debunk, and 'to set [them] beside other works of persuasion in science' so that we can see science not as a new dogma, but as 'thoroughly and respectably part of the old culture' (p. 19). My inquiry suggests that these reasons apply just as appropriately to management theory.

In my scriptive readings I have found many layers of meaning, which have enlarged traditional understandings of management theory. I have also found much to admire. These texts are aesthetically arresting, and there are many moments of exquisite workmanship over which I have hovered with pleasure. At other moments I have taken just as much pleasure in debunking the texts: in exposing some of the buried assumptions that may also give other readers reasons to pause; and in connecting some of the art, the rhetorical devices that I have aesthetically enjoyed, to textual strategies designed to persuade.

My interpretation of root metaphors in the texts suggests that if my *AMR* reviewer correctly believes that we do not read our foundational theory, it may be because every 'new' theorist that we do read supports the notion that we do not need historical knowledge – and in fact recommends that we ignore the past and heed only the text being read. Yet the texts I have read represent 60 years of management theory – and they have much in common. Our theorists seem to be too ready to act like urban developers, forever demolishing the past in order to reinvent (often rude versions of) dignified history. Scriptive reading could reveal the architectural riches, as well as the dry rot in occasional boards, of our theory so that renovation and refurbishment would allow us to retain and respect our treasures, turning museums into pleasantly human habitations.

Discovery: Questioning buried assumptions

Discard of our collective past is just one of the several submerged theory precepts that my scriptive reading surfaced. The assumptions glossed over in dominant readings, are buried too deep for conscious questioning. Ballasted to the surface, brought up for examination, quizzical or challenging, these same assumptions may or may not become espoused values. My inquiry suggests that there are many buried assumptions in management theory, that scriptive reading would reveal them, and that both individually, and as a discipline, we would be enabled by their discovery. When we know what the subterranean messages of our texts are, then we can consciously choose to accept or reject them.

As already noted, one of the more surprising and ultimately rewarding, outcomes of my scriptive reading was the extent to which it surfaced questions and connections which had not spontaneously occurred to me. Follett's distinctive narrative is the most conspicuous and the most revelatory example, but it was not the only surprise. When selecting the texts for analysis I included two texts by women theorists, Follett and Kanter. I was curious to see whether or not these two texts might have more in common with each other than with the other four. They did not. On the contrary, when compared across the first two matrices, Performance and Perspective (as already noted all of the texts featured similar, 'persuasive' elements) they emerged as being markedly unlike.

Furthermore, Kanter's text emerged as having more in common with Taylor's than with the other three. This, to me, was even more surprising given that my dominant readings demonstrate that Taylor's overt concern is 'the efficient system', whereas Kanter's privileged subject is the empowered employee. Apart from one small point of difference (Kanter maintains a personal presence in the text, whereas Taylor plays the omniscient author, objectifying his role and knowledge) my critical reading highlights the profile that they share across all three matrices.

I was equally surprised to find that Drucker, who idealizes and romanticizes managers and management, does not write of problematic management practice, and does not write from a scientist perspective, in all other respects also walks within the imprints of Taylor's footsteps. My scriptive reading showed me that 'what' the text was saying had not moved markedly on from the *Principles of Scientific Management*, and that foundational and contemporary management theory have so much in common as to be almost of one mind.

Already intrigued to find that scriptive reading was throwing up new perceptions of management theory-making on to the screen of my inquiry, I turned my spotlight on to Mintzberg, for his text seemed to me to both belong and not belong, in this company. Because he explicitly and vehemently denies any complicity with other mainstream management theorists and indeed often speaks out against what he sees as the stupidities and self-indulgences of management theorists,[3] I had expected that his text would sit further from the others than it does. Whereas Follett almost invariably walks apart, Mintzberg is sometimes in step with the other three authors, and sometimes walking in the opposite direction. In my dominant reading his 'everyday' prose, and sometimes wearily cynical voice, jars discordantly with the tone and vision of my metanarrative. And yet he walks in step with the other three theorists through the early chapters of my management story, for he would have us discard history while recognizing currently problematic practice, claims discovery of the one important question and corresponding theory, and allows managers to ride on into the future wearing the hero's mantle.

Interestingly, on the third matrix, Persuasion, where I found only one difference across all the texts, and that difference was humour, the two texts that sit apart from the group, are again, those of Follett and Mintzberg. It is tempting to surmise that there is no humour in a management-made

Utopia: that humour makes our familiar world a hospitable environment, and its inhabitants less desperate for escapist romance.

More narratives

My inquiry suggests that exploring diverse interpretations of the texts of our discipline is an exciting and important task. There is an endless vista of fields of inquiry awaiting further research. If, for example, scriptive readers were to provide us with a range of individual interpretations of the same text(s), then the multiple meanings of the endlessly elusive text, text-making as an always on-going process that scriptive reading suggests, would begin to be realized in management scholarship. If, for example, the same five texts that I have read were to be reread many times by many different readers, then the elusive and the controversial discovered could become the on-going subject of multidimensional dialogue as more and more of these texts were opened up for our understanding. This would provide management scholars with a model of multiple readings endlessly revealing more meaning; meaning that is always in the process of being made.

My scriptive readings suggest that the assumptions buried in our theory texts may be more powerfully persuasive than the devices that ornament their expression. Because these assumptions have not all been overtly recognized in the literature to date, I wonder now whether or not open discussion of what has long been taken for granted in management theory will alienate aware readers. And pondering on this I wonder how widely these now unearthed subtexts, will be recognized: are the stories that my scriptive reading tells, the stories that are assumed and accepted by managers and the managed everywhere? Are these the stories retold in the workplace? Are they the stories that managers enact and replay in practice?

I also wonder and worry that my metanarrative of management theory is an indictment of, and part-explanation for, the power-hungry, asset-grabbing, corporatized global giant that, in the eyes of many throughout a shocked world, the USA has now become. My deconstructions were written well before 9/11: they suggest that generations of classical management theory teaching may have played a role in the construction of the policy of the Bush Administration.

The reading outcomes that I have described in the previous section seem to indicate the potential impact that wider uptake of scriptive reading could have on understandings of management theory. I think that at a disciplinary level, scriptive reading would assist the discipline of management to 'know itself' more completely. But it also seems to me that, as with all texts, the stories I have told have left out much, much more than they have included. Many of these untold stories have already made fleeting appearances so, although I have no space to explore them here, I have pulled them just a little further out of the shadows.

I would like to see more historical interpretations of management theory based on scriptive reading. Would scriptive readings of the 1970s, the 1980s, and the 1990s show that fashions in management theory essentially change the message, or would they reveal root metaphor(s) that continue unacknowledged and unchallenged?

Joanne Martin (2000) has suggested that it is time for feminist critical approaches to management to be 'mainstreamed' and to utilize, for example, deconstructive strategies to expose gender bias. Although this was not a specific objective as I designed my inquiry, I hope that my method and analysis will contribute to such a development as I am aware that my gender may sometimes contribute to the outcome of analysis that emerges from the angle of interest that I have instinctively followed.

Is the utopian vision that I have described, subscribed to only in the subtexts of management? I suspect that it has wider currency; that perhaps other readers might not find it as alienating as I do. Scriptive readers could perhaps work in tandem with other research methodologies (an extensive survey, with questions based around the management precepts I have isolated in these texts?) to discover whether or not managers and the managed find them familiar and comforting.

I also, and deeply, wonder if there is no humour in Utopia? If not, and if there is no celebration of anything but material success there, perhaps the Utopias visioned in these texts are really dystopias? Why would we want to live in a world without laughter?

Scriptive reading for writers: A reflexive comment on my scriptive reading

While developing my method of reading, scriptive reading, I monitored a number of its features as they emerged. I was particularly interested in achieving a balance of objective comment, subjective engagement and transparent response, and set out to create this through the overarching design of the three Ps. When, as a dominant reader, I outlined interpretations of the texts that I assume I share with other readers, I was looking to establish grounds for on-going dialogue. As a critical reader I was able to discover meaning in these texts that has not previously been recognized and as a reflexive reader I was able to place my readings within the context of my particular emotive and intellectual responses.

Consistently structuring my reader-responses around this approach to reading achieved a balance of discipline and flexibility that I found valuable. The approach reminded me to regularly assume different reading roles in order to relate to the text in different ways. At the same time it also allowed me, in the critical phase, to spontaneously engage with the text as my responses dictated, in the awareness that this phase would be balanced and explained by its relationship to the other two phases. In all phases of my reading the scriptive approach reassured me that as the scriptive reader travels the text, each experience of the same route is created anew.

Scriptive reading also prompted several discoveries, one of which seems perverse. Popular perceptions of rhetoric as 'empty' are built around a recognition of the emotive power of language devices constructed to persuade: rhetorically powerful language devices may prompt readers to identify with a text, whatever its message. I had thought that effective rhetorical persuasion ('how' the text is presented) might account for reader buy-in to textual messages: that stripped of these eloquent trappings, the 'what' of the text, the theories presented, might seem less appealing.

But it is significant that while all of the texts analysed were discovered to be couched in finely honed rhetorical expressions, only one, Mary Follett's, did not assume nine of the ten precepts around which the other four were built. Because scriptive reading distinguishes the three Ps of rhetoric, performance, perspective and persuasion, I was able to suggest that it is what Mary Follett says that marks out her distinctiveness in this selection of management writings, not how she says it. I was able to seek out the root metaphors in these texts, to discover the assumptions on which the world view they present is predicated, and to expose this to view, even while in the same critical reading commenting on aspects of performance and persuasion.

Root metaphors have not been much explored in management theory – perhaps because management researchers have not had an accessible method with which to work. Looking through the text, pausing long enough at the provoking textual moments encountered in horizontal reading to also discern vertical patterns of meaning hovering below and above the text, has opened up much more of these texts to my close scrutiny. It has enabled me to identify the utopian root metaphor that I see as common to four of these five texts.

The kind of self-conscious awareness that scriptive reading fosters emancipates writers, as well as readers of management theory. Writers are as much bound by the assumptions they may have unconsciously absorbed into their thinking, as are the readers who may unthinkingly adopt the sometimes arcane beliefs, dressed as academic theory, that texts promote. My scriptive reading has prompted me to question my own nationalistic identity, to wonder about utopian visions, to reassess the role of history in our knowledge-making, and to consider (again!) 'which is to be master?': the word, the author or the reader, and how they should best discover and assert 'mastery':

> 'The question is,' said Alice, 'whether you can make words mean so many different things.'
>
> 'The question is,' said Humpty Dumpty, 'which is to be master – that's all.'
>
> (Carroll 1960: 269)

As a scriptive reader, seeing the act of reading as entailing the writing of my own texts, I have begun to read my own texts more critically, searching out my own textual voice, my root metaphors and the persuasive devices I have utilized. I am seeking to become more aware of the perspective that my own text is conveying and of how it is conveyed. This self-consciousness sometimes suggests a revision, a change to the textual message, and/or a change to the rhetoric that conveys it, and sometimes simply provides an insight into the possibilities of diverse reader interpretation, perhaps at some remove from my author-intention.

In my write up of this research journey I have sometimes chosen to express my ideas metaphorically, and I occasionally bring the words of the poets directly into my text. There are times when I think that what language delicately suggests is less ambiguous than the supposedly clear, objective statement. I do not expect that my readers will necessarily agree with this approach to writing up research, but I do think that scriptive readers will become more self-conscious of their own writing practices, and that this developing awareness will lead, as has been my experience, to a modelling of their developing writing processes and expressive modes.

The next step in this merry-go-round could be a scriptive reading of my text by another reader, and then of course a scriptive reading of that text by another reader, and then a scriptive reading of that text. As Robert Graves (1959) warned when he wrote his 'Warning to Children', in the brown paper parcel, into which we have tied our world, there is another neat brown paper parcel containing another world and in that world if we dare untie the string we will find another brown paper parcel . . . and another. If we 'dare' we will face the *mise en abyme*.

This same self-consciousness makes me somewhat uneasy about the terse summaries of my scriptive readings that I have provided in the form of matrices. Although I aimed to avoid a Procrustean synthesis of my scriptive readings, the format in which, to ease my discussion of the critical readings, I have presented these findings, makes them appear tidy and complete. I see the divisions, separations and categorizations that this entailed as a misrepresentation, as well as a representation of my reading outcomes.

I have felt similar constraints in my explanation of the design of my method. Because I am writing in an interdisciplinary environment, I have endeavoured to set out steps in the scriptive reading process, and to isolate the rhetorical elements designated by the three Ps. Yet I see the resulting divisions as somewhat arbitrary. There are so many possible ways of approaching scriptive reading that to some extent I think the method I have described would be best understood if I simply presented examples of my reading strategies in action. This kind of stance, that a poststructuralist 'method' of text analysis can be demonstrated but not explained, is a position commonly held by deconstructionist critics. Nevertheless my intention is that explanation and demonstration effectively complement each other, and that the guidelines to scriptive reading I have provided will not be misunderstood as 'rules'.

I also hoped, as I read my way through the texts, commenting on my interpretations of them, that I could avoid an impression that there might be a mocking, cabbalistic intention informing my recorded responses.

And yet my textual explorations, because they are distinct and separate, are oppositional to the extent that they engage critically with some of the foundational management histories that have been accepted into the canon of classical management theory.

My responses are genuine and I have attempted to record them honestly. If they are provoking or upsetting then I invite other readers to do as I have done, and record their scriptive readings of these same texts. I did not set out on this journey intending to draw critical attention to the constructed nature of management theory texts authored by others while sitting comfortably in some kind of cosily inviolate reader-role. On the contrary, I would both welcome scriptive readings of this, my own text, and readily own my share in the worldview portrayed by the root metaphors I have exposed, for

> The text has no stable identity, no stable origin, no stable end. Each act of reading the text is a preface to the next.
>
> (Spivak 1976: xii)

And would it have been worth it after all,
. . . To have bitten off the matter with a smile,
To have squeezed the universe into a ball
To roll it toward some overwhelming question,
To say . . . 'I shall tell you all' –
If one . . . Should say: 'That is not what I meant at all;
That is not it, at all.'

T.S. Eliot, 'The Love Song of
J. Alfred Prufrock', 1917

Notes

1 Writing what I have written

1 See Pinder and Bourgeois (1982, 1983); and Morgan (1980, 1983b).
2 See Berger and Luckman (1966); Guba and Lincoln (1994); Schwandt (1994).
3 See, for example, Jackson (2001); Clark and Salaman (1996); Watson (1994); Huczynski (1993b); Collins (2000); Furusten (1999).
4 I have followed Czarniawska (1999: 3) in treating management and organization theory as one area. Czarniawska acknowledges that 'there exist organization studies that do not concern themselves with management', but suggests that most of what she has to say can be applied to these also. My subject, like Czarniawska's, is the interpretation of texts. Throughout this research I will assume that all management and organization theory is 'management theory'.
5 Deidre McCloskey's *The Rhetoric of Economics* (1985, 1998) is an outstanding example.
6 Oswick and Grant (1996: 219–20); and see their citation of Ortony (1979).
7 Stanley Fish describes interpretation as 'text-making' (1980: 172).

2 Pre-cedents in management theory

1 'Text' has been reconceptualized in language-based models of knowledge. No longer confined to a 'written representation of reality' it is now generally understood that 'any statement of experience – any oral or written record, any theory or method, any natural or human science – is a discursive practice that can be ẗead". . . Necessarily, then, we are all engaged in textual problems. Texts are no longer the province of English departments, metaphor the business of literary critics, or narratives the stuff of fiction (Klein 1992: 10). Rosenau defines 'text' as 'all phenomena, all events' and notes that postmodernists consider everything a text (1992: xiv).
2 See, for example, Boje *et al.* (1996); Burrell (1996); Calás and Smircich (1997); Grant *et al.* (1998); Hassard and Parker (1993); Hatch (1997); Jacobson and Jacques (1997); Knights (1997); Linstead (1993); Parker 1993; Stablein (1996); Tsoukas (1992).
3 See, for example, the increasingly large and international biennial series of conferences hosted by the Management Centre, King's College, University of London since 1994, and the EGOS subthemes on Discourse 2002 and 2003.
4 See, for example, rhetoric (Czarniawska-Joerges 1995a); discourse (Burrell 2000); texts (Linstead 1999b), and organizational discourse in a special issue of *Organization Studies* edited by Hardy *et al.* planned for 2003.

5 See, for example, Hatch (1996); O'Connor (1995); Kilduff (1993); Calás and Smircich (1991); Chia (1994); Easton and Araujo (1997).
6 See, for example, Clegg *et al.* (1996: 13); Czarniawska (1999); Gergen (1992: 207); Rosenau (1992); Richardson (1994).
7 Morgan (1980, 1981, 1983a, 1983b); Pinder and Bourgeois (1982, 1983).
8 Ricoeur (1978: 13) and Burke (1962: 503–17) restate Aristotle's (1920, 1975) classic definition and description of metaphor, and Hawkes (1972), provides an excellent summary overview of understandings of metaphor through the centuries.
9 To discover applications of these varied terms consult Richards (1936); Black (1962); Lakoff and Johnson (1980); and Ricoeur (1978).
10 See, for example, Alvesson (1993); Cazal and Inns (1998); Grant and Oswick (1996a); Lennie (1999); Morgan (1980, 1983b, 1986); Tsoukas (1991).
11 For the use of all these varied terms, see Davidson (1978: 29); Swanson (1979: 163); Reddy (1993); Schon (1993); Booth (1978); Cohen (1979: 1).
12 For a discussion of how meaning may be constructed through interaction and transference, see Monin and Monin (2001a).
13 Pinder and Bourgeois 1982, 1983; Morgan 1980, 1983b.
14 McCourt (1997, 1998), who sees himself as representative of many in his discipline, insists that a universally acceptable distinction can be made between literal and metaphoric language, while Letiche and Van Uden (1998) counterclaim that theorizing from Ricoeur to Derrida has liberated us from the need to revisit the debate and McCourt's (1998) nonconstructionist position. More recently, Oswick *et al.* (2002), have proposed that metaphor privileges similarity over dissimilarity – a bounded position which ignores the contrived 'shock' value of metaphors which play on dissimilarity – but ensuing dialogue (Marshak 2003; Oswick *et al.* 2003) has opened a door to more profound discussion of what they describe as 'conceptual' [root] metaphors.
15 Of the numerous publications that reflect on interdisciplinary inquiry, four collections of essays on metaphor bring together most of the seminal work immediately relevant to the discipline of management. They are edited by Miall (1982); Ortony (1993); Sacks (1978); and Shibles (1972). Hawkes (1972) provides a succinct and erudite summary history of views of metaphor and also provides a very intelligent select bibliography. Much of my own research into the philosophy and history of metaphor theory has been guided by Warren Shibles (1971), annotated bibliography and history.
16 Turner (1974), and see Ortony (1979: 4).
17 Pepper (1942); Tsoukas (1994b).
18 Putnam *et al.* (1996).
19 Within this literature perhaps the most useful overview of metaphor research in organizations is provided by Alvesson (1993), who lists many of the metaphors that have guided organizational analysis since the 1980s, and some of the authors associated with their use. He also, by focusing on the play of metaphors, moves metaphor analysis in management theory towards recognition of the infinite possibilities of linguistic meaning. The works of Cazal and Inns (1998); Lennie (1999); and the Grant and Oswick (1996b), and Oswick and Grant (1996), edited collection of papers, are also helpful.
20 Plato (1987: 436–9).
21 Readings that have significantly informed and shaped my critical response to papers that comment on metaphor in management studies are as follows. I began my reading with the collections of essays edited by Miall (1982); Ortony (1993); Shibles (1972); and Sacks (1978). Then, partially guided by Hawkes' succinct summary of the history of metaphor theory (1972) I returned to Aristotle's classical work on metaphor in rhetoric, 1920 and 1975, Richards (1936) 'updating'

of metaphor in the so-called 'new rhetoric', and Ricoeur's extensive philosophical discussions (1976, 1978). Black (1962, 1993) distinguished metaphors from models for me, and Empson (1973), opened up ambiguity. De Man (1978) revealed the emotive charge of the powerful metaphor, Burke's (1989) provocative play with metaphorical concepts and the notion of 'perspective' challenged more traditional readings, and Lakoff and Johnson (1980) brought the play and power of metaphor into ordinary, everyday language.

22 In his 'theory of the text' Ricoeur describes the plurivocality of texts as belonging not only to words (polysemy) or even to sentences (ambiguity), but to full works of discourse (1976: 45–69).

23 At a theoretical level postmodern consciousness was introduced to organization studies in 1988 when Robert Cooper and Gibson Burrell began publishing a series of papers in *Organization Studies* (Cooper and Burrell 1988; Burrell 1988, 1994; Cooper 1989). Perhaps these papers had some impact, for in 1992, Martin Parker proclaimed 'Postmodernism is beginning to enter organization studies' (1992b: 1) and then proceeded, after 'introducing the contours of the debate' to critically review 'early contributions', crediting Kenneth Gergen (1992) with opening up the possibilities suggested by the 'new language', the 'emergent discourse', of postmodernism within organization theory (Parker 1992b: 7).

24 Legge (1995) cites 'four French philosophers and the implications of their ideas for the way we look at the world generally and organizations in particular . . . Derrida, Baudrillard, Lyotard and Foucault'.

25 Fuller accounts of the main points Legge covers, are demonstrated in the writings of Burrell (1993, 1996) and echoed in comment by Knights (1997); Hassard (1993); Linstead (1993); Parker (1992a, 1992b); and Tsoukas (1994a) and, some years later, are supported by approaches to teaching management theory in the work of Hatch (1997) and Grint (1995).

26 My comments on Chia's work are primarily based on my reading of his 'The Concept of Decision: A Deconstructive Analysis' (1994) and *Organizational Analysis as Deconstructive Practice* (1996a), see especially pp. 781–804.

27 See Norris (1987).

28 Chia (1996a), see p. 104, and for Watson's review see Watson (1997).

29 Chia (1996a: 2 and 15).

30 Weiskopf and Willmott (1997); and see also van Gils (1999).

31 Tsoukas (1994a: 1), also cites Morgan (1986); Watzlawick (1984); and Weick (1979) in support of this notion.

32 The modernism versus postmodernism debate in the scholarship of management and organization studies has been on-going through the 1990s, as for example in the reply of Martin Parker (1992a) to Haridimos Tsoukas' (1992) critique of Parker's earlier paper (1992b), and was still sometimes polemical as in 1995 when *Organization Studies* published responses to Parker's, 1995a paper, by Stewart Clegg (1995), Norman Jackson (1995), and Pippa Carter (1995), as well as Parker's final responses to his critics (1995b).

33 I discuss reception theory in Chapter 3.

34 Keats (1975: 316–17).

35 An early rhetorical analysis of the writings of Herbert Simon provides an interesting alternative reading to Kilduff's deconstruction. Miller (1990) bases her rhetorical analysis of texts by Simon on her reading of the argument that Simon presents – her analysis ranges across the corpus of Simon's work rather than being restricted (as is Kilduff's analysis of March and Simon's *Organizations*, 1958). She concludes that to see decision-making as intuitive and irrational is paradoxically a more rational stance than is the argument that decision-making is a rational process.

36 See, for example, Eco (1992); Kaplan (1988); Leitch (1996); Parker (1993).
37 John Nelson coined the phrase 'rhetoric of inquiry' (Nelson *et al.* 1987: x; Simons 1990a: vii) to describe what was then an excitingly new interdisciplinary 'turn' in social sciences marked by 'turns': first the 'linguistic turn' (Rorty 1967), then the 'interpretive turn' and, now the 'rhetorical turn' (Simons 1990a: vii). In 1992 Julie Klein confidently described the 'current rhetorical turn in scholarship' as a 'quiet revolution', and linked this phrase to Susan Suleiman's use of it to describe a 'shift in literary theory and criticism from attention to story and storyteller to reader and audience' (Klein 1992: 9).
38 In the scholarship of management this route has also been suggested by Czarniawska (1995b, 1999); Easton and Araujo (1997); O'Connor (1996); and van Maanen (1995).
39 For comment on this movement, and edited collections of papers see Simons (1989b, 1990b); Nelson *et al.* (1987). See also Brown (1987, 1992c). McCloskey's *Rhetoric of Economics* (1985) has been influential across the disciplines and Nelson and McGill's 1986 paper is a particularly powerful position statement. For the Ricoeur quotation (1978) see also Brown (1992a) and Simons (1989a); and on calls for questioning foundational texts see van Maanen (1988); Stablein (1996). The electronic journal of the POROI may be found at http://www.uiowa.edu/~poroi/journal/.
40 Czarniawska, 1999. Czarniawska points out that with the exception of Golden-Biddle and Locke (1997), and the special issue of *Studies in Cultures, Organizations and Societies* edited by Stephen Linstead (1999b), management in this respect lags far behind economics (McCloskey 1985), sociology (Brown 1987; van Maanen 1988; Agger 1990; Capetti 1995) and anthropology (Clifford and Marcus 1986; Geertz 1988).
41 O'Connor (1995, 1996, 1999); O'Connor *et al.* (1995).
42 Novels as 'case studies' of management practice (1994); rhetoric as already noted (1995a); narrative as an analytic mode (1997, 1998), and management theory as a literary genre (1999).
43 Ricoeur (1981: 211).
44 See Czarniawska (1999: 25); supported by Iser (1978) and Rorty (1992).
45 Linstead (1999a: 3). As expected, Linstead cites Calás and Smircich (1991) and Kilduff (1993), as examples of deconstruction; and he cites Hatch (1998), Watson (1996) and Oswick and Grant (1996) on tropes.

3 Pre-scripts in literary theory

1 Ruskin (1903–1912) provided the philosophical arguments for this position and F.R. Leavis (1976) furnished examples of its workings in practice.
2 See, for example, Richards (1924, 1929) and John Crowe Ransome's *The New Criticism* (1941); and also Brooks and Warren (1938); Eliot (1951); Wimsatt (1963); Empson (1973). For his essay, written in 1968, on the 'death of the author' see Barthes (1977a).
3 Hamlet's words were: 'The play's the thing' (III, i, 600).
4 See Abrams (1989b: 241–4) for a helpful discussion of these ideas.
5 See, for example, *Ariadne's Thread*, 1992.
6 Barthes (1977a: 147); and (1988: 193); and in the following paragraphs, for the botanical image (1982: 254–60, specifically p. 255); and on intertextuality (1977a: 148).
7 Miller (1976b) elucidates this notion. See especially pp. 11–13.
8 See, for example, Iser (1978); Fish (1980); Abrams (1989a).
9 Following Goffman (1974).

10 Barthes, 1974, 1977b, 1982. I have explained Barthes' author/writer distinction because I think it illuminates the twentieth century swing to reader-response theories of textual meaning-making; but because this distinction is not widely understood (or even perhaps accepted where it is understood) I have continued to write conventionally of the 'authors' of texts, but sometimes refer to them as writers in order to provide currency for both terms.

11 Reader-response theorists are loosely grouped together around their positioning of the reader at the centre of meaning-making. There is however, wide diversity among them (Holub 1984: xii–xiii). Iser, see my comments later in this chapter, has nevertheless earned his 'right to the title of the total' or complete reader-response critic' (Freund 1987: 135), and his theory has particularly influenced the development of my method. *Rezeption-aesthetik*, a distinctively German school of modern criticism, is known as reception theory.

12 Freund (1987: 164); and see also Fish (1970).

13 On this problematic Culler (1982: 75).

14 The paper has since been published: see Monin *et al.* (2003).

15 See the volume of diverse essays representing reader-response positionings edited by Suleiman and Crosman (1980b); and also Freund (1987).

16 Hopkins (1967: 69–70). Hopkins poetry is, above all else, a celebration of the unique, of the 'inscape', or individuality, of all phenomena.

17 See Richards (1936); Foss *et al.* (1991); Gill and Whedbee (1997).

18 Gaonkar (1990: 349–50); and Burke (1969: 50).

19 Foss *et al.* (1991), who follow Fisher (1978) and Brockriede (1982).

20 Aristotle (1991), cited in Gill and Whedbee (1997: 159).

21 Abrams (1989c: 272, 294–5).

4 Scriptive reading: A method of text analysis

1 Aporia is derived from the Greek word meaning an 'unpassable path'. In Derridean usage it is a 'conceptual cover-term for the effects of *differance* . . . what deconstruction persistently reveals is an ultimate impasse of thought engendered by a rhetoric that always insinuates its own textual workings into the truth claims of philosophy' (Norris 1982: 49).

2 De Man (1986: 22–3); Caputo (1997: 38–44).

3 See Belsey (1980); Caputo (1997: 74–82); Eco (1990).

4 Micklethwait and Wooldridge (1996: 27–9); and see, for example, Crainer (1997, 1998); Boyett and Boyett (1998); Clutterbuck and Crainer (1990), Duncan (1989); Boone and Bowen (1987).

5 Bowring (2000); Calás (1993); Calás and Smircich (1991); Chia (1994); Kilduff (1993); Mumby and Putnam (1992).

6 Clark and Greatbatch (2000); Clark and Salaman (1998); Grint and Case (1998); Case (1999); Jackson (1996, 1999, 2000, 2001); Kieser 1997.

7 Huczynski (1993b).

8 Clutterbuck and Crainer (1990: 235); Good Guru Guide (1994).

9 Huczynski (1993b: 1–10).

10 See Graham (1995a); and Ettorre (1995).

11 See Hart (1997) for further discussion of Burke on this.

5 Scriptive readings

1 Through each of the five analyses in this chapter I have noted the title and author of the selected text in the 'Overview' section. Thereafter quotations from the selected text are referenced by page number only.

2 See, for example, Kristeva (1980); Culler (1982); Johnson (1987).
3 A substantial defence has been mounted by his supporters (Boddewyn (1961); Drucker (1976); Fry (1976); Locke (1982)) and for attacks on his ideology see particularly Banta (1993); and Merkle (1980). See Wren (1979) on early critical comment. For my own further contribution to this debate see Monin *et al.* (2003).
4 This intertextual reading of Plato and Follett is forthcoming in Monin and Monin (2003).
5 See Monin and Monin (2003) for my further exploration of the 'forgetting' of Mary Follett.
6 'Continent without gurus' (1994: 62). For Drucker's comment on this label see Clutterbuck and Crainer (1990: 235); and for the negative view of popular gurus, academic or not, that academic management theorists tend to have of them, see Jackson (2001).
7 A paper (Monin and Monin 1998) based on this reading was presented at a conference on Organizational Discourse hosted by the Management Centre, King's College, University of London; and Mintzberg responded to a copy of the paper I sent to him (H. Mintzberg, personal communication, 27 October 1999).

7 A metanarrative of management theory and a differing voice

1 In *Deconstruction in a Nutshell*, Caputo (1997: 31–6) plays with the paradoxical notion that texts, which do not have definable meanings and determinable missions, and always exceed the boundaries they seem to occupy, can be contained in 'nutshells'. Hamlet visioned his life so.
2 This is a gendered story, which assumes a masculine hero.
3 There are numerous descriptions of Utopia in detailed prescriptive and descriptive literatures; but utopian notions also theme through histories, political treatises, religious beliefs, and the promotions of commercial enterprises. For a very readable translation of Thomas More's original composition, which dates back to 1515, see More (2001). Kumar (1991) provides an excellent summary of the utopian concept its history and universality; Manuel (1966) also makes pertinent comment on utopian themes, history and practice; Carey (1999) has collected an interesting selection of utopian literature; and Parker (2002) has edited a book of comment on Utopia and organizations.
4 For further comment on management theory as a fairy story see Monin and Monin (2001a).
5 I have discussed twentieth-century discard of Follett in much greater detail in Monin and Monin (2003).

8 Post-scriptive reading

1 O'Connor's (1996) close reading of theory texts; rhetorical analysis and dramatistic inquiry into guru texts (Case 1999; Grint and Case 1998; Jackson 2000); and deconstructions of management theory texts (Calás and Smircich 1991; Kilduff 1993; Chia 1994).
2 The paper I referred to in Chapter 3, which has since appeared as Monin *et al.*, 2003.
3 His theorizing ranges from the mainstream (Mintzberg 1973) to the popularist (Mintzberg 1996), to the provocative (Mintzberg 1991), to the cynical (Mintzberg 1978) and the unhappy (Mintzberg 2001).

Bibliography

Abrams, M.H. (1953) *The Mirror and the Lamp: Romantic Theory and the Critical Tradition*. New York: Oxford University Press.

Abrams, M.H. (1989a) *Doing Things with Texts: Essays in Criticism and Critical Theory* (M. Fischer, ed.). New York: W.W. Norton & Co.

Abrams, M.H. (1989b) 'The deconstructive angel', in *Doing Things with Texts: Essays in Criticism and Critical Theory* (M. Fischer, ed.) (pp. 237–52). New York: W.W. Norton & Co.

Abrams, M.H. (1989c) 'How to do things with text', in *Doing Things with Texts: Essays in Criticism and Critical Theory* (M. Fischer, ed.) (pp. 269–96). New York: W.W. Norton & Co.

Agger, B. (1990) *The Decline of Discourse: Reading, Writing and Resistance in Postmodern Capitalism*. New York: Falmer Press.

Alvesson, M. (1993) 'The play of metaphors', in J. Hassard and M. Parker (eds), *Postmodernism and Organisation* (pp. 114–31). London: Sage.

Alvesson, M. (1995) 'The meaning and meaningless of postmodernism: Some ironic remarks', *Organizational Studies* 16(6): 1047–675.

Aristotle (1920) *On the Art of Poetry*, trans. I. Bywater. London: Oxford University Press.

Aristotle (1975) *The Art of Rhetoric*, trans. J. Freese. London: Heinemann.

Aristotle (1991) *On Rhetoric: A Theory of Civil Discourse*, trans. G. Kennedy. New York: Oxford University Press.

Banta, M. (1993) *Taylored Lives: Narrative Productions in the Age of Taylor, Veblen, and Ford*. Chicago: University of Chicago Press.

Barley, S.R. and Kunda, G. (1992) 'Design and devotion: Surges of rational and normative ideologies of control in managerial discourse', *Administrative Science Quarterly* 37: 367–99.

Barthes, R. (1974) *S/Z*, trans. R. Miller. Oxford: Basil Blackwell.

Barthes, R. (1977a) 'The death of the author', in *Image–Music–Text*, trans. S. Heath, (pp. 142–8). New York: Hill & Wang.

Barthes, R. (1977b) *Image–Music–Text*, trans. S. Heath. New York: Hill & Wang.

Barthes, R. (1982) 'Introduction to the structural analysis of narratives', in S. Sontag (ed.) *A Barthes Reader* (pp. 251–95). New York: Hill & Wang.

Barthes, R. (1988) 'Textual analysis: Poe's Valdemar", in D. Lodge (ed.) *Modern Criticism and Theory* (pp. 172–95). London: Longman.

Belsey, C. (1980) *Critical Practice*. London: Routledge.

Berger, P.L. and Luckmann, T. (1966) *The Social Construction of Reality: A Treatise in the Sociology of Knowledge*. New York: Doubleday.

Black, M. (1962) *Models and Metaphors: Studies in Language and Philosophy*. Ithaca, NY: Cornell University Press.

Black, M. (1993) 'More about metaphor', in A. Ortony (ed.) *Metaphor and Thought*, 2nd edn (pp. 19–41). Cambridge: Cambridge University Press.

Boddewyn, J. (1961) 'Frederick Winslow Taylor revisited', *Academy of Management Journal* 4: 100–7.

Boje, D.M., Gephart, R.P. Jr. and Thatchenkery, T.J. (eds) (1996) *Postmodern Management and Organization Theory*. Thousand Oaks, CA: Sage.

Boone, L.E. and Bowen, D. (1987) *The Great Writings in Management and Organizational Behaviour*, 2nd edn. New York: McGraw-Hill.

Booth, W. (1974) *Modern Dogma and the Rhetoric of Assent*. Chicago: University of Chicago Press.

Booth, W.C. (1978) 'Metaphor as rhetoric: The problem of evaluation', in S. Sacks (ed.) *On Metaphor* (pp. 47–70). Chicago and London: University of Chicago Press.

Bowring, M.A. (2000) 'De/constructing theory: A look at the institutional theory that positivism built', *Journal of Management Inquiry* 9(3): 258–70.

Boyett, J.H. and Boyett, J.T. (1998) *The Guru Guide: The Best Ideas of the Top Management Thinkers*. New York: John Wiley & Sons.

Brockriede, W. (1982) 'Arguing about human understanding', *Communication Monographs* 49 (September): 137–47.

Brooks, C. and Warren, R.P. (1938) *Understanding Poetry*. New York: Henry Holt.

Brooks, C. (1947) *The Well-Wrought Urn: Studies in the Structure of Poetry*. London: Methuen.

Brown, R. (1987) *Society as Text*. Chicago: University of Chicago Press.

Brown, R.H. (1992a) 'Preface', in R.H. Brown (ed.) *Writing the Social Text: Poetics and Politics in Social Science Discourse* (pp. ix–x). New York: Aldine de Gruyter.

Brown, R.H. (1992b) 'From suspicion to affirmation: Postmodernism and the challenges of rhetorical analysis', in R.H. Brown (ed.) *Writing the Social Text: Poetics and Politics in Social Science Discourse* (pp. 219–27). New York: Aldine de Gruyter.

Brown, R.H. (ed.) (1992c) *Writing the Social Text: Poetics and Politics in Social Science Discourse*. New York: Aldine de Gruyter.

Bruns, G.L. (1987) 'On the weakness of language in the human sciences', in J.S. Nelson, A. Megill and D.N. McCloskey (eds) *The Rhetoric of the Human Sciences: Language and Argument in Scholarship and Public Affairs* (pp. 239–62). Madison, WI: University of Wisconsin Press.

Burke, K. (1962) *A Grammar of Motives and a Rhetoric of Motives*. Cleveland, OH: The World Publishing Company.

Burke, K. (1969) *A Rhetoric of Motives*. Berkeley, CA: University of California Press.

Burke, K. (1989) *On Symbols and Society* (J.R. Gusfield, ed.). Chicago: University of Chicago Press.

Burrell, G. (1988) 'Modernism, post-modernism and organizational analysis. 2: The contribution of Michael Foucault', *Organization Studies* 9(2): 221–35.

Burrell, G. (1989) 'The absent centre: The neglect of philosophy in Anglo-American management theory', *Human Systems Management* 8: 307–12.

Burrell, G. (1993) 'Eco and the bunnymen', in J. Hassard and M. Parker (eds) *Postmodernism and Organizations*. London: Sage.

Burrell, G. (1994) 'Modernism, post modernism and organizational analysis. 4: The contribution of Jurgen Habermas', *Organization Studies* 15: 1–19.

Burrell, G. (1996) 'Normal science, paradigms, metaphors, discourses and genealogies of analysis', in S.R. Clegg, C. Hardy and W.R. Nord (eds) *Handbook of Organization Studies* (pp. 642–58). London: Sage.

Burrell, G. (ed.) (2000) 'Time and talk' (Special issue). *Organization* 7(3) (August).

Byrne, J.A. (1992) 'Management's new gurus', *Business Week* (August 31): 42–50.

Calás, M.B. (1993) 'Deconstructing charismatic leadership: Re-reading Weber from the darker side', *Leadership Quarterly* 4: 305–28.

Calás, M.B. and Smircich, L. (1991) 'Voicing seduction to silence leadership', *Organization Studies* 12(4): 567–602.

Calás, M.B. and Smircich, L. (1996) 'Not ahead of her time: Reflections on Mary Parker Follett as prophet of management', *Organization* 3: 147–52.

Calás, M.B. and Smircich, L. (1997) *Postmodern Management Theory*. Aldershot, Hampshire: Ashgate/Dartmouth.

Calás, M.B. and Smircich, L. (1999) 'Past postmodernism? Reflections and tentative directions', *Academy of Management Review* 24(4): 649–71.

Capetti, C. (1995) *Writing Chicago: Modernism, Ethnography and the Novel*. New York: Columbia University Press.

Caputo, J.D. (ed.) (1997) *Deconstruction in a Nutshell: A Conversation with Jacques Derrida*. New York: Fordham University Press.

Carey, J. (ed.) (1999) *The Faber Book of Utopias*. London: Faber & Faber.

Carroll, L. (1960) *The Annotated Alice: Alice's Adventures in Wonderland and Alice Through the Looking Glass*. London: Anthony Blond.

Carter, P. (1995) 'Writing the wrongs', *Organization Studies* 16(4): 573–5.

Case, P. (1999) 'Remember re-engineering? The rhetorical appeal of a managerial salvation device', *Journal of Management Studies* 36(4): 419–41.

Cazal, D. and Inns, D. (1998) 'Metaphor, language and meaning', in D. Grant, T. Keenoy and C. Oswick (eds) *Discourse and Organization* (pp. 177–92). London: Sage.

Chia, R. (1994) 'The concept of decision: A deconstructive analysis', *Journal of Management Studies* 31(6): 781–806.

Chia, R. (1996a) *Organizational Analysis as Deconstructive Practice*. Berlin: de Gruyter.

Chia, R. (1996b) 'Metaphors and metaphorization in organizational analysis: Thinking beyond the thinkable', in D. Grant and C. Oswick (eds) *Metaphor and Organizations* (pp. 127–45). London: Sage.

Chia, R. (1997) 'Essai: Thirty years on: From organizational structures to the organization of thought', *Organization Studies* 18: 685–707.

Clark, T. and Greatbatch, D. (2000) 'Maintaining audience affiliation through story-telling: The case of management gurus', paper presented at the 4th International Conference on Organisational Discourse: Wordviews, Workviews and Worldviews, King's College London.

Clark, T. and Salaman, G. (1996) 'The management guru as organizational witchdoctor', *Organization* 3(1): 85–107.

Clark, T. and Salaman, G. (1998) 'Re-imagining the corporation: Guru theory narratives, the flew organisation and the heroic leader', in C. Combes, D. Grant,

T. Keenoy and C. Oswick (eds) *Organizational Discourse: Pretexts, Subtexts and Contexts* (pp. 76–8). London: KMPC.

Clegg, S. (1995) 'Parker's mood', *Organization Studies* 16(4): 568–71.

Clegg, S. and Hardy, C. (1996) 'Introduction: Organizations, organization and organizing', in S.R. Clegg, C. Hardy and W. Nord (eds) *Handbook of Organization Studies* (pp. 1–28). London: Sage.

Clifford, J. (1986) 'Introduction: Partial truths', in J. Clifford and G.E. Marcus (eds) *Writing Culture: The Poetics and Politics of Ethnography* (pp. 1–26). Berkeley, CA: University of California Press.

Clifford, J. and Marcus, G.E. (eds) (1986) *Writing Culture: The Poetics and Politics of Ethnography*. Berkeley, CA: University of California Press.

Clutterbuck, D. and Crainer, S. (1990) *Makers of Management*. London: Macmillan.

Cohen, T. (1979) 'Metaphor and the cultivation of intimacy', in S. Sacks (ed.) *On Metaphor* (pp. 1–10). Chicago and London: University of Chicago Press.

Collins, D. (2000) *Management Fads and Buzzwords: Critical–Practical Perspectives*. London: Routledge.

Continent without gurus (1994) *Economist* 331 (7866) (June 4): 62.

Cooper, R. (1989) 'Modernism, post modernism and organizational analysis. 3: The contribution of Jacques Derrida', *Organization Studies* 10(4): 479–502.

Cooper, R. and Burrell, G. (1988) 'Modernism, post modernism and organizational analysis: An introduction', *Organization Studies* 9(1): 91–112.

Covino, W.A. (1994) *Magic, Rhetoric and Literacy: An Eccentric History of the Composing Imagination*. New York: State University of New York Press.

Crainer, S. (1997) *The Ultimate Business Library: 50 Books that Made Management*. Oxford: Capstone Publishing.

Crainer, S. (1998) *The Ultimate Book of Business Gurus: 110 Thinkers who Really Made a Difference*. New York: AMACOM (American Management Association).

Culler, J. (1982) *On Deconstruction: Theory and Criticism after Structuralism*. Ithaca, NY: Cornell University Press.

Czarniawska, B. (1997) 'A four times told tale: Combining narrative and scientific knowledge in organisation studies', *Organization* 4(1): 7–30.

Czarniawska, B. (1998) *A Narrative Approach to Organization Studies*. London: Sage.

Czarniawska, B. (1999) *Writing Management: Organization Theory as a Literary Genre*. Oxford: Oxford University Press.

Czarniawska-Joerges, B. (ed.) (1995a) 'Managerial and organizational rhetoric' (Special issue). *Studies in Cultures, Organizations and Societies* 1.

Czarniawska-Joerges, B. (1995b) 'Rhetoric and modern organizations', *Studies in Cultures, Organizations and Societies* 1: 147–52.

Davidson, D. (1978) 'What metaphors mean', in S. Sacks (ed.) *On Metaphor* (pp. 29–45). Chicago and London: University of Chicago Press.

Deetz, S. (1996) 'Commentary: The positioning of the researcher in studies of organizations: De-Hatching literary theory', *Journal of Management Inquiry* 5(4): 387–91.

De Man, P. (1978) 'The epistemology of metaphor', in S. Sacks (ed.) *On Metaphor* (pp. 11–28). Chicago and London: University of Chicago Press.

De Man, P. (1986) *The Resistance to Theory*. Manchester: Manchester University Press.

Derrida, J. (1972) *La Dissemination*. Paris: Seuil.

Derrida, J. (1976) *Of Grammatology*, trans. G.C. Spivak. Baltimore, MD: Johns Hopkins University Press.

Derrida, J. (1978) *Writing and Difference*, trans. A. Bass. London: Routledge & Kegan Paul.

De Saussure, F. (1974) *Course in General Linguistics*, trans. W. Baskin. London: Fontana.

Drucker, P. (1955) *The Practice of Management*. London: Heinemann.

Drucker, P.F. (1976) 'The coming rediscovery of scientific management', *Conference Board Record* 13: 23–7.

Drucker, P.F. (1995) 'Introduction: Mary Parker Follett: Prophet of management', in P. Graham (ed.) *Mary Parker Follett – Prophet of Management: A Celebration of Writings* (pp. 1–9). Boston, MA: Harvard Business School Press.

Duncan, W.J. (1989) *Great Ideas in Management: Lessons from the Founders and Foundations of Managerial Practice*. San Francisco: Jossey-Bass.

Dunford, R. and Palmer, I. (1996) 'Metaphors in popular management discourse: The case of corporate restructuring', in D. Grant and C. Oswick (eds) *Metaphor and Organizations* (pp. 95–109). London: Sage.

Eagleton, T. (1983) *Literary Theory: An Introduction*. Minneapolis, MN: University of Minnesota Press.

Easton, G. and Araujo, L. (1997) 'Management research and literary criticism', *British Journal of Management* 8: 99–106.

Eco, U. (1990) *The Limits of Interpretation*. Bloomington, IN: Indiana University Press.

Eco, U. with Rorty, R., Culler, J., Brooke-Rose, C. (1992) *Interpretation and Overinterpretation* (S. Collini, ed.). Cambridge and New York: Cambridge University Press.

Elias, N. (1992) *The Symbol Theory*. London: Sage.

Eliot, T.S. (1951) *Selected Essays*, 3rd edn. London: Faber & Faber.

Empson, W. (1973) *Seven Types of Ambiguity*, 3rd edn. London: Chatto & Windus.

Ettorre, B. (1995) 'A woman for all seasons', *Management Review* 84(6): 7.

Feldman, S.P. (1998) 'Playing with the pieces: Deconstruction and the loss of moral culture', *Journal of Management Studies* 35(1): 59–79.

Fenollosa, E. (1969) 'The Chinese written character as a medium for poetry', in E. Pound (ed.) *Instigations*. Freeport, NY: Books for Libraries Press.

Fish, S. (1970) 'Literature in the reader: Affective stylistics', *New Literary History* 2: 123–62.

Fish, S. (1980) *Is There a Text in this Class? The Authority of Interpretive Communities*. Cambridge, MA: Harvard University Press.

Fish, S. (1989) *Doing What Comes Naturally: Change, Rhetoric and the Practice of Theory in Literary and Legal Studies*. Oxford: Clarendon Press.

Fisher, B.A. (1978) *Perspectives on Human Communication*. New York: Macmillan.

Follett, M.P. (1987) *Freedom and Co-ordination: Lectures in Business Organization*. New York: Garland Publications.

Foss, S.K., Foss, K.A. and Trapp, R. (1991) *Contemporary Perspectives on Rhetoric*, 2nd edn. Prospect Heights, IL: Waveland Press.

Freund, E. (1987) *The Return of the Reader: Reader-Response Criticism*. London: Methuen.

Fry, L.W. (1976) 'The maligned F.W. Taylor: A reply to his many critics', *Academy of Management Review* 1(30): 124–39.

Furusten, S. (1999) *Popular Management Books: How They are Made and What They Mean for Organizations*. London: Routledge.

Gaonkar, D.P. (1990) 'Rhetoric and its double: Reflections on the rhetorical turn in the human sciences', in H.W. Simons (ed.) *The Rhetorical Turn: Invention and Persuasion in the Conduct of Inquiry* (pp. 341–66). Chicago: University of Chicago Press.

Geertz, C. (1988) *Works and Lives: The Anthropologist as Author*. Stanford, CA: Stanford University Press.

Gergen, K.J. (1991) *The Saturated Self: Dilemmas of Identity in Contemporary Life*. New York: Basic Books.

Gergen, K. (1992) 'Organisational theory in the postmodern era', in M. Reed and M. Hughes (eds) *Rethinking Organization: New Directions in Organization Theory and Analysis* (pp. 207–26). London: Sage.

Gibbs, R.W. (1993) 'Process and products in making sense of tropes', in A. Ortony (ed.) *Metaphor and Thought*, 2nd edn (pp. 252–76). Cambridge: Cambridge University Press.

Gill, A.M. and Whedbee, K. (1997) 'Rhetoric', in T.A. van Dijk (ed.) *Discourse as Structure and Process*, vol. 1 (pp. 157–84). London: Sage.

Goffman, E. (1974) *Frame Analysis: An Essay on the Organization of Experience*. Cambridge, MA: Harvard University Press.

Golden-Biddle, K. and Locke, K. (1997) *Composing Qualitative Research*. Thousand Oaks, CA: Sage.

Good guru guide: Take me to your leader (1994) *Economist* 329 (7843) (December 25): 21–6.

Graham, P. (1995a) 'Editor's note', in P. Graham (ed.) *Mary Parker Follett – Prophet of Management: A Celebration of Writings* (pp. vii–ix). Boston, MA: Harvard Business School Press.

Graham, P. (ed.) (1995b) *Mary Parker Follett – Prophet of Management: A Celebration of Writings*. Boston, MA: Harvard Business School Press.

Grant, D., Keenoy, T. and Oswick, C. (eds) (1998) *Discourse and Organization*. London: Sage.

Grant, D. and Oswick, C. (1996a) 'Introduction: Getting the measure of metaphors', in D. Grant and C. Oswick (eds) *Metaphor and Organizations* (pp. 1–20). London: Sage.

Grant, D. and Oswick, C. (eds) (1996b) *Metaphor and Organizations*. London: Sage.

Graves, R. (1959) *Collected Poems*. London: Cassell & Company.

Grint, K. (1994) 'Reengineering history: Social resonances and business process reengineering', *Organization* 1: 179–201.

Grint, K. (1995) *Management: A Sociological Introduction*. Oxford: Polity Press.

Grint, K. and Case, P. (1998) 'The violent rhetoric of re-engineering: Management consultancy on the offensive', *Journal of Management Studies* 35(5): 557–77.

Guba, E.G. and Lincoln, Y.S. (1994) 'Competing paradigms in qualitative research', in N.K. Denzin and Y.S. Lincoln (eds) *Handbook of Qualitative Research* (pp. 105–17). Thousand Oaks, CA: Sage.

Guillen, M.F. (1997) 'Scientific management's lost aesthetic: Architecture, organization, and the Taylorized beauty of the mechanical', *Administrative Science Quarterly* 42: 682–715.

Gusfield, J.R. (1989) *Kenneth Burke on Symbols and Society*. Chicago: University of Chicago Press.

Hart, R.P. (1997) *Modern Rhetorical Criticism*, 2nd edn. Boston, MA: Allyn and Bacon.

Hartman, G.H. (1980) *Criticism in the Wilderness: The Study of Literature Today*. New Haven, CT: Yale University Press.

Hassard, J. (1993) 'Postmodernism and organizational analysis: An overview', in J. Hassard and M. Parker (eds) *Postmodernism and Organizations* (pp. 1–23). London: Sage.

Hassard, J. and Parker, M. (eds) (1993) *Postmodernism and Organizations*. London: Sage.

Hatch, M.J. (1996) 'The role of the researcher: An analysis of narrative position in organisation theory', *Journal of Management Inquiry* 5(4): 359–74.

Hatch, M.J. (1997) *Organization Theory: Modern, Symbolic and Postmodern Perspectives*. Oxford: Oxford University Press.

Hatch, M.J. (1998) 'Irony and the social construction of contradiction in the humour of a management team', *Organization Science* 8(3): 275–88.

Hawkes, T. (1972) *Metaphor*. London: Routledge.

Hernadi, P. (1987) 'Literary interpretation and the rhetoric of the human sciences', in J.S. Nelson, A. Megill and D.N. McCloskey (eds) *The Rhetoric of the Human Sciences: Language and Argument in Scholarship and Public Affairs* (pp. 263–75). Madison, WI: University of Wisconsin Press.

Holub, R.C. (1984) *Reception Theory: A Critical Introduction*. London: Methuen.

Hopkins, G.M. (1967) 'Pied beauty', in W.H. Garner and N.H. MacKenzie (eds) *The Poems of Gerard Manley Hopkins*, 4th edn (pp. 69–70). London: Oxford University Press.

House, H. (1956) *Aristotle's Poetics*. London: Rupert Hart-Davis.

Huczynski, A. (1993a) 'Explaining the succession of management fads', *International Journal of Human Resource Management* 4: 443–63.

Huczynski, A. (1993b) *Management Gurus: What Makes Them and How to Become One*. London: Routledge.

Hughes, T. (1995) 'The thought-fox', in *Ted Hughes: New Selected Poems 1957–1994* (p. 3). London: Faber & Faber.

Inns, D. (2002) 'Metaphor in the literature of organizational analysis: A preliminary taxonomy and a glimpse of a humanities-based perspective', *Organization* 9(2): 305–30.

Iser, W. (1972) 'The reading process: A phenomenological approach', *New Literary History: A Journal of Theory and Interpretation* 3: 279–99.

Iser, W. (1978) *The Act of Reading: A Theory of Aesthetic Response*. Baltimore, MD: Johns Hopkins University Press.

Iser, W. (1980) 'Interaction between text and reader', in S.R. Suleiman and I. Crosman (eds) *The Reader in the Text: Essays on Audience and Interpretation* (pp. 106–19). Princeton, NJ: Princeton University Press.

Jackson, B. (1996) 'Re-engineering the sense of self: The manager and the management guru', *Journal of Management Studies* 33(5): 571–90.

Jackson, B.G. (1999) 'The goose that laid the golden egg? A rhetorical critique of Stephen Covey and the effectiveness movement', *Journal of Management Studies* 36(3): 253–376.

Jackson, B.G. (2000) 'A fantasy theme analysis of Peter Senge's learning organization', *Journal of Applied Behavioral Science* 36(2): 193–209.

Jackson, B.G. (2001) *Management Gurus and Management Fashions: A Dramatistic Inquiry*. London: Routledge.

Jackson, N. (1995) 'To write, or not to right?', *Organization Studies* 16(4): 571–3.

Jacobson, S. and Jacques, R. (1997) 'Destablising the field: Poststructuralist strategies in a postmodern era', *Journal of Management Inquiry* 6: 42–59.

Johnson, B. (1987) *A World of Difference*. Baltimore, MD: Johns Hopkins University Press.

Kanter, R.M. (1984) *The Change Masters: Corporate Entrepreneurs at Work*. London: Routledge.

Kanter, R.M. (1995) 'Preface', in P. Graham (ed.) *Mary Parker Follett – Prophet of Management: A Celebration of Writings* (pp. xiii–xix). Boston, MA: Harvard Business School Press.

Kapland, E.A. (ed.) (1988) *Postmoderism and its Discontents: Theories, Practices*. London: Verso.

Keats, J. (1975) 'Ode on a Grecian urn', in A.W. Allison, H. Barrows, C.R. Blake, A.J. Carr, A.M. Eastman and H.M. English Jr. (eds) *The Norton Anthology of Poetry* (revised shorter edition) (pp. 316–17). New York: W.W. Norton & Co.

Keenoy, T., Oswick, C. and Grant, D. (2000) 'Discourse, epistemology and organization: A discursive footnote', *Organization* 7(3): 542–4.

Kieser, A. (1997) 'Rhetoric and myth in management fashion', *Organization* 4(1): 49–74.

Kilduff, M. (1993) 'Deconstructing organisations', *Academy of Management Review* 18(1): 13–31.

Klamer, A. (1987) 'As if economists and their subjects were rational', in J.S. Nelson, A. Megill and D.N. McCloskey (eds) *The Rhetoric of the Human Sciences: Language and Argument in Scholarship and Public Affairs* (pp. 163–83). Madison, WI: University of Wisconsin Press.

Klein, J.T. (1992) 'Text/context: The rhetoric of the human sciences', in R.H. Brown (ed.) *Writing the Social Text: Poetics and Politics in Social Science Discourse* (pp. 9–27). New York: Aldine de Gruyter.

Knights, D. (1997) 'Organizational theory in the age of deconstruction: Dualism, gender and postmodernism revisited', *Organizations Studies* 18(1): 1–19.

Kristeva, J. (1980) *Desire in Language: A Semiotic Approach to Literature and Art*, trans. T. Gora, A. Jardine and L.S. Roudiez, ed. L.S. Roudiez. New York: Columbia University Press.

Kumar, K. (1991) *Utopianism*. Milton Keynes: Open University Press.

Lacan, J. (1977) *Écrits: A Selection*, trans. A. Sheridan. New York: W.W. Norton & Co.

Lakoff, G. and Johnson, M. (1980) *Metaphors We Live By*. Chicago and London: University of Chicago Press.

Lanham, R. (1993) *The Electronic Word: Democracy, Technology and the Arts*. Chicago: University of Chicago Press.

Leavis, F.R. (1976) *The Common Pursuit*. Harmondsworth: Penguin Books.

Legge, K. (1995) *Human Resource Management: Rhetorics and Realities*. Basingstoke, Hampshire: Macmillan.

Leitch, V. (1996) *Postmodernism: Local Effects, Global Flows*. Albany, NY: SUNY Press.

Lemaire, A. (1977) *Jacques Lacan*, trans. D. Macey. London: Routledge & Kegan Paul.

Lennie, I. (1999) 'Managing metaphorically', *Studies in Cultures, Organizations and Societies* 5: 43–59.

Letiche, H. and Van Uden, J. (1998) 'Answers to a discussion note: On the fhetaphor of the metaphor", *Organization Studies* 19(6): 1029–33.

Levi-Strauss, C. (1962) *The Savage Mind (La Pensée Sauvage)*. London: Weidenfeld and Nicolson.

Lilley, S. (1997) 'Stuck in the middle with you?', *British Journal of Management* 8: 51–9.

Linstead, S. (1993) 'Deconstruction in the study of organizations', in J. Hassard and M. Parker (eds) *Postmodernism and Organizations* (pp. 49–70). London: Sage.

Linstead, S. (1999a) 'An introduction to the textuality of organizations', *Studies in Cultures, Organizations and Societies* 5: 1–10.

Linstead, S. (ed.) (1999b) 'The textuality of organizations' (Special issue), *Studies in Cultures, Organizations and Societies* 5.

Locke, E.A. (1982) 'The ideas of Frederick W. Taylor: An evaluation', *Academy of Management Review* 7(1): 14–24.

Lodge, D. (1988a) 'Foreword', in D. Lodge (ed.) *Modern Criticism and Theory: A Reader* (pp. x–xiii). London: Longman.

Lodge, D. (1988b) 'Ferdinand de Saussure', in D. Lodge (ed.) *Modern Criticism and Theory: A Reader* (pp. 1–2). London: Longman.

McCloskey, D.N. (1985) *The Rhetoric of Economics*. Madison, WI: University of Wisconsin Press.

McCloskey, D.N. (1988) 'The consequences of rhetoric', in A. Klamer, D.N. McCloskey and R.M. Solow (eds) *The Consequences of Human Rhetoric* (pp. vii–x). New York: Cambridge University Press.

McCloskey, D.N. (1998) *The Rhetoric of Economics*, 2nd edn. Madison, WI: University of Wisconsin Press.

McCourt, W. (1997) 'Discussion note: Using metaphors to understand and to change organisations: A critique of Gareth Morgan's approach', *Organization Studies* 18(3): 511–22.

McCourt, W. (1998) 'Rejoinder: On the fhetaphor of the metaphor", *Organization Studies* 19(6): 1035–7.

Manuel, F.E. (ed.) (1966) *Utopias and Utopian Thought*. Boston, MA: Houghton Mifflin.

March, J.G. and Simon, H.A. (1958) *Organizations*. New York: John Wiley & Sons.

Marshak, R.J. (2003) 'Metaphor and analogical reasoning in organization theory: Further extensions', *Academy of Review* 28(1): 9–10.

Martin, J. (1990) 'Deconstructing organizational taboos: The suppression of gender conflict in organizations', *Organization Science* 1: 339–59.

Martin, J. (2000) 'Hidden gendered assumptions in mainstream organizational theory and research', *Journal of Management Inquiry* 9(2): 207–16.

Martin, J. and Knopoff, K. (1997) 'The gendered implications of apparently gender-neutral theory: Re-reading Max Weber', in A. Larson and R.E. Freeman (eds) *Women's Studies and Business Ethics: Towards a New Conversation* (pp. 30–49). New York: Oxford University Press.

Merkle, J.A. (1980) *Management and Ideology: The Legacy of the International Scientific Management Movement*. Berkeley, CA: University of California Press.

Merriden, T. (1998) 'Knocking the theory', *Management Today* (March): 105–6.

Metcalf, H.C. (ed.) (1926) *Scientific Foundations of Business Administration*. Baltimore, MD: Williams and Wilkins Company.

Metcalf, H.C. and Urwick, L. (eds) (1941) *Dynamic Administration: The Collected Papers of Mary Parker Follett.* London: Pitman & Sons.

Miall, D.S. (ed.) (1982) *Metaphor: Problems and Perspectives.* Hassocks, Sussex: Harvester Press.

Micklethwait, J. and Wooldridge, A. (1996) *The Witch Doctors: What the Management Gurus are Saying, Why it Matters and How to Make Sense of it.* London: Heinemann.

Miller, C.R. (1990) 'The rhetoric of decision science, or Herbert A. Simon says', in H.W. Simons (ed.) *The Rhetorical Turn: Invention and Persuasion in the Conduct of Inquiry* (pp. 162–84). Chicago: University of Chicago Press.

Miller, J.H. (1976a) 'Ariadne's thread: Repetition and the narrative line', *Critical Inquiry* III: 57–77.

Miller, J.H. (1976b) 'Stevens' rock and criticism as cure, I', *Georgia Review* 30: 6–11.

Miller, J.H. (1980) 'The figure in the carpet', *Poetics Today* 1(3): 107–18.

Miller, J.H. (1992) *Ariadne's Thread: Story Lines.* New Haven, CT: Yale University Press.

Mintzberg, H. (1973) *The Nature of Managerial Work.* Englewood Cliffs, NJ: Prentice-Hall.

Mintzberg, H. (1978) 'Mintzberg's final paradigm', *Administrative Science Quarterly* 23(4): 635–6.

Mintzberg, H. (1991) 'A letter to Marta Calás and Linda Smircich', *Organization Studies* 12(4): 602.

Mintzberg, H. (1995) 'Some fresh air for management', in P. Graham (ed.) *Mary Parker Follett – Prophet of Management: A Celebration of Writings* (pp. 199–205). Boston, MA: Harvard Business School Press.

Mintzberg, H. (1996) 'Musings on management: Ten ideas to rile everyone who cares about management', *Harvard Business Review* (July–August): 61–7.

Mintzberg, H. (2001) *Why I Hate Flying: Tales for the Tormented Traveller.* New York: Texere.

Monin, N. and Monin, D.J. (1998) 'Rhetoric and managerial discourse: A rhetorical analysis of a text by Henry Mintzberg', in C. Combes, D. Grant, T. Keenoy and C. Oswick (eds) *Organizational Discourse: Pretexts, Subtexts and Contexts* (p. 241). London: KMPC.

Monin, N. and Monin, J. (2001a) 'The rape of the machine metaphor', in W. Smith, M. Higgins, M. Parker and G. Lightfoot (eds) *Science Fiction and Organization* (pp. 61–72). London: Routledge.

Monin, N. and Monin, J. (2001b) 'Does genre matter? Management theory as a fairy tale', paper presented at the 13th ANZAM Conference, 5–7 December, Auckland, NZ.

Monin, N. and Monin, D.J. (2003) 'Re-navigating management theory: Steering by the star of Mary Follett', in B. Czarniawska and P. Gagliardi (eds) *Narratives We Organize By* (pp. 57–74). Amsterdam: John Benjamins.

Monin, N., Monin, D.J. and Barry, D. (2003) 'Toggling with Taylor: A different approach to reading a management theory text', *Journal of Management Studies* 40(3): 377–401.

More, T. (2001) *Utopia*, trans. C.H. Miller. New Haven, CT: Yale University Press.

Morgan, G. (1980) 'Paradigms, metaphors and puzzle solving in organization theory', *Administrative Science Quarterly* 25: 605–22.

Morgan, G. (1981) 'The schismatic metaphor and its implications for organisational analysis', *Organization Studies* 2: 23–41.

Morgan, G. (1983a) 'In research as in conversation, we meet ourselves', in G. Morgan (ed.) *Beyond Method: Strategies for Social Research.* London: Sage.

Morgan, G. (1983b) 'More on metaphor: Why we cannot control tropes in administrative science', *Administrative Science Quarterly* 28: 601–7.

Morgan, G. (1986) *Images of Organizations.* Thousand Oaks, CA: Sage.

Morgan, G. (1996) 'An afterword: Is there anything more to be said about metaphor?', in D. Grant and C. Oswick (eds) *Metaphor and Organizations* (pp. 227–40). London: Sage.

Mumby, D.K. and Putnam, L.L. (1992) 'The politics of emotion: A feminist reading of bounded rationality', *Academy of Management Review* 17: 465–86.

Nelson, J.S. (1993) 'Account and acknowledge, or represent and control? Postmodern politics and economics of collective responsibility', *Accounting, Organizations and Society* 18: 207–29.

Nelson, J.S. and Megill, A. (1986) 'Rhetoric of inquiry: Projects and prospects', *Quarterly Journal of Speech* 72: 20–37.

Nelson, J.S., Megill, A. and McCloskey, D.N. (eds) (1987) *The Rhetoric of the Human Sciences: Language and Argument in Scholarship and Public Affairs.* Madison, WI: University of Wisconsin Press.

Nietzsche, F.W. (1972) 'On truth and falsity in their extramoral sense', in W. Shibles (ed.) *Essays on Metaphor* (pp. 1–13). Whitewater, WI: The Language Press.

Norris, C. (1987) *Derrida.* London: Fontana.

Norris, C. (1988) *Deconstruction and the Interests of Theory.* Leicester: Leicester University Press.

O'Connor, E.S. (1995) 'Paradoxes of participation: Textual analysis and organisational change', *Organization Studies* 16(5): 769–803.

O'Connor, E.S. with Hatch, M.J., White, H.V. and Zald, N. (1995) 'Undisciplining organisational studies: A conversation across domains, methods and beliefs', *Journal of Management Inquiry* 4(2): 119–36.

O'Connor, E.S. (1996) 'Lines of authority: Readings of foundational texts on the profession of management', *Journal of Management History* 2(3): 26–49.

O'Connor, E.S. (1999) 'The politics of management thought: A case study of the Harvard Business School and the Human Relations School', *Academy of Management Review* 24(1): 117–31.

Ortony, A. (1979) 'Metaphor a multidimensional problem', in A. Ortony (ed.) *Metaphor and Thought* (pp. 1–16). Cambridge: Cambridge University Press.

Ortony, A. (ed.) (1993) *Metaphor and Thought,* 2nd edn. Cambridge: Cambridge University Press.

Oswick, C. and Grant, D. (1996) 'The organization of metaphors and the metaphors of organization: Where are we and where do we go from here?', in D. Grant and C. Oswick (eds) *Metaphor and Organizations* (pp. 213–26). London: Sage.

Oswick, C., Keenoy, T. and Grant, D. (2002) 'Metaphor and analogical reasoning in organization theory: Beyond orthodoxy', *Academy of Management Review* 27(2): 294–304.

Oswick, C., Keenoy, T. and Grant, D. (2003) 'More on metaphor: Revisiting analogical reasoning in organization theory', *Academy of Management Review* 28(1): 10–12.

Palmer, I. and Dunford, R. (1996) 'Conflicting use of metaphors: Reconceptualising their use in the field of organisational change', *Academy of Management Review* 21(3): 691–717.

Parker, M. (1992a) 'Getting down from the fence: A reply to Haridimos Tsoukas', *Organization Studies* 13(4): 651–3.

Parker, M. (1992b) 'Post-modern organizations or postmodern organization theory?', *Organization Studies* 13(1): 1–19.

Parker, M. (1993) 'Life after Jean-Francois', in J. Hassard and M. Parker (eds) *Postmodernism and Organizations* (pp. 204–12). London: Sage.

Parker, M. (1995a) 'Critique in the name of what? Postmodernism and critical approaches to organization', *Organization Studies* 16(4): 553–68.

Parker, M. (1995b) 'Angry young man has egotistic tantrum', *Organization Studies* 16(4): 575–7.

Parker, M. (ed.) (2002) *Utopia and Organization*. Oxford: Blackwell.

Pepper, S.C. (1942) *World Hypotheses: A Study in Evidence*. Berkeley, CA: University of California Press.

Pepper, S.C. (1972) 'The root metaphor theory of metaphysics', in W. Shibles (ed.) *Essays on Metaphor* (pp. 15–39). Whitewater, WI: The Language Press.

Pinder, C.C. and Bourgeois, V.W. (1982) 'Controlling tropes in administrative science', *Administrative Science Quarterly* 27: 641–52.

Pinder, C.C. and Bourgeois, V.W. (1983) 'Contrasting philosophical perspectives in Administrative Science: A reply to Morgan', *Administrative Science Quarterly* 28: 608–13.

Plato (1987) *The Republic*, trans. D. Lee, 2nd edn. London: Penguin Books.

Putnam, L.L., Phillips, N. and Chapman, P. (1996) 'Metaphors of communication in organization', in S.R. Clegg, C. Hardy and W.R. Nord (eds) *Handbook of Organization Studies* (pp. 375–408). London: Sage.

Ransom, J.C. (1941) *The New Criticism*. Norfolk, CT: New Directions.

Reddy, M.J. (1993) 'The conduit metaphor: A case for frame conflict in our language about language', in A. Ortony (ed.) *Metaphor and Thought*, 2nd edn (pp. 164–201). Cambridge: Cambridge University Press.

Reed, M. (1990) 'From paradigms to images: The paradigm warrior turns post-modernist guru', *Personnel Review* 19(3): 35–40.

Richards, I.A. (1924) *Principles of Literary Criticism*. London: Routledge & Kegan Paul.

Richards, I.A. (1929) *Practical Criticism: A Study of Literary Judgement*. London: Routledge & Kegan Paul.

Richards, I.A. (1936) *The Philosophy of Rhetoric*. New York: Oxford University Press.

Richardson, L. (1994) 'Writing: A method of inquiry', in N.K. Denzin and Y.S. Lincoln (eds) *Handbook of Qualitative Research* (pp. 516–29). Thousand Oaks, CA: Sage.

Ricoeur, P. (1976) *Interpretation Theory: Discourse and the Surplus of Meaning*. Fort Worth, TX: Texas Christian University Press.

Ricoeur, P. (1978) *The Rule of Metaphor: Multi-disciplinary Studies of the Creation of Meaning in Language*, trans. R. Czerny with K. McLaughlin and S.J. Costello. London: Routledge & Kegan Paul.

Ricoeur, P. (1981) 'The model of the text: Meaningful action considered as text', in J.B. Thompson (ed. and trans.) *Hermeneutics and the Human Sciences* (pp. 197–221). Cambridge: Cambridge University Press.

Rosenau, P.M. (1992) *Postmodernism and the Social Sciences.* Princeton, NJ: Princeton University Press.

Rorty, R. (ed.) (1967) *The Linguistic Turn: Recent Essays in Philosophical Method.* Chicago: University of Chicago Press.

Rorty, R. (1992) 'The pragmatist's progress', in S. Collini (ed.) *Interpretation and Overinterpretation/Umberto Eco with Richard Rorty, Jonathan Culler, Christine Brooke-Rose* (pp. 89–108). Cambridge: Cambridge University Press.

Ruskin, J. (1903–12) *Works,* 39 vols (E.T. Cook and A. Wedderburn, eds). London: George Allen.

Sacks, S. (ed.) (1978) *On Metaphor.* Chicago and London: University of Chicago Press.

Schlender, B. (1998) 'Peter Drucker takes the long view', *Fortune* 138(6): 162–73.

Schon, D.A. (1993) 'Generative metaphor: A perspective on problem-setting in social policy', in A. Ortony (ed.) *Metaphor and Thought,* 2nd edn (pp. 137–63). Cambridge: Cambridge University Press.

Schwandt, T.A. (1994) 'Constructivist, interpretivist approaches to human inquiry', in N.K. Denzin and Y.S. Lincoln (eds) *Handbook of Qualitative Research* (pp. 118–37). Thousand Oaks, CA: Sage.

Shelley, P.B. (1975) 'Ode to the west wind', in A.W. Allison, H. Barrows, C.R. Blake, A.J. Carr, A.M. Eastman and H.M. English Jr. (eds) *The Norton Anthology of Poetry* (revised shorter edition) (pp. 282–4). New York: W.W. Norton & Co.

Shibles, W. (1971) *Metaphor: An Annoted Bibliography.* Whitewater, WI: The Language Press.

Shibles, W. (ed.) (1972) *Essays on Metaphor.* Whitewater, WI: The Language Press.

Simons, H.W. (1989a) 'Introduction', in H.W. Simons (ed.) *Rhetoric in the Human Sciences* (pp. 1–9). Newbury Park, CA: Sage.

Simons, H.W. (ed.) (1989b) *Rhetoric in the Human Sciences.* Newbury Park, CA: Sage.

Simons, H.W. (1990a) 'Preface', in H.W. Simons (ed.) *The Rhetorical Turn: Invention and Persuasion in the Conduct of Inquiry* (pp. vii–xii). Chicago: University of Chicago Press.

Simons, H.W. (ed.) (1990b) *The Rhetorical Turn: Invention and Persuasion in the Conduct of Inquiry.* Chicago: University of Chicago Press.

Spivak, G.C. (1976) 'Translator's preface', in J. Derrida (ed.) *Of Grammatology,* trans. G.C. Spivak. Baltimore, MD: Johns Hopkins University Press.

Stablein, R. (1996) 'Data in organization studies', in S.R. Clegg, C. Hardy and W.R. Nord (eds) *Handbook of Organization Studies* (pp. 509–25). London: Sage.

Suleiman, S.R. and Crosman, I. (1980a) 'Preface', in S.R. Suleiman and I. Crosman (eds) *The Reader in the Text: Essays on Audience and Interpretation* (pp. vii–viii). Princeton, NJ: Princeton University Press.

Suleiman, S.R. and Crosman, I. (eds) (1980b) *The Reader in the Text: Essays on Audience and Interpretation.* Princeton, NJ: Princeton University Press.

Swanson, D.R. (1979) 'Toward a psychology of metaphor', in S. Sacks (ed.) *On Metaphor* (pp. 161–4). Chicago: University of Chicago Press.

Taylor, F.W. (1967) *The Principles of Scientific Management.* New York: W.W. Norton & Co.

Tsoukas, H. (1991) 'The missing link: A transformational view of metaphors in organizational science', *Academy of Management Review* 16: 566–85.

Tsoukas, H. (1992) 'Postmodernism, reflexive rationalism and organizational studies', *Organization Studies* 13(4): 643–50.

Tsoukas, H. (1994a) *New Thinking in Organizational Behaviour*. Oxford: Butterworth-Heinemann.

Tsoukas, H. (1994b) 'Refining common sense: Types of knowledge in management studies', *Journal of Management Studies* 31(6): 761–80.

Turner, V. (1974) *Dramas, Fields and Metaphors: Symbolic Action in Human Society*. Ithaca, NY: Cornell University Press.

van Gils, M. (1999) 'Organizational analysis as deconstructive practice', *Organization Studies* 20(3): 547–50.

van Maanen, J. (1988) *Tales of the Field: On Writing Ethnography*. Chicago: University of Chicago Press.

van Maanen, J. (1995) 'Style as theory', *Organization Science* 6(1): 133–43.

van Maanen, J. (1996) 'On the matter of voice', *Journal of Management Inquiry* 5(4): 375–81.

van Noppen, J.P. and Hols, E. (eds) (1990) *Metaphor II: A Classified Bibliography of Publications from 1985–1990*. Philadelphia: John Benjamins.

Voltaire, J.F. (1937) *Candide and other Tales*, trans. T. Smollett. London: Dent.

Watson, T.J. (1994) 'Management flavours of the month?'their role in managers' lives', *The International Journal of Human Resource Management* 5(4): 893–909.

Watson, T.J. (1996) 'Rhetoric, discourse and argument in organizational sense-making: A reflexive tale', *Organization Studies* 16(5): 805–21.

Watson, T.J. (1997) 'Organizational analysis as deconstructive practice/managing knowledge: Perspectives on cooperation and competition', *Journal of Applied Management Studies* 6(1): 103–5.

Watzlawick, P. (ed.) (1984) *The Invented Reality*. New York: W.W. Norton & Co.

Weick, K. (1979) *The Social Psychology of Organizing*, 2nd edn. Reading, MA: Addison-Wesley.

Weick, K.E. (1989) 'Theory construction as disciplined imagination', *Academy of Management Review* 14: 516–31.

Weick, K.E. (1995) *Sensemaking in Organizations*. Thousand Oaks, CA: Sage.

Weick, K.E. (1999) 'Theory construction as disciplined reflexivity: Tradeoffs in the 90s', *Academy of Management Review* 24(4): 797–806.

Weiskopf, P. and Willmott, H. (1997) 'Turning the given into a question: A critical discussion of Chia's organizational analysis as deconstructive practice 1996', *ERJOT* 3(2): 1–8. Retrieved 20 November 1999 [http://www.apa.org/journals/webref.html#website].

Wimsatt, W.K. (ed.) (1963) *Explication as Criticism*. New York: Columbia University Press.

Wood, D. and Bernasconi, R. (1985) *Derrida and Différance*. Coventry, Warwickshire: Parousia Press.

Wordsworth, W. (1936) 'Intimations of immortality', in T. Hutchinson (ed.) *The Poetical Works of Wordsworth* (pp. 460–2). London: Oxford University Press.

Wren, D.A. (1979) *The Evolution of Management Thought*, 2nd edn. New York: John Wiley & Sons.

Index